Susan du Toit
02-01-2024

SESOTHO made easy

A step-by-step guide to learning and mastering Sesotho

Examples also provided in Afrikaans

AUBREY D. MOKOENA
B.A., H.ED., B.ED., M.D.P (S.A.)

Part of
African Languages Made Easy
Series

JL van Schaik

Published by J L van Schaik Publishers
A division of Media24 Books
1059 Francis Baard Street, Hatfield, Pretoria

First edition 1998
Second impression 2006
Third impression 2007
Fourth impression 2008
Fifth impression 2009
Sixth impression 2010
Seventh impression 2011
Eighth impression 2012
Ninth impression 2013
Tenth impression 2014
Eleventh impression 2015
Twelfth impression 2016
Thirteenth impression 2016
Fourteenth impression 2017
Fifteenth impression 2017
Sixteenth impression 2018
Seventeenth impression 2018
Eighteenth impression 2019
Nineteenth impression 2020
Twentieth impression 2020
Twenty first impression 2021
Twenty second impression 2021
Twenty third impression 2021
Twenty fourth impression 2022

10-digit ISBN 0627 02301 0
13-digit ISBN 978 0 627 02301 9

Cover design by Blue apple Design House
Typesetting in 10 ½ /12 ½ pt New Century Schoolbook by A1 Graphics

Printed and bound by Novus Print, Cape Town

Contents
(Inhoud)

About the author
(Inligting oor die outeur)

The author, Aubrey Mokoena, was born on 12 April 1948 in Orlando West, Soweto. He received his lower primary education at Tlhoreng School and then proceeded to Belle Higher Primary School. Thereafter, he went to the Orlando West Secondary School where he did forms I and II in one year. In 1966 he obtained his Junior Certificate with a first-class pass. He matriculated at the same school in 1968 and was a student teacher the following year. In 1970 he went to the University of the North to study for a Bachelor of Arts Degree, which he ultimately completed through UNISA in 1975.

He pursued his studies through UNISA and in 1978 obtained the Higher Education Diploma and in 1980 a Bachelor of Education degree. He also completed the Management Development Programme with the UNISA School of Business Leadership. Thereafter, he taught Sesotho and other subjects at the Orlando North Secondary School and pioneered an Adult Education School in 1974 in Soweto. At the time of publishing this book, Aubrey is a Member of Parliament and holds the position of Chairperson of Committees of the National Assembly. He is married to Maleshane and has a son, Mandela (18), and daughter, Naledi (11).

Introduction
(Inleiding)

Human beings communicate with one another through language. Human language is that aspect of human behaviour that separates us from animals as far as intelligible communication is concerned. An important attribute of language is that it has a tremendous capacity to bring people together and thus enable them to understand one another better. It is well known that nations have gone to war on account of misunderstanding or poor communication. In our country, poor human relations have existed because of the legacy of a racial divide and the inability of one racial group to understand and speak the language of the other.

Despite the difficulties we, the South African nation, have experienced, we are indeed blessed by the enormous goodwill that exists amongst us. The goodwill emanates, inter alia, from the stark realisation that although we come from different racial backgrounds, we have a common destiny. Our fate is inextricably intertwined. We must make a success of this country. Language may serve to maintain that goodwill and, in fact, nurture it to grow further.

After the democratic general elections in April 1994, South Africa entered a new era, which offered its citizens numerous opportunities and challenges. Among these are the eleven official languages which we South Africans have the opportunity of learning. English and Afrikaans were the only official languages and the other nine were relatively unknown. Now the constitution of the country has elevated them to an equal status with English and Afrikaans. These nine languages are (with estimated speakers):

IsiZulu	8 million people
IsiXhosa	6,5 million people
Sesotho	4,5 million people
Sepedi	3 million people
Setswana	2 million people
Xitsonga	2 million people
Tshivenḓa	1,6 million people
IsiNdebele	1,2 million people
SiSwati	1 million people
Estimated total:	29,8 million

The total South African population (according to the 1996 preliminary census) is 37,9 million. Approximately 29.8 million people speak nine African languages. This means that roughly 10 million South Africans cannot speak any of the nine languages of their compatriots. By contrast, the 29.8 million can speak either English or Afrikaans with relative ease. This book is aimed at bridging that gap. A few Whites speak African languages with admirable fluency. While others struggle with what is commonly known as "Fanakalo", which is a bastardisation of English and Zulu. This is clearly unacceptable because it demeans all those speaking it as well as those spoken to. This book is therefore aimed at those Whites who speak Fanakalo to teach them to speak correct Sesotho. It also aims to stimulate interest along all non-Sesotho speakers to learn Sesotho.

The book is a step-by-step guide, written methodically in order to reveal the structure of Sesotho. We have tried to present the learning material in an enlightening manner. The approach is not academic. However, for those studying Sesotho formally, this book may be used as a textbook. It contains both informal and formal learning material. Stop using Fanakalo. Learn to speak Sesotho correctly. You will be surprised how many people will admire and respect you!

Sesotho Made Easy is part of the *African Languages Made Easy* series. The idea is to cover the entire spectrum of the nine official African languages so that, as South Africans, we can all communicate with one another.

Aubrey D. Mokoena

Acknowledgements
(Erkennings)

I am grateful to my former teachers, especially those who taught me Sesotho at different educational stages, inter alia, Miss Moletsane (now Mrs Tenza), Mr Phetjudi, Mrs O. Ntshalintshali (B.A. UNIN), Mrs Mary Jacobs (formerly Nontolwane) (B.A. S.A), Dr Alusi Moloi (who taught me at the University of the North), Prof J.M. Lenake (who taught me at UNISA) and Dr S.K. Matseke who was Principal at Orlando West High School and enabled me to do std. 6 and std. 7 in one year. Credit also goes to the Mmampodi series, jointly authored by B.T. Khoali, I. Moephuli, J.M. Lenake, A.M. Moleleki, J.R. Masiea and C.F. Swanepoel. They all instilled in me the love for and understanding of Sesotho.

I acknowledge S.M. Mofokeng and C.M. Doke for their *Textbook of the Southern Sotho grammar* and the many authors of Sesotho literature for having enriched my vocabulary. Among these are K.E. Ntsane, S.M. Guma with *An outline structure of Southern Sotho,* J.J. Moiloa, B.M. Khaketla and T. Mofolo.

I also express my gratitude to Ntsiepe Maine (B.A., STD) and Lefu Leemisa for assisting me in certain technical aspects of the book and Dr Magauta Dube, senior lecturer in Sesotho at Vista University (Soweto Campus) for proof-reading the manuscript. She made critical and helpful comments. I also thank Peter Skefu, an art teacher, for providing an earlier set of illustrations for chapter 1.

Mandla Matimba (B.A. STD) developed the concept and network of ALSC (African Languages Study Centres) which is under the umbrella of the ALAS Franchise (African Languages Advancement Services).

A warm word of gratitude goes to Zulfiekar Umar who is a final-year student in engineering, for designing the original front cover of this book.

I pay tribute to my grandmother, Anna Khomo, who raised me, developed me spiritually and nurtured me in the language. I am deeply indebted to her!

Finally I thank Amanda Steyn (Head of African Languages) and Tebello Masima (Publisher and Marketer) of J.L. van Schaik Publishers for their assistance and encouragement.

Aubrey D. Mokoena

1

Pictorial vocabulary

(Prente-woordeskat)

In the first chapter of the book we provide 181 pictures as a means of exposing you, the Sesotho learner, to basic words and concepts that are used in daily experience.

This pictorial vocabulary is an attempt to make you feel at home in your interesting and fulfilling journey to learn Sesotho more easily.

In these illustrations we also supply you with associated words or concepts in addition to the one depicted. The idea here is to gradually enable you to accumulate the Sesotho vocabulary effortlessly and without being aware of it! This chapter will also be useful to children.

batho – people (mense)
motho – person (persoon)

jara – carry (dra)
morwalo – burden (las)
phahlo – luggage (bagasie)

hlooho – head (kop)
moriri – hair (hare)
molala – neck (nek)
sefaha – necklace (halsketting)
sefuba – breast (bors)

phomolo – rest (rus)
ho phomola – to rest (om te rus)
robala – sleep (slaap)
lora – dream (droom)
bethe – bed (bed)
mosamo – pillow (kussing)

matha – run (hardloop)
mokokotlo – back (rug)

bashemane – boys (seuns)
lwana – fight (baklei)
otla – hit (slaan)
nko – nose (neus)

kgaitsedi – sister (suster)
ausi – sister (suster)

morena – king (koning)
setjhaba – nation (nasie)

mofumahadi – queen (koningin)
ho rena – to rule (om te regeer)

ngwana – child (kind)
ho ithuta – to learn, to teach oneself (om te leer)
thuto – education (opvoeding, opvoedkunde)

moruti – minister (predikant)
ho rera – to preach (om te preek)

nkgono – grandmother (ouma)
ho tsofala – to become old (om oud te word)

mme – mother (moeder, ma)
lesea – baby (baba)
ho pepa ngwana – to carry child on the back (om te abba)

monna – man (man)
ho ema – to stand (om te staan)

lepolesa – policeman (polisieman)
ho tshwara – to arrest (om te vang)

jase – coat (jas)
ho apara – to wear (om aan te trek)

patsi – wood (hout)
ho ratha – to chop (om te kap)

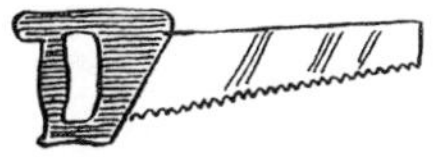

sakga – saw (saag)
lepolanka – plank (plank)

thae – tie (das)

hempe – shirt (hemp)
tshweu – white (wit)
ho tena/apara – to dress (om aan te trek)
ho tsola – to undress (om die klere uit te trek)

jeresi – jersey (trui)
ho futhumala – to be warm (om warm te kry)

baki – jacket (baadjie)
monna – man (man)

borikgwe – trousers (broek)

mose – dress (rok)

dikausi – socks (sokkies)

dieta – shoes (skoene)
ho rwala – to wear (om te dra/om aan te trek)

katiba – hat (hoed)
ho rwala – to wear (om te dra)

kepisi – cap (pet)

nale – needle (naald)
kgareng – cotton (garing)

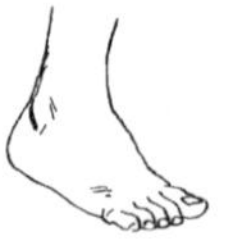

leoto – foot (voet)
serethe – heel (hak)
menwana – toes (tone)

letsoho – hand (hand)
monwana – finger (vinger)
ho supa – to point at (om aan te dui)

leihlo – eye (oog)
mahlo – eyes (oë)
ho sheba – to look (om te kyk)
ho bona – to see (om te sien)
dintshi – eyelashes (ooghare)
sefahleho – face (gesig)

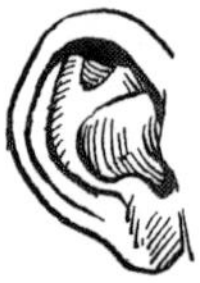

tsebe – ear (oor)
ho utlwa – to hear (om te hoor)

molomo – mouth (mond)
leleme – tongue (tong)
dipounama – lips (lippe)

monwana – finger (vinger)
lenala – nail (nael)

sephaka – arm (arm)
setswe – elbow (elmboog)

leino – tooth (tand)
meno – teeth (tande)
ho bososela – to smile (om te glimlag)

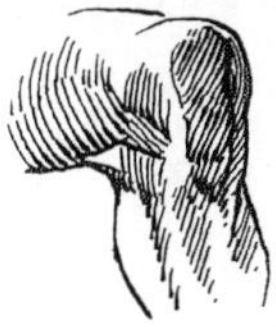

lengole – knee (knie)
tlhafu – calf (kuit)

nko – nose (neus)
seledu – chin (ken)
molala – neck (nek)
motho – person (persoon)
letsoho – hand (hand)
mpa – stomach (maag)
seatla – palm, hand (palm, hand)

setofo – stove (stoof)
ho tjhesa – to be hot (om warm te kry)
ho tuka – to burn (om te brand)
ho bata – to be cold (om koud te kry)

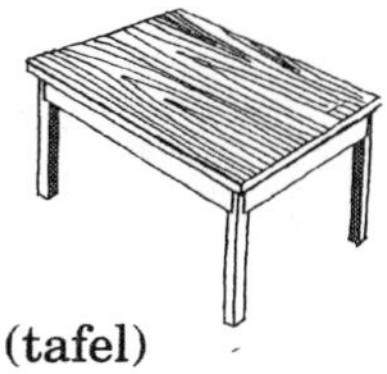

tafole – table (tafel)
e sephara – a broad one (breed)

sehatsetsi/foritjhi – fridge (yskas)
ho baballa – to preserve (om te bewaar)

setulo – chair (stoel)
ho dula – to sit (om te sit)

ho fuduwa – to stir (om te roer)
ho nwa – to drink (om te drink)

lebese – milk (melk)

botlolo – bottle (bottel)

mokopu – pumpkin (pampoen)
monate – delicious (lekker)

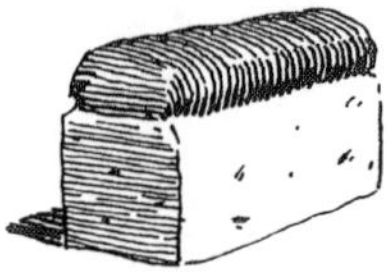

borotho – bread (brood)
ho ja – to eat (om te eet)

kerese – candle (kers)
lebone – light (lig)

sekgele – umbrella (sambreel)
ho sireletsa – to protect (om te beskerm)

lefielo – broom (besem)
fiela – sweep (om te vee)
hlwekisa – clean (om skoon te maak)
kgothala – to be industrious (om fluks te wees)

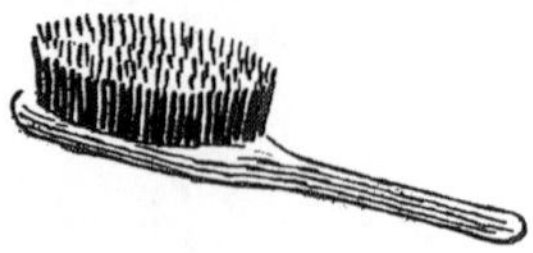

borosolo – brush (borsel)
lerole – dust (stof)

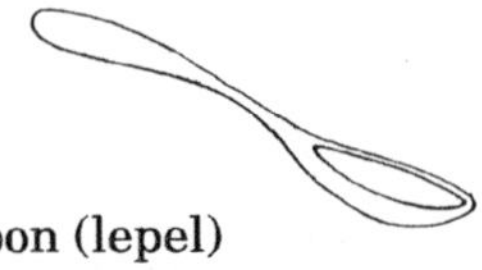

kgaba – spoon (lepel)
ho fuduwa – to stir (om te roer)

thipa – knife (mes)
ho seha – to cut (om te sny)
ho hlaba – to stab, pierce (om te steek)

aene – iron (strykyster)
ho sidila/aena – to iron (om te stryk)

sekere – a pair of scissors ('n skêr)
ho seha – to cut (om te sny)

ketlele – kettle (ketel)
ho tshela – to pour (om te skink)
kofi – coffee (koffie)
teye – tea (tee)
tswekere – sugar (suiker)
lebese – milk (melk)
metsi – water (water)
kgaba – spoon (lepel)
ho nwa – to drink (om te drink)

pitsa – pot (pot)
ho pheha/ho apeha – to cook (om te kook)
dijana – dishes (borde)
dikotlolo – dishes (skottelgoed)
ho ja – to eat (om te eet)
ho tshola – to dish up (om op te skep)

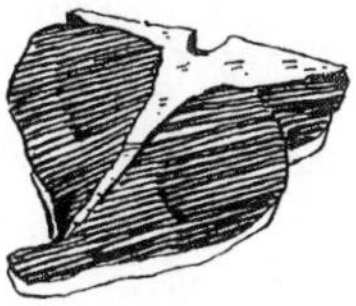

nama – meat (vleis)
sehwapa – biltong (biltong)

fereko/foroko – fork (vurk)
ho hlaba – to pierce (om te steek)

tleloko/tshepe – bell (klok)
ho lla – to ring (om te lui)

jeke – jug (beker)

kgalase – glass (glas)

lebone – lamp (lamp)
lesedi – light (lig)

emere – bucket (emmer)
ho tlala – to be full (om vol te wees)

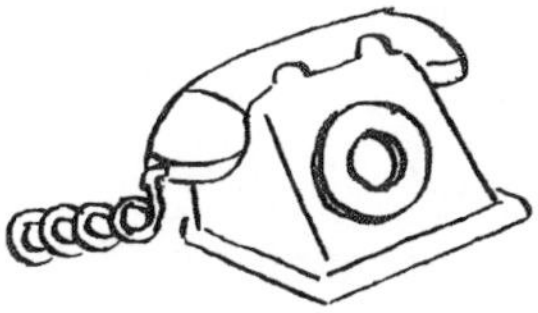

founu – telephone (telefoon)
ho founa – to telephone (om te bel)

morara – grapes (druiwe)
o babang – the sour one (die suur een)
o tswekere – the sweet one (die soet een)

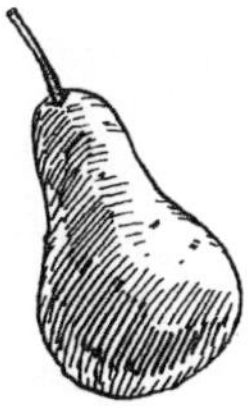

pere/piyere – pear (peer)
tala – green (groen)

apole – apple (appel)
ho butswa – to ripen (om ryp te word)

ditholwana – fruit (vrugte)
monate – delicious (lekker)

anyanese/eie – onion (ui)

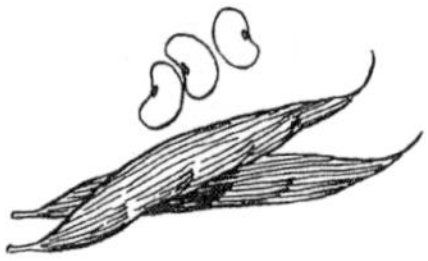

dinawa – beans (boontjies)
ho pheha – to cook (om te kook)

tjhisi/kase – cheese (kaas)

sereledi/botoro – butter (botter)
tlotsa – smear, apply (om te smeer)
selaye – slice (sny)
thipa – knife (mes)

tapole – potato (aartappel)
ditapole – potatoes (aartappels)

dipompong – sweets (lekkers)
ho momona – to suck (om te suig)
monate – delicious (lekker)

panana – banana (piesang)

lamunu – orange (lemoen)
lekgapetla – peel (skil)
ho eboha – to peel (afskil)

perekisi – peach (perske)
ho hlabosa – to be delicious (om smaaklik te wees)

palesa – flower (blom)
ho mela – to grow (om te groei)
ho hloma – to blossom (om te blom)
ho jala – to plant (om te plant)
ho kgabisa – to decorate (om te versier)

mabele – wheat (koring)
ho ja – to eat (om te eet)
dijo – food (kos)
monate – delicious (lekker)
ho lapa – to be hungry (om honger te wees)
ho kgora – to be full (om versadig te wees)

sefate – tree (boom)
difate – trees (bome)
palama – climb (opklim)
theoha – come down (afklim)
katse – cat (kat)
moriti – shade (skaduwee)
kutu – stem (stam)
lekala – branch (tak)
mahlaku/matlhare – leaves (blare)

poone – mealies (mielies)
phofo – mealie-meal (mieliemeel)

koto – bludgeon (knopkierie)
ho otla – to hit (om te slaan)

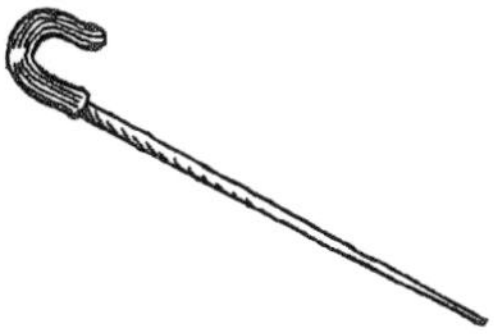

lere – staff (staf)
ho ikokotlela – to support oneself (om jouself te ondersteun)

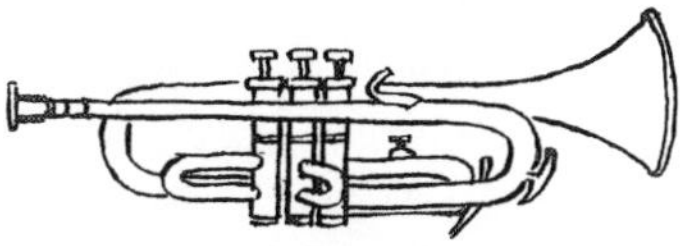

terompeta – trumpet (trompet)
ho butswela – to blow (om te blaas)

phafa/kubu – whip (sweep)
ho shapa – to thrash (om 'n pak slae te gee)

sethunya – gun (geweer)
ho thunya – to shoot (om te skiet)

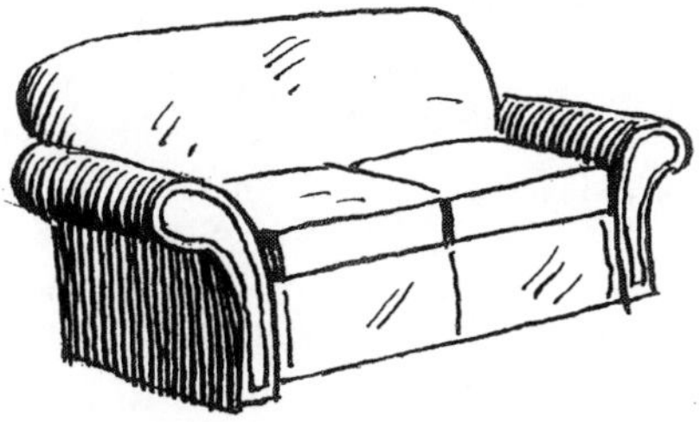

soufa – couch (sofa)
ho phomola – to rest (om te rus)

ntlo – house (huis)
ntle – beautiful (mooi)
kgolo – big (groot)
tjhemele – chimney (skoorsteen)
mosi – smoke (rook)
marulelo – roof (dak)

koloi – car (motor (kar))
ho palama – to ride (om te ry)

kariki – cart (kar)
pere – horse (perd)
mohatla – tail (stert)
lebidi – wheel (wiel)
moetse – mane (maanhare)

mpho – present, gift (geskenk)
ho fana – to be generous (om vrygewig te wees)
ho timana – to be stingy (om suinig te wees)

ntja – dog (hond)
ho loma – to bite (om te byt)
ho bohola – to bark (om te blaf)

katse – cat (kat)
ngwapa – scratch (krap)
mohatla – tail (stert)
ditedu – whiskers (snorbaard)
boya – fur, wool (pels)

mmutla – hare (haas)
ho matha – to run (om te hardloop)

kgoho – fowl (hoender)
sethole – hen (hen)
mokoko – cock (haan)

tshephe – springbok (springbok)
lebelo – speed (spoed)
ho tlola – to jump (om te spring)

tlou – elephant (olifant)
e kgolo – a big one ('n groot een)
nko – nose (neus)

kgomo – cow (koei)
lebese – milk (melk)
ho hama – to milk (om te melk)
lesaka – kraal (kraal)

pere – horse (perd)
ho matha – to run (om te hardloop)
ho palama – to ride (om te ry)
ho jara – to carry (om te dra)
morwalo – load, burden (vrag)
boima – heaviness (swaarheid)
phahlo – parcel (pakkie)

nku – sheep (skaap)
manaka – horns (horing)

qwaha – zebra (sebra)

kwena – crocodile (krokodil)
sehahabi – reptile (reptiel, kruipende dier)

senqanqane – frog (padda)
ho tlola – to jump (om te spring)

hlapi – fish (vis)
ho sesa – to swim (om te swem)
lewatle – sea (see)
noka – river (rivier)
lebopo – river bank (rivierwal)

leobu – chameleon (trapsoetjies)
lenama – slow (stadig)
butle – slow (stadig)

lekgala – crab (krap)

sekgo – spider (spinnekop)
ditshila – dirt (vuil)
bohloko – disease (siekte)
dikokwanahloko – germs (kieme)

phokojwe – fox (jakkals)
leqheka – trick (skelmstreek)
masene – craftiness (geslepenheid)

tsie – locust (sprinkaan)
ho tlola – to jump (om te spring)

serurubele – butterfly (skoenlapper)
ho fofa – to fly (om te vlieg)

nonyana – bird (voël)
ho fofa – to fly (om te vlieg)

letata – duck (eend)
ho sesa – to swim (om te swem)

podi – goat (bok)

thuhlo – giraffe (kameelperd)
telele – tall (lank)

kolobe – pig (vark)
fariki – pig (vark)
seretse – mud (modder)
ho pitika – to wade in the mud (om in die modder te rol)

tshukudu – rhinoceros (renoster)

kubu – hippopotamus (seekoei)

mankgane – bat (vlermuis)

mokgodutswane – lizard (akkedis)
ho hahaba – to crawl (om te kruip)

tweba – mouse (muis)
ho tlola – to jump (om te spring)
ho matha – to run (om te hardloop)

lengau – leopard (luiperd)
e bohale – a fierce one ('n verwoede een)

notshi – bee (by)
manepe – honey (heuning)

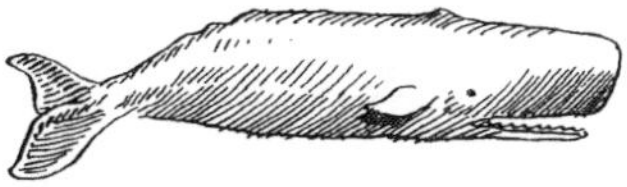

leruwaruwa – whale (walvis)
hlapi – fish (vis)
kgolo – big (groot)

noha – snake (slang)
ho loma – to bite (om te byt)

mpshe – ostrich (volstruis)
mahe – eggs (eiers)
ho hadika – to fry (om te braai)

leeba – dove (duif)

kamele – camel (kameel)

buka – book (boek)
ho bala – to read (om te lees)
leqephe – page (bladsy)

enke – ink (ink)

pene – pen (pen)
ho ngola – to write (om te skryf)
mongolo – handwriting (handskrif)

potloloto/pentshele – pencil (potlood)
lengolo – letter (brief)

lebanta – belt (gordel)
ho tlama – to tie, fasten (om vas te maak)

bolo – ball (bal)
ho bapala – to play (om te speel)
ho raha – to kick (om te skop)
papadi – game, match (spel)
sebapadi – player (speler)

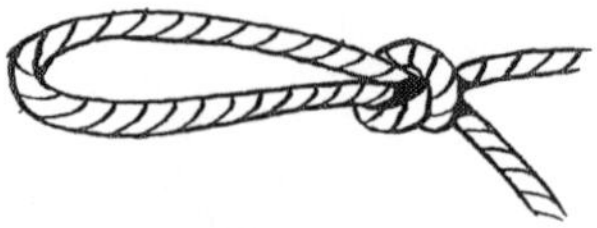

mohala – string (lyn)
thapo – rope (tou)
ho tlama – to tie (om vas te maak)
ho lokolla – to untie (om los te maak)

konopo – button (knoop)
hempe – shirt (hemp)

lebenkele – shop (winkel)
ho reka – to buy (om te koop)

bese – bus (bus)
palama – to board (in- of opklim)
kganna – to drive (bestuur)
batsamai – travellers, commuters (passasiers)

sefofane – aeroplane (vliegtuig)
hodimo – high, up (hoog, op)

kanono – cannon (kanon)
ho thunya – to shoot (om te skiet)

haraka – rake (hark)
jwang – grass (gras)

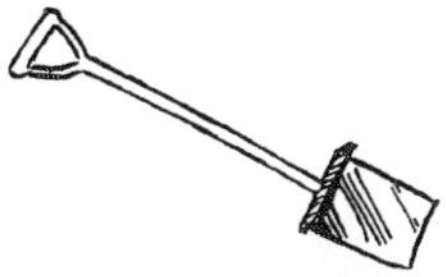

kgarafu – spade (graaf)
ho tjheka – to dig (om te grawe)

kereke – church (kerk)
sefapano – cross (kruis)
tumelo – religion (godsdiens)
tora – tower (toring)

seyalemoya – radio (radio)
ho hasa – to broadcast (om uit te saai)
bamamedi – listeners (luisteraars)
sebohodi – broadcaster (uitsaaier)

setshwantsho – picture (prent)

senotlolo – key (sleutel)
ho bula – to open (om oop te maak)
ho notlela – to lock (om te sluit)

nkgo – vase (blompot)
ho kgabisa – to decorate (om te versier)

kopi – cup (koppie)
mohwele – handle (handvatsel)
ho nwa – to drink (om te drink)
ho petsoha – to crack (om te bars)
ho peperana – to crack (om te kraak)
sosare/pirinki – saucer (piering)

pompo – tap (kraan)
ho nosetsa – to water (om nat te lei)

lebokose la poso – a postbox ('n posbus)
lengolo – letter (brief)
ho posa – to send by post (om deur die pos te stuur)

watjhe/tshupanako – watch (horlosie)
nako – time (tyd)
lenaka – arm, horn (arm, horing)
hora – hour (uur)
motsotso – minute (minuut)
motsotwana – second (sekonde)

peipi – pipe (pyp)
ho tsuba – to smoke (om te rook)

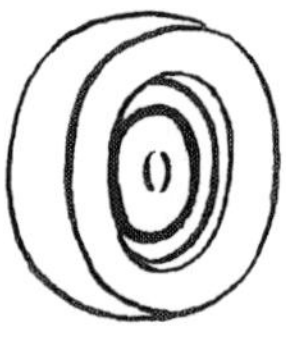

lebidi – wheel (wiel)
ho bidika – to roll (om te rol)

tjhemele – chimney (skoorsteen)
mosi – smoke (rook)
mollo – fire (vuur)
tjhesa – burn (brand)
patsi – wood (hout)
lelakabe – flame (vlam)

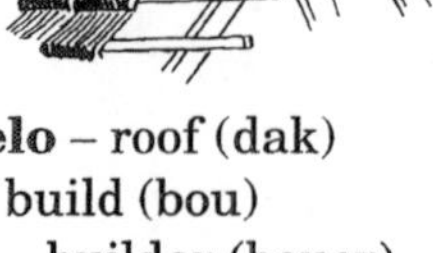

marulelo – roof (dak)
haha – build (bou)
sehahi – builder (bouer)

hamore – hammer (hamer)**hamore** – hammer (hamer)
sepekere – nail (spyker)
ho kgokgothela – to nail (om die spyker in te slaan)

monyako – door (deur)
lemati – door (deur)
lehlafi – door – inside panel (deur – binne-paneel)
ho kwala – to close (om toe te maak)
ho bula – open (om oop te maak)

fenstere – window (venster)
lebone – light (lig)
setshwantsho – picture (prent)

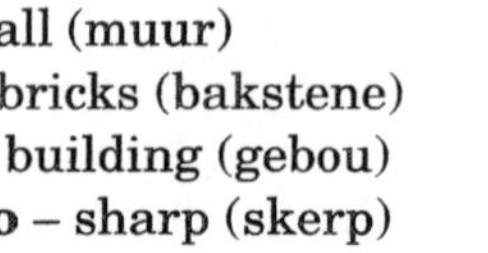

lebota wall (muur)
ditene – bricks (bakstene)
moaho – building (gebou)
ntjhotjho – sharp (skerp)

sekolo – school (skool)
ho bala – to read (om te lees)
ho ithuta – to learn (om te leer)
ho nahana – to think (om te dink)

tente – tent (tent)
ho hloma – to pitch (om op te slaan)

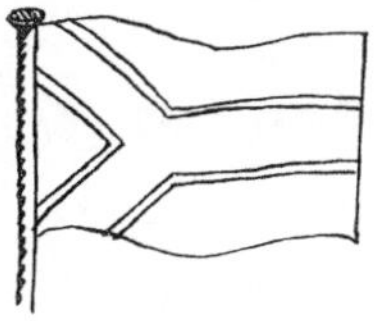

folakga – flag (vlag)
ho fefolwa – to be blown by the wind (om deur die wind gewaai te word)

semela – plant (plant)
jwang – grass (gras)
tala – green (groen)
makgulo – pastures (weiveld)

lehlaku/lehlare – leaf (blaar)
le letala – green one (groen een)

sefate – tree (boom)

kgwedi – moon (maan)
ho kganya – to shine (om te skyn)

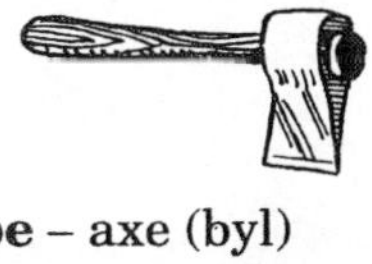

selepe – axe (byl)
ho ratha – to chop (om te kap)

terene – train (trein)
diterene – trains (treine)

seporo – railway (treinspoor)

sekepe – ship (skip)
ho sesa – to nagivate (om te vaar)

tekesi – taxi (taxi)
koloi – car (kar)
mokganni – driver (bestuurder)

baesekele – bicycle (fiets)
dibaesekele – bicycles (fietse)

maru – clouds (wolke)
pula – rain (reën)
ho na – to rain (om te reën)

lejwe – stone (klip)
lefika – rock (rots)

mmila – road (pad)
terata/fentshe – wire fence (heining)

tsela – road (pad)
mmila – road, pathway (weg)
seterata – street (straat)

letsatsi – sun (son)
ho tjhaba – to rise (om op te kom)
hoseng – in the morning (in die oggend)
ho dikela – to set – sun (om onder te gaan)
mantsiboya – sunset (sonsondergang)
bosiu – night (in die nag)
motsheare – daytime (gedurende die dag)

lehadima – lightning (weerlig)
ho duma – to thunder (om te dreun)

lewatle – sea (see)
maqhubu – waves (golwe)

thaba – mountain (berg)
difate – trees (bome)

2

An overview of the Sesotho sentence construction

('n Oorsig van die samestelling van die Sesotho-sin)

Sesotho, like many African languages, is highly noun-based. This means that in the construction of a sentence, focus is placed on the noun. The noun is divided into fifteen classes as elaborated on in Chapter 5. The noun then relates to the rest of the sentence through its prefix i.e. the part-word that is attached to the noun in terms of its classification. Thereafter, the noun is linked to the verb, adjective or adverb through a concordial agreement. This is illustrated as follows:

1. ***se*fate *se se*tala**
   tree which is green
   ('n groen boom, die boom wat groen is)
2. ***bo*hobe *bo bo*holo**
   bread which is big
   ('n groot brood, die brood wat groot is)
3. ***le*bone *le le*tle**
   light which is beautiful
   ('n mooi lig, 'n lig wat mooi is)

The three examples are of a descriptive nature. Adjectives **-tala, -holo** and **-letle** have had the prefix ***se, bo*** and ***le*** attached to them in order to create harmony or a concordial agreement. This means it is wrong to write or say the following:

1. ***se*fate *bo* tala**
2. ***bo*hobe *le* holo**
3. ***le*bone *se* setle**

The above examples are wrong because, in the case of sentence 1, the noun **sefate** (tree) is linked to colour **tala** (green) by the concord ***bo*** which does not belong to the same class as ***sefate.*** Similarly, in sentence 2, the noun **bohobe** (bread) is linked to size **holo** (big) by the concord ***le*** which does not belong to the same noun class as ***bohobe.*** The same applies to sentence 3 where **lebone** (light) is linked to the adjective **letle** (beautiful) by the concord ***se*** which does not belong to the same noun class as **lebone.** We continue to use the same three sentences in a verbal form as compared to the first instance when we discussed them in a descriptive or adjectival form. However, please note that in the use of the verbal form, the verb does not conform to the noun class, as illustrated below:

1. ***Se*****fate** ***se*** **a hola.**
   Tree *it is* growing.
   ('n Boom groei.)
2. ***Bo*****hobe** ***bo a*** **jewa.**
   Bread *it is being* eaten.
   ('n Brood word geëet.)
3. ***Le*****bone** ***le*** **a fela.**
   Light *it is* getting finished.
   (Die lig word klaar.)

In the same way as shown in the previous three examples, there must be a matching of the prefix to the noun, stem and the verbal form. Below are further examples that will help you develop a broader understanding of the above-mentioned explanation:

1. ***se*****lepe** ***se selelele*** (descriptive/adjectival form)
   an axe which is long
   ('n lang byl, die byl wat lank is)
2. ***se*****ledu** ***se*** **sephara**
   a chin which is broad
   ('n breë ken, die ken wat breed is)
3. ***se*****fapano** ***se*** **seholo**
   a cross which is big
   ('n groot kruis, die kruis wat groot is)
4. ***Se*****lepe** ***se*** **a ratha.** (verbal form)
   An axe is chopping.
   ('n Byl kap.)
5. ***Se*****ledu** ***se*** **a hlaba.**
   A chin is sharp.
   ('n Ken is skerp.)

6. ***Sefapano se* a imela.**
   A cross is heavy.
   ('n Kruis is swaar.)

The foregoing explanation will serve as a friendly basis for introducing you to a more detailed treatment of the noun in Chapter 5.

Another feature of African languages is that they are highly tonal in nature, i.e. tone plays an important role in the meaning of a word. In Sesotho, words that have the same spelling often have different meanings. Examples are:

(i) **diphiri** – secrets (geheime)
(ii) **diphiri** – hyenas (hiënas)

In the case of (ii) the last two syllables are uttered with a high tone, whereas in the case of (i) they are uttered with a lower tone.

Other examples are:

(iii) **lelala** – grinding stone (maalklip)
(iv) **ho lelala** – to look up (kyk op)
(v) **rona** (the **o** is lowered) – we (ons)
(vi) **ho rona** (the **o** is raised) – not to be suitable (nie geskik nie)
(vii) **bona** (**o** is lowered) – them (hulle)
(viii) **bona!** (the **o** is raised) – look! (kyk!)
(ix) **ho sebetsa** (the **se** is raised) – to work (om te werk)
(x) **sebetsa** (the **se** is lowered) – weapon (wapen)

The above ten words are just an illustration out of many words, including synonyms, antonyms, homophones etc. that the student will come across in the course of the book. Chapter 3 deals with the phenomenom of raised and lowered vowels.

A significant point to note is that Sesotho has a disjunctive orthography, i.e. not joined or combined as in the case of Zulu. By comparison the writing of Sesotho is similar to that of English while that of Zulu is similar to Afrikaans, i.e. in joining up words.

Another interesting feature of Sesotho is that it is a highly evocative language, i.e. its words are expressive as compared with Tshivenda which is characterised by many subdued or "swallowed" sounds.

3

The sound (phonetical) structure of Sesotho

(Die klank- (fonetiese) struktuur van Sesotho)

Introduction (Inleiding)

As a beginner in learning Sesotho, we do not wish to confuse you with the complexities of the sound system of Sesotho. However, we need to be fair to you by giving you a basic understanding of how speech sounds are produced in Sesotho. This will help you not to speak in such a way that a Mosotho, who hears you speak, will immediately know that you were not properly introduced to the phonetics (science of the speech sound) or phonology (sound system) of Sesotho. The Sesotho speech sounds, like those of many other languages, are divided into vowels and consonants. When we articulate sounds, we use air. Depending on the kind of sound, the air can be initiated from the lungs, from the glottis or it can be initiated in the mouth cavity. As a result, when we classify our sounds we identify the kind of air we use and we look at the direction that it takes to either go out or be sucked in. In certain instances, the air may cause some kind of vibration and again we would use that to classify sounds differently.

The manner in which the air is released brings about the differences between the vowels and the consonants and this enables us to define the two kinds of sounds differently. Vowels are sounds in which, when articulated, there is no obstruction of air release, whereas consonants are sounds in which, when articulated, there is partial or complete obstruction of air release. Examples of vowels are: a, e, i, o and u.

Examples of consonants are, among others, b, d, k, m, p, r, s, t etc. There is only one click sound in Sesotho. A click is a consonant that is pronounced with an explosive sound. Our click is "q", but not pronounced like in queen, but like a sound of a tiny stone dropping into water or like the sound produced by the high heel of a woman's shoe!

Below we briefly discuss the vowels and the consonants.

Vowels (Klinkers)

In Sesotho, there are seven main vowels, called cardinal vowels. We present them in the following chart. This chart is structured to resemble the shape of the human mouth. These vowels are produced at positions of the mouth assisted by the tongue, the teeth and other organs.

The vowel chart: Table 1

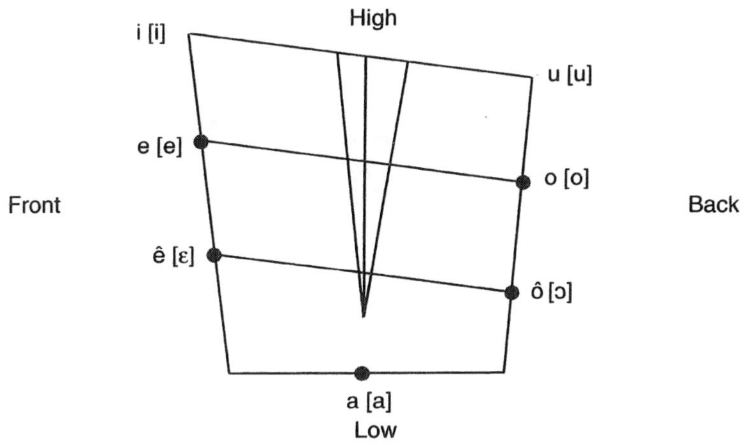

We will briefly explain each one of them and give you practical examples:

1. **i:** This is described as the high front vowel. Here, the tongue is pushed towards the front of the teeth and pressed against the roof of the mouth (the palate).

   Examples are:

   pitika – to roll (rol)

   hadika – to fry (braai)

   sidila – to massage (masseer)

2. **e:** This is described as a mid-high front vowel. Here, the tongue is relatively lower than in the position of cardinal vowel **i.**

   Examples are:

   pela – hedgehog (krimpvarkie)

   tena – to dress (aantrek)

   leka – to try (probeer)

3. **ê:** This is called the mid-low front vowel. This sound is written like this for phonetic purposes. In writing, it appears like an ordinary "e" but is pronounced with the tongue in a lower position than in the case of the half-close front **e**.

Examples are:

thebe – shield (skild)

dibebe – festering wounds (sere)

ema – to stand up (om op te staan)

4. **a:** This is described simply as an open low vowel, with the tongue lowered to the floor of the mouth but slightly withdrawn to the back of the mouth.

Examples are:

bana – children (kinders)
nama – meat (vleis)
na – to rain (om te reën)

5. **ô:** This is called the mid-low back vowel, with the tongue lowered but withdrawn. It is just a phonetic manner of writing this sound. In practical orthography, it is simply written as an o.

Examples are:

kokota – to knock on the door (om aan die deur te klop)
koto – bludgeon (knopkierie)
oma – to dry (om droog te word)

6. **o:** This is called the closed mid-high back vowel. Here the tongue is relatively raised but withdrawn to the back of the mouth.

Examples are:

thoto – luggage (bagasie)
pola – to hit, thrash (om te slaan)
totobatsa – to emphasise (beklemtoon)

7. **u:** This is described as the closed high back vowel. Here the tongue occupies the position directly opposite that of the vowel i.

Examples are:

utulla – to unearth, expose (om uit te haal, te onthul)
lekunutu – secret (geheim)
tutubala – to close one's eyes (om jou oë toe te maak)

8. Semi-vowels. These are half-vowels that generally look like consonants. There are only two semi-vowels in Sesotho, namely, **w** and **y**, e.g.

wa – of (van)
wena – you (jy)
weso – ours (ons s'n)
ya – of (van)
yena – he, she (hy, sy)
yeso – ours (ons s'n)

Consonants (Medeklinkers)

We have already mentioned a few examples of consonants like **b, d, k, m,** etc. In Sesotho, consonants occur in various combinations. As a learner of Sesotho, we will not delve too much into the intricate permutations. As mentioned earlier, in the articulation of consonants there is an obstruction of the air that is released. We use and look at the manner of air release to classify and describe consonants. This brings us to the following classifications:

Broadly speaking in Sesotho, consonants may be classified as follows:

1. Voiced consonants: These are produced with great effort, pressure or vibration of the vocal chords.

   Examples of these are: **b, d, r** etc.

   e.g. **bina** – to sing (sing)

   dula – to sit (om te sit)

   mema – to invite (om uit te nooi)

   loha – to knit (om te brei)

   rata – to love (om vir iemand lief te wees)

2. Unvoiced consonants: These are pronounced without a great deal of vibration of the vocal chords.

   Examples are: **k, t,** e.g.

   kuta – to cut (om te sny)

   taba – talk (gesprek)

3. Nasal consonants: These are produced with pressure exerted on the nose. In their articulation, the air escapes through the nose.

   Examples are **m, n, ng, ny**:

   nala – prosperity (voorspoed)

   mme – mother (moeder)

   ngwana – child (kind)

   nyala – to marry (om te trou)

4. Lateral consonants: These are produced with the air going out along the side of the mouth.

   Examples are **hl, tl**:

   hlala – to divorce (laat skei)

   tlama – to tie (om vas te bind)

5. Aspirated consonants: In Sesotho speech, consonants are followed by vowels. All vowels are voiced and normally they would be voiced immediately. But it happens that with the articulation of aspirated consonants, there is no immediate voicing of the vowel following. When this happens, the consonant is said to

have an aspirated sound. Phonetically, aspirated sounds are written with an **[h]** on top. For example **ph** – **[p^h]**, **th** – **[t^h]**, **tlh** – **[tl^h]**.

phamola – to grab (om te gryp)

thiba – to block (om te versper)

tlhapa – a swear-word (vloekwoord)

tshaba – to be afraid (om bang te wees)

Note that it does not necessarily mean that when a consonant is followed by an **[h]**, that consonant is an aspirated consonant. For example:

shapa – to beat (om te slaan)

Rather, the sound is a sound without an **[h]** on top as can be seen from the phonetic script.

6. Rolled consonants: There is only one rolled consonant in Sesotho, namely **r**. In this articulation, a series of obstructions is followed by a series of air releases. Examples are:

rata – to love (om vir iemand lief te wees)

ruta – to teach (om te onderrig)

rora – to roar, a lion (om te brul)

ritela – to brew liquor (om te brou)

rarella – to intertwine (om deurmekaar te vleg)

7. The click: This has already been dealt with in the introduction, i.e. the sound **q** and **qh.** A few examples are:

qapa – to compose (om te komponeer)

qoqa – to discuss, converse (om te bespreek)

qeta – to finish (om klaar te maak)

qhaqha – to unbundle, demolish, undo (om af te breek)

qhowa – a top of a mountain, peak, pinnacle (hoogste punt, piek)

It might interest you as a learner of Sesotho to note that, while Sesotho has only one click sound, isiZulu and isiXhosa have more clicks and in various combinations. There are a few interesting examples:

c, ch, x, gx

4

Vocabulary for specific life situations

(Woordeskat vir spesifieke lewensomstandighede)

Examples of words in common speech usage (Voorbeelde van woorde in gewone spraakgebruik)

In order to help you develop a feel for Sesotho, we will give you words used in daily speech, and also provide simple applications and associated concepts in nineteen life situations:

Greetings and general conversation (Groet en gewone gesprekvoering)

1. **Dumela** (singular, i.e. when greeting one person). – Hello, good morning, good day, good afternoon. (Goeiemôre, goeiedag, goeiemiddag.)
2. **Dumelang** (plural, i.e. when greeting more than one person). – Hello, good morning, good day, good afternoon. (Goeiemôre, goeiedag, goeiemiddag.)
3. **O kae?** (singular) – How are you? (Hoe gaan dit?)
   O a phela? (singular) – Are you alright? (Is jy wel?)
4. **Le kae?** (plural) – How are you? (Hoe gaan dit?)
   Le a phela? (plural) – Are you alright? (Is julle wel?)
5. **Ke a o dumedisa.** – I am greeting you. (Ek groet jou.)
   Ke a le dumedisa. – I am greeting you (many). (Ek groet julle.)
6. **Re a le dumedisa.** – We are greeting you. (Ons groet julle.)
7. **Ke nako mang?** – What time is it? (Hoe laat is dit?)
8. **Ke hokae moo?** – Which place is this? (Watter plek is hierdie?)
9. **Ke kopa dijo.** – I am asking for food. (Ek vra kos.)

10. **Ke nyorilwe.** – I am thirsty. (Ek is dors.)
11. **Ke batla tekesi.** – I would like to have a taxi. (Ek wil 'n taxi hê.)
12. **Ke a kula.** – I am sick or not well. (Ek is siek.)
13. **Ke lahlehile.** – I am lost. (Ek het verdwaal.)
14. **Mapolesa a kae?** – Where are the police? (Waar is die polisie?)
15. **Tjhelete ya ka e fedile.** – My money is finished. (My geld is klaar.)
16. **Diaparo tsa ka di tabohile.** – My clothes are torn. (My klere is geskeur.)
17. **Koloi ena ha e tsamae.** – This car is not moving. (Hierdie kar beweeg nie.)
18. **Ke rata batho.** – I love people. (Ek hou van mense.)
19. **Ha ke rate dintwa.** – I do not like fights. (Ek hou nie van bakleiery nie.)
20. **Bana ba bapala seterateng.** – The children are playing in the street. (Die kinders speel in die straat.)
21. **Ntja e a bohola.** – A dog barks. ('n Hond blaf.)
22. **Nonyana e a fofa.** – A bird flies. ('n Voël vlieg.)
23. **Lerole le lengata.** – There is a lot of dust. (Daar is baie stof.)
24. **Ntlo e kgolo.** – A big house. ('n Groot huis.)
25. **Ho a bata.** – It is cold. (Dit is koud.)
26. **Ho phodile.** – It is cool. (Dit is koel.)
27. **Ho a tjhesa.** – It is hot. (Dit is (baie) warm.)
28. **Ho futhumetse.** – It is warm. (Dit is warm.)
29. **Jwang bo botala.** – The grass is green. (Die gras is groen.)
30. **Maru a thibile.** – It is overcast or cloudy. (Dit is bewolk.)
31. **Ke bua le wena.** – I am talking to you. (Ek praat met jou.)
32. **Ke a o rata.** – I love you. (Ek is lief vir jou.)
33. **Ha ke o rate.** – I do not love (like) you. (Ek hou nie van jou nie.)
34. **Pere e a raha.** – A horse kicks. ('n Perd skop.)
35. **Kgomo e a fula.** – A cow grazes. ('n Koei wei.)
36. **Modimo o lerato.** – God is love. (God is liefde.)

37. **Ke o bone moketeng.** – I saw you at a function. (Ek het jou by 'n funksie gesien.)

38. **Ke lenyalo.** – It is a wedding. (Dit is 'n bruilof.)

39. **Ke lefu.** – It is a funeral or death. (Dit is 'n begrafnis of dood.)

Transport and travel (Vervoer en reis)

1. **koloi** – car (kar)
2. **mokganni** – driver (bestuurder)
   ho kganna (verb) – to drive (om te bestuur)
3. **lebidi** – wheel (wiel)
4. **seipone** – mirror (spieël)
   ho sheba seipone (verb) – to look into the mirror (om in die spieël te kyk)
5. **fenstere** – window (venster)
6. **monyako** – door (deur)
   ho bula (verb) – to open (om oop te maak)
7. **setulo** – seat (sitplek)
   ho dula (verb) – to sit (om te sit)
8. **ho thella** (verb) – to skid (om te gly)
9. **mariki** – brakes (remme)
   ho kgina mariki – to apply brakes (om die rem te trap)
10. **tsela** – road, way (pad, weg)
11. **mmila** – road, way (pad, weg)
12. **seterata** – street (straat)
13. **peterole** – petrol (petrol, brandstof)
14. **oli** – oil (olie)
15. **metsi** – water (water)
16. **terene** – train (trein)
17. **seteishene** – station (stasie)
18. **motsamai** – traveller (reisiger)
19. **phahlo** – luggage (bagasie)

20. **tekete** – ticket (kaartjie)
21. **tjhelete** – money (geld)
22. **ho lefa** (verb) – to pay (om te betaal)
23. **ho palama** (verb) – to board, ride (om op of in te klim, om te ry)
24. **ho theoha** (verb) – to alight, disembark (om af te klim)
25. **mofaho** – provisions, refreshments for the journey (padkos)
26. **leeto** – journey, trip (reis, rit)
27. **sefofane** – flight, aeroplane (vlug, vliegtuig)

Parts of the (human) body (Dele van die liggaam)

1. **mmele** – body (liggaam)
   Mmele wa ka o bohloko. – My body is painful. (My liggaam is seer.)
2. **hlooho** – head (kop)
   hlooho e kgolo – a big head ('n groot kop)
   Ke tshwerwe ke hlooho. – I have a headache. (Ek het hoofpyn.)
3. **moriri** – hair (hare)
   O na le moriri o motle. – You have beautiful hair. (Jy het mooi hare.)
4. **letlalo** – skin (vel)
   Letlalo le bonolo – a soft skin ('n sagte vel)
5. **leihlo** – eye (oog)
   Leihlo la ka le bohloko. – My eye is aching. (My oog is seer.)
6. **nko** – nose (neus)
   Nko ya ka e thibane. – My nose is blocked. (My neus is toe.)
7. **molomo** – mouth (mond)
   Bula molomo. – Open your mouth. (Maak jou mond oop.)
8. **leino** – tooth (tand)
   meno (plural) – teeth (tande)
   O na le meno a matle. – You have beautiful teeth or a fine set of teeth. (Jy het mooi tande.)
9. **leleme** – tongue (tong)
   Ke latswa ka leleme. – I taste with a tongue. (Ek proe met 'n tong.)

10. **mathe** – saliva (speeksel)

O se ke wa tshwela mathe. – Do not spit. (Moenie spoeg nie.)

11. **seledu** – chin (ken)

seledu se seholo – a big chin ('n groot ken)

12. **lerama** – cheek (wang)

lerama le lefubedu – a red cheek ('n rooi wang)

13. **tsebe** – ear (oor)

Tsebe ya ngwana e bohloko. – The child's ear is aching. (Die kind se oor is seer.)

14. **phatla** – forehead (voorkop)

Podi e thula ka phatla. – A goat hits with its forehead. ('n Bok stamp met sy voorkop.)

15. **molala** – neck (nek)

Ke robehile molala. – I broke my neck. (Ek het my nek gebreek.)

16. **lehetla** – shoulder (skouer)

mahetla (plural) – shoulders (skouers)

Ke jara ka mahetla. – I carry on my shoulders. (Ek dra op my skouers.)

17. **sefuba** – breast or chest (bors)

Ke rata sefuba sa kgoho. – I like the breast of a chicken. (Ek hou van 'n hoenderbors.)

Ke tshwerwe ke sefuba. – I have a cough or sore chest. (Ek hoes of het las van my bors.)

18. **kgopo** – rib (rib)

dikgopo (plural) – ribs (ribbes)

Dikgopo tsa hao di a bonahala hobane o otile haholo. – Your ribs are visible because you are too thin. (Jou ribbes is sigbaar want jy is te maer.)

19. **mala** – intestines (derm)

Mala a hlwekile. – My intestines are clean. (My derm is skoon.)

20. **mpa** – stomach (pens)

Ngwana o ngwaya mpa. – The child scratches his/her stomach. (Die kind krap sy/haar maag.)

21. **letheka** – waist (middellyf)

Ngwanana o sotha letheka. – The girl twists her waist. (Die meisie draai haar middellyf.)

22. **serope** – thigh (dy)

    Ke ja serope sa kgoho. – I am eating a thigh of a chicken. (Ek eet 'n hoenderdy.)

23. **lengole** – knee (knie)

    mangole (plural) – knees (knieë)

    Re koba mangole ha re rapela. – We bend our knees when we pray. (Ons buig ons knieë wanneer ons bid.)

24. **lesapo** – bone (been)

    lesapo le lesweu – a white bone ('n wit been)

25. **madi** – blood (bloed)

    sediba sa madi – a fountain of blood ('n fontein van bloed)

26. **leqaqailane** – ankle (enkel)

    Leqaqailane la ka le bohloko. – My ankle is painful. (My enkel is seer.)

27. **serethe** – heel (hak)

    Ke raha ka serethe. – I kick with my heel. (Ek skop met my hak.)

28. **leoto** – foot (voet)

    leoto le sephara – a flat foot ('n plat voet)

29. **monwana** – finger (vinger)

    Monwana wa letsoho o molelele. – The finger is long. (Die vinger is lank.)

    Monwana wa leoto o mokgutshwanyane. – The toe is short. (Die toon is kort.)

30. **letsoho** – hand (hand)

    letsoho le lelelele – a long hand ('n lang hand)

31. **sephaka** – arm (arm)

    Sephaka se bohloko. – The arm is painful. (Die arm is seer.)

32. **setswe/sejabana** – elbow (elmboog)

    Sebapadi se kgitla se seng ka setswe. – The player nudges another one (with an elbow). (Die speler stamp die ander met 'n elmboog.)

33. **seatla** – palm (palm)

    seatla se bonolo – a soft palm ('n sagte palm)

34. **lenala** – nail (nael)

    manala or dinala (plural) – nails (naels)

    Katse e ngwapa ha bohloko ka dinala. – The cat scratches painfully with the nails. (Die kat krap seer met die naels.)

35. **boko** – brain (brein)

Sebedisa boko ba hao. – Use your brains. (Gebruik jou verstand.)

Church (Kerk)

1. **Modimo** – God (God)

   Modimo o lerato. – God is love. (God is liefde.)

2. **Jesu** – Jesus (Jesus)

   Jesu o re shwetse sefapanong. – Jesus died for us on the cross. (Jesus het vir ons aan die kruis gesterf.)

3. **lehodimo** – heaven (hemel)

   Modimo o hlodile mahodimo le lefatshe. – God created heaven and earth. (God het hemel en aarde geskape.)

4. **lengeloi** – angel (engel)

   Lengeloi la bua le Maria. – The angel spoke to Mary. (Die engel het met Maria gepraat.)

5. **tumelo** – faith (geloof)

   E ba le tumelo – Have faith. (Jy moet geloof hê.)

6. **Bebele** – Bible (Bybel)

   Ke bala Bebele – I am reading the Bible. (Ek lees die Bybel.)

7. **sefela** – hymn (gesang)

   Sefela se phahamisa moya wa ka. – The hymn raises my spirit. (Die gesang bemoedig my.)

8. **thero** – sermon (preek)

   thero e sisimosang maikutlo – an inspiring sermon ('n preek wat inspireer)

9. **kereke** – church (kerk)

   Ke kena kereke. – I attend church. (Ek gaan kerk toe.)

10. **rapela** (verb) – pray (bid)

    Ke rapela ka mehla. – I pray daily. (Ek bid elke dag.)

11. **moruti** – minister (predikant)

    Moruti o a rera. – The minister preaches. (Die predikant preek.)

12. **phutheho** – congregation (gemeente)

    phutheho e kgolo – a large congregation ('n groot gemeente)

13. **selallo** – Holy Communion (nagmaal)

Re ja selallo. – We partake of Holy Communion. (Ons neem deel aan die nagmaal.)

14. **sebe** – sin (sonde)

    dibe (plural) – sins (sondes)

    Re tshwarele dibe tsa rona. – Forgive us our sins. (Vergewe ons ons sondes.)

15. **ditlolo** – trespasses (oortredings)

    Re leballe ditlolo tsa rona. – Forgive us our trespasses. (Vergewe ons ons oortredings.)

16. **sefapano** – cross (kruis)

    Jesu o ile a thakgiswa sefapanong. – Jesus was crucified on the cross. (Jesus is gekruisig aan die kruis.)

17. **nyolohelo** – ascension (opvaring/bestyging)

    Ke letsatsi la nyolohelo. – It is Ascension day. (Dit is Hemelvaartdag.)

18. **kahlolo** – judgement (oordeel)

    Bohle re tla fumana kahlolo. – All of us shall receive judgment. (Almal van ons sal geoordeel word.)

19. **mohau** – grace (genade)

    Re phela ka mohau. – We live by grace. (Ons lewe deur (Gods) genade.)

20. **tshenolo** – revelation (openbaring)

    Tshenolo ke buka ya ho qetela ya Bebele. – Revelations is the last book of the Bible. (Openbaring is die laaste boek van die Bybel.)

Education (Opvoeding)

1. **thuto** – education (opvoeding)

   Thuto e molemo. – Education is beneficial. (Opvoeding is voordelig.)

2. **sekolo** – school (skool)

   Bana ba kena sekolo. – Children attend school. (Kinders gaan skool toe.)

3. **buka** – book (boek)

   Ke bala buka. – I read a book. (Ek lees 'n boek.)

4. **mosuwe** – teacher (onderwyser)

   Mosuwe wa rona ke Tshepo. – Our teacher is Tshepo. (Ons onderwyser is Tshepo.)

5. **mosuwetsana** – female teacher (onderwyseres)

   mesuwetsana (plural) – female teachers (onderwyseresse)

Re rutwa ke mesuwetsana feela. – We are being taught by female teachers only. (Ons word deur onderwyseresse alleenlik geleer.)

6. **hlooho ya sekolo** – principal (hoof)

   Hlooho ya sekolo sa rona e mafolofolo. – Our school principal is energetic. (Ons hoof is bedrywig.)

7. **tlhahlobo** – examination (eksamen)

   Re ngola tlhahlobo hosane. – We are writing the examination tomorrow. (Ons skryf die eksamen môre)

8. **thothokiso** – poem (gedig)

   Bana ba sekolo ba ithuta thothokiso. – Pupils are learning a poem. (Leerlinge leer 'n gedig.)

9. **ngola** – write (skryf)

   Ke ngola hantle. – I write well. (Ek skryf goed.)

10. **lengolo** – letter (brief)

    Ke fumane lengolo la hao. – I have received your letter. (Ek het jou brief ontvang.)

11. **moqoqo** – essay (opstel)

    Ke ngotse moqoqo o monate. – I have written an interesting essay. (Ek het 'n interessante opstel geskryf.)

12. **mohlahlobi** – inspector (inspekteur)

    Mohlahlobi o a tla. – The inspector is coming. (Die inspekteur kom.)

13. **atleha** (verb) – pass, succeed (slaag, sukses behaal)

    Ha o etsa mosebetsi wa hao, o tla atleha. – If you do your work, you will pass, succeed. (As jy jou werk doen, sal jy slaag, sukses behaal.)

14. **ho se atlehe** – not to succeed, to fail (om te druip of nie te slaag nie)

    Ha o sa etse mosebetsi wa hao, o ke ke wa atleha. – If you do not do your work, you will not pass, succeed. (As jy nie jou werk doen nie, sal jy nie slaag nie.)

15. **ho tshwaya buka** – to mark the book (written work) (om die boek na te sien (skryfwerk))

    Mosuwe o tshwaya buka ya Pitso. – The teacher marks Pitso's book (written work). (Die onderwyser merk Pitso se boek d.w.s. skryfwerk.)

Agriculture (Landbou)

1. **lema** (verb) – plough (ploeg)

   Ke rata ho lema. – I like ploughing. (Ek hou daarvan om te ploeg.)

2. **tshimo** – farm (plaas)

   Tshimo ya ntate e kgolo .– My father's farm is big. (My vader se plaas is groot.)

3. **poone** – mealies (mielies)

   Ke ja poone. – I eat mealies. (Ek eet mielies.)

4. **jala** – plant (plant)

   Molemi o jala mabele. – The farmer plants wheat. (Die boer plant koring.)

5. **ditholwana** – fruit (vrugte)

   Ditholwana di a hlabosa. – Fruit is delicious. (Vrugte is lekker.)

6. **morara** – grapes (druiwe)

   Veine e ritelwa ka morara. – Wine is produced from grapes. (Wyn word van druiwe gemaak.)

7. **mohoma** (noun) – plough (ploeg)

   Mohoma o robehile. – The plough is broken. (Die ploeg is gebreek.)

8. **pula** – rain (reën)

   Ha pula e nele, balemi ba a lema. – After the rain, farmers plough. (Na die reën, ploeg die boere.)

9. **dikgomo** – cattle (beeste)

   Dikgomo di hula mohoma. – The cattle pull the plough. (Die beeste trek die ploeg.)

10. **monontsha** – manure (mis)

    Mobu o hloka monontsha. – The soil requires manure. (Die grond benodig mis.)

11. **kotula** (verb) – reap (oes)

    Nako ya ho kotula e fihlile. – The time to reap has arrived. (Die tyd om te oes het aangebreek.)

12. **letsema** – team ploughing (spanploeg)

    Letsema le bebofatsa ho lema. – Team ploughing makes ploughing easy. (Spanploeg maak ploeg maklik.)

13. **hama** (verb) – milk (melk)

    Moshemane o hama kgomo. – The boy milks the cow. (Die seun melk die koei.)

14. **lehola** – weeds (onkruid)

    Lehola le sitisa dijalo. – Weeds hinder plants. (Onkruid hinder plante.)

15. **medupe** – soft soaking rain (sagte reën/motreën)

    Pula ya medupe e amohelehile haholo. – The soft soaking rain is most welcome. (Die sagte reën is welkom.)

16. **komello** – drought (droogte)

    Komello e sehloho. – Drought is cruel. (Droogte is wreed.)

17. **lehadima** – lightning (weerlig)

    Lehadima le kotsi. – Lightning is dangerous. (Die weerlig is gevaarlik.)

18. **mohlape** – flock (trop)

    mohlape wa dinku o motle – a beautiful flock of sheep ('n mooi trop skape)

Animals (wild) and associated concepts (Wilde diere en verwante konsepte)

1. **phoofolo** – animal (dier)

   diphoofolo (plural) – animals (diere)

   Diphoofolo di ngata. – Animals are many. (Diere is baie.)

2. **hlaha** (adjective) – wild (wild)

   phoofolo e hlaha – a wild animal ('n wildè dier)

3. **moru** – forest (bos)

   moru o motenya – a thick/dense forest ('n digte bos)

4. **lengau** – leopard (luiperd)

   Lengau le ipata morung. – The leopard hides itself in the forest. (Die luiperd kruip in die bos weg.)

5. **tlou** – elephant (olifant)

   Tlou e na le manaka a mabedi. – An elephant has tusks (horns) being two, i.e. an elephant has two tusks (horns). ('n Olifant het twee tande.)

6. **nare** – buffalo (buffel)

   Nare e hlaba motho ka lenaka. – A buffalo pierces a person with a horn. ('n Buffel steek 'n mens met 'n horing.)

7. **kwena** – crocodile (krokodil)

   Kwena ke sehahabi. – A crocodile is a reptile. ('n Krokodil is 'n kruipende dier/ reptiel.)

8. **kubu** – hippopotamus (seekoei)

   Kubu e phela metsing. – A hippopotamus lives in the water. ('n Seekoei lewe in die water.)

9. **hlapi** – fish (vis)

   Hlapi e sesa nokeng. – A fish swims in the river. ('n Vis swem in die rivier.)

10. **noha** – snake (slang)

    Ke tshaba noha. – I fear a snake. (Ek is bang vir 'n slang.)

11. **mmutla** – hare (haas)

    Mmutla o na le lebelo. – A hare has speed, i.e. a hare runs fast. ('n Haas hardloop vinnig.)

12. **phokojwe** – fox (jakkals)

    Phokojwe e masene. – A fox is clever. ('n Jakkals is slim.)

13. **phiri** – hyena (hiëna)

    O robala jwalo ka phiri. – You sleep like a hyena. (Jy slaap soos 'n hiëna.)

14. **tshephe** – springbok (springbok)

    Leshodu le tlola jwalo ka tshephe. – A thief jumps like a springbok. ('n Dief spring soos 'n springbok.)

15. **tshukudu** – rhinoceros (renoster)

    Tshukudu e na le lenaka le ntjhotjho. – A rhinoceros has a horn which is sharp. ('n Renoster het 'n skerp horing.)

16. **tshwene** – monkey, baboon (bobbejaan)

    Tshwene e makgisa. – A monkey, baboon is shaggy. ('n Bobbejaan is harig.)

17. **thakadi** – hedgehog (krimpvarkie)

    Thakadi e tjheka mokoti. – A hedgehog digs a hole. ('n Krimpvarkie grawe 'n gat.)

18. **kamele** – camel (kameel)

    Kamele e na le molala o molelele. – A camel has a neck which is long. ('n Kameel het 'n lang nek.)

Animals (domestic) (Huisdiere)

1. **ya hae** – of home, i.e. domestic (huislik)

   phoofolo ya hae – an animal of home, i.e. domestic animal ('n huisdier)

2. **kgomo** – cow (koei)

   Moshemane o hama kgomo. – A boy milks a cow. ('n Seun melk 'n koei.)

3. **nku** – sheep (skaap)

   Boya ba nku bo mofuthu. – Wool of a sheep is warm. (Die wol van 'n skaap is warm.)

4. **pere** – horse (perd)

   Pere e hula kariki. – A horse pulls a cart. ('n Perd trek 'n kar.)

5. **podi** – goat (bok)

   Ha ke je nama ya podi. – I do not eat the meat of a goat. (Ek eet nie die vleis van 'n bok nie.)

6. **kolobe** – pig (vark)

   Kolobe e nonne haholo. – A pig is too fat. ('n Vark is te vet.)

7. **kgoho** – hen, fowl (hoender)

   Ke rata nama ya kgoho. – I like the meat of a fowl, i.e. I like chicken. (Ek hou van hoendervleis.)

8. **lehe** – egg (eier)

   Kgoho e behela lehe. – A hen lays an egg. ('n Hen lê 'n eier.)

9. **ntja** – dog (hond)

   Ntja e a loma. – A dog bites. ('n Hond byt.)

10. **katse** – cat (kat)

    Katse e a ngwapa. – A cat scratches, i.e. people and things. ('n Kat krap mense en dinge.)

11. **letata/pidipidi** – duck (eend)

    Letata le a sesa. – A duck swims. ('n Eend swem.)

12. **kalakune** – turkey (kalkoen)

    Re ja kalakune ka Keresemese. – We eat a turkey at Christmas. (Ons eet 'n kalkoen met Kersfees.)

Birds (Voëls)

1. **nonyana** – bird (voël)

   Nonyana e a fofa. – A bird flies. ('n Voël vlieg.)

2. **leeba** – dove (duif)

   Leeba ke nonyana ya mohau. – A dove is a bird of peace. ('n Duif is 'n voël van vrede.)

3. **lekgwaba** – white-necked crow ('n witnekkraai)

4. **phakwe** – hawk (valk)

   Phakwe e fofa le tsuonyana molomong. – A hawk flies (away) with a chicken in its beak. ('n Valk vlieg weg met 'n kuiken in sy bek.)

5. **tshemedi** – butcher-bird (laksman)
6. **thaha** – bishop-bird (wewervoël)
7. **serobele** – sparrow (mossie)
8. **motinyane** – grass warbler (tinktinkie)
9. **kgaka** – guinea fowl (tarentaal)

   Kgaka e tshwana le kgoho. – A guinea fowl resembles a hen. ('n Tarentaal lyk soos 'n hoenderhen.)
10. **lenong** – vulture (aasvoël)

    Lenong le ja setopo sa phoofolo. – A vulture eats a carcass. ('n Aasvoël vreet 'n karkas.)
11. **ntsu** – eagle (arend)

    Ntsu e fofela marung. – An eagle flies towards the clouds. ('n Arend vlieg in die rigting van die wolke.)

Insects and rodents (Insekte en knaagdiere)

1. **kokwana** – insect (insek)

   Kokwana e nyenyane. – An insect is small. ('n Insek is klein.)
2. **seboko** – worm (wurm)

   seboko sa morara – a worm of grape, i.e. a grape worm ('n druiwe-wurm)
3. **letsetse** – flea (vlooi)

   Letsetse le a loma. – A flea bites. ('n Vlooi byt.)
4. **nta** – louse (luis)

   Nta e rata ditshila. – A louse is fond of dirt. ('n Luis is lief vir vuilgoed.)
5. **lephela** – cockroach (kokkerot, kakkerlak)

   Lephela le mathaka dijong. – A cockroach runs all over the food. ('n Kokkerot hardloop oor die kos.)
6. **tshitshidi** – bug (weeluis)

   Tshitshidi e monya madi. – A bug sucks the blood. ('n Weeluis suig die bloed.)
7. **bohlwa** – ant (mier)

   Bohlwa bo kgothetse. – The ant is industrious. ('n Mier is vlytig.)
8. **lefokolodi** – millipede (duisendpoot)

   Lefokolodi le na le maoto a mangata. – A millepede has feet which are many (it has many feet). ('n Duisendpoot het baie pote.)

9. **notshi** – bee (by)

   Notshi e etsa manepe. – A bee makes honey. ('n By maak heuning.)

10. **phepheng** – scorpion (skerpioen)

    Phepheng e a hlaba. – A scorpion stings. ('n Skerpioen steek.)

11. **seboba** – wasp (perdeby)

    Seboba se loma ha bohloko. – A wasp stings painfully. ('n Perdeby steek seer.)

12. **serurubele** – butterfly (skoenlapper)

    Serurubele se na le mebala e metle. – A butterfly has colours which are beautiful, i.e. it has beautiful colours. ('n Skoenlapper het mooi kleure.)

13. **Lerwana** – red ant (rooimier)

14. **tshintshi** – fly (vlieg)

    Mme o bolaya tshintshi. – Mother swats a fly. (Moeder klap die vlieg.)

15. **tweba** – mouse (muis)

    Katse e lelekisa tweba. – A cat chases a mouse. ('n Kat jaag 'n muis.)

16. **kgoto** – rat (rot)

    Kgoto e kgolo ho tweba. – A rat is bigger than a mouse. ('n Rot is groter as 'n muis.)

17. **letlametlo/senqanqane** – frog (padda)

    Letlametlo le a tlola. – A frog leaps. ('n Padda spring.)

    Senqanqane se a tlola. – A frog leaps. ('n Padda spring.)

Sports, athletics and recreation (Sport, atletiek en ontspanning)

1. **bolo** – ball (bal)

   Sebapadi se raha bolo. – A player kicks the ball. ('n Speler skop die bal.)

2. **lebala** – ground (grond)

   lebala la dipapadi – ground of sports, i.e. sports ground/field (sportveld)

3. **tenese** – tennis (tennis)

   Papadi ya tenese e makgethe. – A game of tennis is decent. ('n Spel tennis is ordentlik.)

4. **ditebele** – boxing (boks)

   Papadi ya ditebele e bohloko. – A match of boxing is painful. ('n Boksgeveg is pynlik.)

5. **betjha** (v) – to gamble (om te dobbel)

   Ke betjha ka R10,00. – I gamble with R10,00. (Ek dobbel met R10,00.)

6. **O se ke wa bapala ka bophelo ba hao.** – Do not gamble with your life. (Moenie met jou lewe dobbel nie.)

7. **beisa** (v) – race (resies jaag)

   Ho beisa ke ho matha ka ho hlodisana. – To race is to run in a competition. (Om resies te jaag is om te kompeteer.)

8. **mojaho** – racing (wedren)

   Mojaho wa dipere o a qabola. – Racing of horses is fascinating. ('n Perdewedren is boeiend.)

9. **matha** (v) – to run (om te hardloop)

   Moshemane o matha haholo. – A boy runs a lot. ('n Seun hardloop baie.)

10. **Lebelo** – speed (haastig)

    Ngwana enwa o lebelo. – This child is speedy. (Hierdie kind is haastig.)

11. **mokoka** – stamina (uithouvermoë)

    Hore o mathe halelele, o hloka mokoka. – In order to run a long distance, you need stamina. (Om 'n lang afstand te hardloop moet jy uithouvermoë hê.)

12. **phomola** (v) – rest (rus)

    Ho phomola ho monate. – To rest is pleasurable. (Om te rus is aangenaam.)

13. **qhanolla** (v) – relax (ontspan)

    Ra fihla ra qhanolla. – We arrived and relaxed. (Ons het aangekom en toe ontspan.)

14. **mofufutso** – sweat, perspiration (sweet)

    Sebapadi se qhitsa mofufutso. – A player is sweating/perspiring. (Die speler sweet.)

15. **sesa** (v) – swim (swem)

    Papadi eo ke e ratang ke ho sesa. – A sport that I like is swimming. ('n Sport waarvan ek hou, is swem.)

16. **kwetlisa** (v) – exercise, i.e. physical training (oefeninge doen)

    Ke tsoha hoseng ho kwetlisa bana. – I wake up in the morning to let the children exercise. (Ek staan vroeg in die môre op om die kinders te laat oefeninge doen.)

17. **moletsaphala** – referee (skeidsregter)

    Moletsaphala a qeta papadi. – The referee ended the match/play. (Die skeidsregter het die wedstryd beeïndig.)

Culture (Kultuur)

1. **moetlo** – custom (gewoonte)

   Ke moetlo wa Basotho ho ntsha bohadi. – It is a custom of the Basotho to pay lobola (money paid by a groom to the bride's parents for the marriage). (Dit is die gewoonte van die Basotho om lobola te betaal.)

2. **mohobelo** – dance (dans)

   Banna ba etsa mohobelo. – The men are dancing. (Die manne dans.)

3. **moropa** – drum (tamboer)

   Moropa ona o duma ha monate. – A drum this one sounds well, i.e. this drum sounds well. (Hierdie tamboer klink goed.)

4. **modidietsane** – ululation (gehuil)

   Mosadi o hlaba modidietsane. – A woman ululates well. ('n Vrou weeklaag.)

5. **molodi** – whistle (fluit)

   Tsotsi e letsa molodi bosiu. – A thug sounds a whistle at night, i.e. a thug whistles at night. ('n Boef fluit in die nag.)

6. **kgiba** – gyrate (draai)

   Barwetsana ba a kgiba. – Little girls gyrate. (Die meisies draai in die rondte.)

7. **bina** (v) – sing (sing)

   Bana ba sekolo ba bina ha monate. – Children at school sing harmoniously, i.e. school children sing harmoniously. (Die skoolkinders sing lekker.)

8. **badimo** – spiritual media/guardian angels (geestelike beskermers)

   Ke lorile badimo. – I dreamed about spiritual media/guardian angels. (Ek het van geestelike beskermers gedroom.)

9. **letsopa** – clay (klei)

   Ke bopa pitsa ya letsopa. – I am making a pot of clay. (Ek maak 'n pot van klei.)

10. **letsholo** – group hunting (groep-jagtog)

    Banna ba motse ba tswa letsholo. – Men of the village go out on group hunting. (Die manne van die dorp gaan uit op 'n groep-jagtog.)

11. **letsema** – communal ploughing (gemeenskaplike ploeëry)

    Letsema le thusa batho ba fokolang. – Communal ploughing helps people who are weak, i.e. people who struggle to plough on their own. (Gemeenskaplike ploeëry help die mense wat sukkel.)

12. **Diphehiso** – collective food contribution (gemeenskaplike voedselvoorsiening)

Basadi ba motse ba etsa diphehiso ho thusana. – Women of a community contribute food collectively to help one another. (Die vrouens van 'n gemeenskap dra kos by om mekaar te help.)

13. **lebollo** – initiation (inisiasie, stamskool)

    Lebollo ke sekolo sa thabeng. – Initiation is a traditional school (usuallly on the mountain) where customs and other cultural rites are taught, i.e. the initiation school is usually held on the mountain. (Lebollo is 'n tradisionele skool wat op die berg gehou word.)

14. **dithothokiso** – poems (gedigte)

    Ke rata dithothokiso tse ngotsweng ke Ntsane. – I like the poems which have been written by Ntsane. (Ek hou van die gedigte wat deur Ntsane geskryf is.)

15. **dithoko** – praise songs (lofgedigte)

    Bana ba ithuta dithoko tsa Morena Moshweshwe. – Children are learning the praise songs of King Moshweshwe. (Kinders leer die lofgedigte van koning Mosjesj.)

16. **maele** – proverbs (spreekwoorde)

    Maele a nontsha puo. – Proverbs enrich a language. (Spreekwoorde verryk 'n taal.)

17. **mosollane** – solo (solo)

    Ngwanana o bina mosollane o motle. – A girl sings a beautiful solo. ('n Meisie sing 'n mooi solo.)

Wedding (Bruilof)

1. **lenyalo** – wedding (bruilof)

   E ne e le lenyalo le letle. – It was a wedding which is beautiful, i.e. a beautiful wedding. (Dit was 'n mooi bruilof.)

2. **mokete** – feast/function (funksie)

   Ke lokisetsa mokete wa kolobetso. – I am preparing for a baptismal function. (Ek berei voor vir 'n doopfunksie.)

3. **dijo** – food (kos)

   Dijo di monate. – The food is delicious. (Die kos is lekker.)

4. **dino** – drinks/beverages (drankies)

   Dino tsena di a taha. – These drinks are intoxicating, i.e. these drinks intoxicate. (Hierdie drankies is bedwelmend.)

5. **jwala** – liquor (sterk drank)

   Monna o nwa jwala. – A man drinks liquor. ('n Man drink sterk drank.)

6. **nama** – meat (vleis)

   Ke rekile nama e ngata. – I bought meat which is a lot (i.e. I have bought a lot of meat). (Ek het baie vleis gekoop.)

7. **monyadi** – groom (bruidegom)

   Pitso ke monyadi wa Dimakatso. – Pitso is Dimakatso's groom. (Pitso is Dimakatso se bruidegom.)

8. **monyaduwa** – bride (bruid)

   Dimakatso ke monyaduwa wa Pitso. – Dimakatso is a bride of Pitso (i.e. she is Pitso's bride). (Dimakatso is die bruid van Pitso (d.w.s. sy is Pitso se bruid.)

9. **moetsana** – bridesmaid (strooimeisie)

   Moetsana o felehetsa monyaduwa. – A bridesmaid accompanies the bride. ('n Strooimeisie vergesel die bruid.)

10. **kereke** – church (kerk)

    Banyalani ba kena kerekeng. – The bridal couple enter the church. (Die bruidspaar kom die kerk binne.)

11. **moruti** – minister/pastor (predikant)

    Moruti o hlohonolofatsa banyalani. – The minister blesses the couple. (Die predikant seën die paartjie.)

12. **batswadi** – parents (ouers)

    Batswadi ba boha banyalani. – The parents are looking at the bridal couple. (Die ouers kyk na die bruidspaar.)

13. **reng** – ring (ring)

    Pitso o rekile reng e turang. – Pitso has bought a ring which is expensive. (Pitso het 'n duur ring gekoop.)

14. **kuku** – cake (koek)

    Banyalani ba rekile kuku e maemo a mararo. – The bridal couple have bought a three-layered cake. (Die troupaar het `n koek met drie lae gekoop.)

15. **dinepe/ditshwantsho** – photos (foto's)

    Banyalani ba nka ditshwantsho. – The bridal couple have photographs taken. (Die troupaar laat foto's neem.)

16. **mollo** – fire (vuur)

    Ntate o besa mollo. – Daddy makes a fire. (Pa maak vuur.)

17. **kgomo** – cow (koei)

    Ba hlaba kgomo. – They slaughter a cow. (Hulle slag 'n koei.)

18. **nku** – sheep (skaap)

    Letlalo la nku le a oma. – The skin of a sheep is drying up. (Die vel van 'n skaap word droog.)

19. **bua** (v) – skin (die vel afstroop)

    Banna ba bua kgomo le nku. – The men are skinning a cow and a sheep. (Die manne slag 'n koei en 'n skaap.)

20. **Mmino wa lenyalo o monate.** – Music of a wedding is enjoyable/beautiful. (Die musiek van 'n bruilof is aangenaam.)

21. **ditholwana** – fruit (vrugte)

    Basadi ba ebola ditholwana. – The women are peeling the fruit. (Die vrouens skil die vrugte af.)

22. **mafura** – fat (vet)

    Nama ena e mafura. – Meat this is fat, i.e. this meat is fat. (Hierdie vleis is vetterig.)

23. **tswekere** – sugar (suiker)

    Dikuku tsena ha di na tswekere. – The cakes these have no sugar, i.e. these cakes have no sugar. (Hierdie koekies bevat nie suiker nie.)

24. **letswai** – salt (sout)

    Letswai le fedile. – The salt is finished. (Die sout is klaar.)

25. **mose** – dress (rok)

    Mose wa monyaduwa o motle. – The dress of the bride is beautiful. (Die rok van die bruid is mooi.)

26. **sutu** – suit (pak klere)

    Sutu ya monyadi e ntle. – The suit of the groom is beautiful. (Die pak klere van die bruidegom is mooi.)

27. **dieta** – shoes (skoene)

    Dieta tsa mosadi di ntle. – The shoes of the woman are beautiful. (Die skoene van die vrou is mooi.)

28. **tafole** – table (tafel)

    Tafole e makgethe. – The table is neat. (Die tafel is netjies.)

29. **tente** – tent (tent)

    Tente e a dutla. – The tent is leaking. (Die tent lek.)

30. **hlaba** – slaughter (slag)

    Basadi ba hlaba dikgoho. – Women are slaughtering the fowls. (Die vrouens slag die hoenders.)

31. **ja** (v) – eat (eat)

    O ja haholo. – You eat a lot. (Jy eet baie.)

32. **nwa** – drink (drink)

    Moeti o nwa metsi. – The visitor is drinking water. (Die besoeker drink water.)

33. **metsi** – water (water)

    Tlisang metsi a ho apeha/pheha. – Bring the water for cooking. (Bring water om mee te kook.)

34. **lebese** – milk (melk)

    Tshela lebese teyeng. – Pour milk into the tea. (Gooi melk in die tee.)

35. **bohobe** – bread (brood)

    A re jeng bohobe. – Let us eat bread. (Laat ons brood eet.)

36. **kgemere** – ginger beer (gemmerbier)

    Kgemere e phodile. – The ginger beer is cool. (Die gemmerbier is koel.)

37. **dikahare** – tripe (afval)

    Dikahare tsa nku di monate. – The tripe of a sheep is delicious. (Die afval van `n skaap is lekker.)

Funeral (Begrafnis)

1. **shwa** (v) – die (sterf)

   Ho shwa ho bohloko. – To die is painful i.e. dying is sad. (Om te sterf is hartseer.)

2. **mofu** – dead person (oorledene)

   Mofu o isitswe tlong ya kgatsetso. – The dead person has been taken to the morgue. (Die oorledene is na die dodehuis gevat.)

3. **Lebitla** – grave (graf)

   Lebitla ha le na tlholo. – A grave has no victory. ('n Graf het geen oorwinning nie.)

4. **setsha sa bafu/mabitla** – cemetery, graveyard (begraafplaas)

   Mabitla ana a se a tletse. – A graveyard this one is already full, i.e. this cemetery is already full. (Hierdie begraafplaas is reeds vol.)

5. **phupu** – funeral (begrafnis)

   Phupu e tla tshwarelwa kerekeng. – The funeral service will be conducted in church. (Die begrafnisdiens sal in die kerk gehou word.)

6. **setopo** – corpse (lyk)

Setopo se fumanwe hoseng. – The corpse was found in the morning. (Die lyk is in die oggend gevind.)

7. **lekese** – coffin (doodskis)

   Lekese la ngwana le lesweu. – A child's coffin is white. ('n Doodskis vir 'n kind is wit.)

8. **mohlolohadi** – widow (weduwee)

   Mantshebo e se e le mohlolohadi. – Mantshebo is now a widow. (Mantshebo is nou 'n weduwee.)

9. **kgutsana** – orphan (weeskind)

   Kgutsana e a hlokomelwa. – An orphan is looked after. ('n Weeskind word versorg.)

10. **tshedisa** – console (vertroos)

    Phutheho e tshedisa Mantshebo. – The congregation consoles Mantshebo. (Die gemeente vertroos Mantshebo.)

11. **lla** (v) – cry (huil)

    Batho ba hlokahaletsweng ba a lla. – People who are bereaved cry. (Mense wat bedroef is, huil.)

12. **maswabi** – sadness (droefheid)

    Ka maswabi a maholo ke lla le wena. – With sadness which is great I cry with you, i.e. with great sadness I cry or sympathize with you. (Met groot droefheid huil ek saam met jou.)

13. **kotsi** – accident, danger (ongeluk)

    kotsi ya koloi – an accident of a car, i.e. a car accident ('n motorongeluk)

14. **nehela moya** (v) – give up the ghost (die gees gee)

    Mokudi a nehela moya. – The patient gave up the ghost. (Die pasiënt het die gees gegee.)

15. **ila** (v) – fast, deny oneself, mourn (vas, rou)

    Batho ba hlokahaletsweng ba a ila. – People who are bereaved mourn. (Mense wat bedroef is, rou.)

16. **sesila** – bad luck (ongelukkigheid, teëspoed)

    Ba hlatswa sesila. – They get rid of bad luck. (Hulle raak ontslae van teëspoed.)

17. **bohloko** – pain (pyn)

    Ke utlwa bohloko. – I feel pain. (Ek voel die pyn.)

18. **mahlomola** – grief, misery (leed)

Ke mahlomola a maholo ho lahlehelwa ke mme. – It is grief which is great to lose one's mother, i.e. it is great grief to lose one's mother. (Dit is groot leed om 'n mens se moeder te verloor.)

19. **tsoho** – resurrection (opstanding)

    Ke dumela ho tsoho ya bafu. – I believe in the resurrection of the dead. (Ek glo aan die opstanding uit die dood.)

20. **bolaya** – kill (doodmaak)

    O se ke wa bolaya. – Thou shall not kill. (Jy mag niedoodmaak nie.)

21. **thapo** – weeds, i.e. mourning attire – usually black (weduweedrag/rouklere)

    Mohlolohadi o apere thapo. – A widow is dressed in weeds. ('n Weduwee het rouklere aangetrek.)

Trade, commerce and industry (Handel, koophandel en nywerheid)

1. **kgwebo** – trade (handel)

   Kgwebo e a ata. – Trade is increasing. (Handel vermeerder.)

2. **moruo** – economy (ekonomie)

   Moruo wa naha ya rona o tsitsitse. – The economy of our country is sound. (Die ekonomie van ons land is gesond.)

3. **rekisa** – sell (verkoop)

   Ke rekisa matokomane. – I sell peanuts. (Ek verkoop grondboontjies.)

4. **hweba** – to trade (om handel te dryf)

   Dinaha di hweba ka kgauta. – Countries they trade in gold, i.e. countries trade in gold. (Lande dryf handel met goud.)

5. **thepa** – goods (goedere)

   Thepa ena e ngata. – The goods these are too much, i.e. there are too many goods. (Die goedere is te veel.)

6. **phahlo** – parcel (pakkie)

   Ke phahlo ya mang ee? – It is a parcel for who this one? i.e. whose parcel is this? (Wie se pakkie is hierdie?)

7. **tjhelete** – money (geld)

   Ha ke na tjhelete. – I do not have money. (Ek het nie geld nie.)

8. **nyollelo** – increase (verhoging)

   Basebetsi ba kopa nyollelo. – The workers are asking for an increase. (Die werkers vra vir 'n verhoging.)

9. **theolelo** – decrease (vermindering)

   Baahi ba thabetse theolelo ya tefo ya motlakase. – The residents are happy about the reduction in electricity charges. (Die inwoners is bly oor die vermindering van die elektrisiteitstariewe.)

10. **mosebetsi** – work (werk)

    Mosebetsi ha o yo. – Work is not available. (Daar is geen werk nie.)

11. **lekgetho** – tax (belasting)

    Ke lefa lekgetho. – I pay tax. (Ek betaal belasting.)

12. **phaello** – interest (rente)

    Tjhelete ya ka e hodisitswe ke phaello bankeng. – Money of mine is increased by interest at the bank, i.e. my money has grown because of interest at the bank. (My geld het meer geword by die bank as gevolg van rente.)

13. **banka** – bank (bank)

    Banka e boloka tjhelete. – A bank keeps money. ('n Bank hou geld.)

14. **boloka** (v) – save (spaar)

    Ke boloka tjhelete bankeng. – I save money at the bank. (Ek spaar my geld by die bank.)

15. **hula** (v) – withdraw (onttrek)

    Seipati o hula lekgolo la diranta. – Seipati withdraws one hundred rand. (Seipati onttrek een honderd rand.)

16. **matsete** – investments (beleggings)

    Matsete a a hola. – Investments are growing. (Beleggings groei.)

17. **phelekanyetsa** – cheat (verneuk)

    O se ke wa phelekanyetsa sefofu. – Do not cheat a blind person. (Jy moet nie 'n blinde verneuk nie.)

18. **tjhona** – become broke (om platsak te wees)

    Ha o sa sebetse o a tjhona. – If you do not work you get broke. (As jy nie werk nie, sal jy platsak raak.)

19. **hloma** (v) – become successful (om suksesvol te wees)

    Ke fumane mosebetsi mme ke a hloma. – I got work, as a result I became successful. (Ek het werk gekry, as gevolg daarvan is ek suksesvol.)

20. **ranta** – rand (rand)

    Ke lefile ranta. – I paid one rand. (Ek het 'n rand betaal.)

21. **sente** – cent (sent)

    Nkgono o lahlile sente. – Granny has lost a cent. (Ouma het 'n sent verloor.)

22. **feme** – firm (firma)

    Ke feme e kgolo. – It is a firm which is big, i.e. it is a big firm. (Dit is 'n groot firma.)

Law and order (Wet en orde)

1. **molao** – law (wet)

   Molao o thata. – the law is strict. (Die wet is streng.)

2. **lepolesa** – police (polisie)

   Lepolesa le tshwara leshodu. – A policeman arrests a thief. ('n Polisieman arresteer 'n dief.)

3. **kgotla** – court (hof)

   Sesenyi se isitswe kgotla. – A wrongdoer has been taken to court. ('n Kwaaddoener is hof toe geneem.)

4. **tjhankane, teronko** – prison, jail (tronk)

   Tjhankane ha e monate – prison is not pleasant (die tronk is nie aangenaam nie)

5. **mahlahahlela** – handcuffs, chains (handboeie)

   Moqosuwa o tlangwa ka mahlahahlela. – The accused is fastened with handcuffs. (Die aangeklaagde is met handboeie geboei.)

6. **tshwara** (v) – arrest, hold (arresteer)

   Ke tla o tshwarisa mapoleseng. – I will have you charged by the police. (Ek sal jou laat aankla deur die polisie.)

7. **ahlola** (v) – judge (oordeel)

   Sesenyi se a ahlolwa. – A wrongdoer is being judged. ('n Kwaaddoener word veroordeel.)

8. **ahlola** – sentence (vonnis)

   Moahlodi o ahlola mmolai. – The magistrate sentences the murderer. (Die landdros vonnis die moordenaar.)

9. **nyewe** – case (saak)

   Nyewe ya hao e boima. – Case of yours is heavy, i.e. your case is heavy. (Jou saak is moeilik.)

10. **qosa** (v) – accuse, charge (aankla)

    Lepolesa le qosa Mpho ka boshodu. – A policeman accuses Mpho of theft. ('n Polisieman kla Mpho aan vir diefstal.)

11. **sotla** (v) – punish (straf)

Molebedi wa teronko o sotla batshwaruwa. – A warder punishes the prisoners. (Die tronkbewaarder straf die gevangenes.)

12. **leta** – wait (wag)

    Moqosuwa o leta hore a bitswe. – The accused waits to be called. (Die aangeklaagde wag om geroep te word.)

13. **lokolla** (v) – release (vrylaat)

    Motshwaruwa o a lokollwa hona jwale. – The prisoner is being released just now. (Die gevangene word nou vrygelaat.)

14. **kwalla** (v) – lock up, imprison (toesluit)

    Sesenyi se a kwallwa hona jwale. – The wrongdoer is being locked up. (Die kwaaddoener word toegesluit.)

15. **boipiletso** – appeal (appèl)

    Motshwaruwa o etsa boipiletso. .– The prisoner lodges an appeal. (Die gevangene teken appèl aan.)

16. **fanyeha** (v) – hang (hang)

    Ba fanyeha sesenyi. – They hang the wrongdoer. (Hulle hang die kwaaddoener.)

17. **thapo** – rope (galgtou)

    Moqosuwa o ahloletswe thapo. – The accused has been sentenced to death by hanging. (Die beskuldigde is tot 'n galgdood gevonnis.)

18. **toka** – justice (regverdigheid)

    Ha ho be le toka lefatsheng. – Let there be justice in the world. (Laat daar regverdigheid op aarde wees.)

19. **botlokotsebe** – crime, deliquency (misdaad)

    Baahi ba sebetsa le mapolesa ho fedisa botlokotsebe. – Residents are working with the police to stop crime. (Inwoners werk saam met die polisie om misdaad stop te sit.)

20. **tsotsi** – thug (boef)

    Tsotsi e kgathatsa batho. – A thug harasses people. ('n Boef pla mense.)

21. **lelaeta** – hooligan, ruffian (skurk)

    Lelaeta le solla bosiu. – A hooligan roams at night. ('n Skurk loop in die nag rond.)

22. **beta** (v) – rape, outrage (verkrag)

    Lelaeta le beta basadi naheng. – A hooligan rapes women in the veld. ('n Skurk verkrag vrouens in die veld.)

23. **tsuba** (v) – smoke (rook)

    O se ke wa tsuba. – Do not smoke. (Moenie rook nie.)

24. **matekwane** – dagga (dagga)

    O se ke wa tsuba matekwane. – Do not smoke dagga. (Moenie dagga rook nie.)

25. **leqwetha/akgente/moemedi** – lawyer (prokureur)

    Leqwetha la ka le hlalefile. – My lawyer is brilliant. (My prokureur is slim.)

26. **sesenyi** – wrongdoer (kwaaddoener)

    Sesenyi se senyetsa batho. – The wrongdoer wrongs people. ('n Kwaaddoener doen mense 'n onreg aan.)

27. **motjhotjhisi** – prosecutor (staatsaanklaer)

    Ke motjhotjhisi ya bohlale. – He/she is a sharp prosecutor. (Hy/sy is 'n knap staatsaanklaer.)

28. **mahlodi** – judge (regter)

    Ke moahlodi ya sedi. – He/she is a judge who is clever. (Hy/sy is 'n slim regter.)

29. **makgistrata/moahlodi** – magistrate (landdros)

    Makgistrata/moahlodi o halefile. – The magistrate is angry. (Die landdros is kwaad.)

Social matters (Maatskaplike sake)

1. **atamela** – approach, come nearer to (benader)

   Atamela ho Jehova. – Come nearer to Jehova. (Kom nader aan God.)

2. **atisa** – increase, multiply (vermenigvuldig)

   Atisa mahobe. – Increase the bread. (Vermenigvuldig die brood.)

3. **ahlama** (v) – to open the mouth (om die mond oop te maak)

   Ke a ahlama. – I am opening my mouth. (Ek maak my mond oop.)

4. **ahlamisa** (v) – cause to open (maak dat die mond oop is)

   Kwena e ahlamisa molomo wa yona. – A crocodile opens mouth of its, i.e. a crocodile opens its mouth. (Die krokodil maak sy mond oop.)

5. **amohela** – receive (ontvang)

   Ke amohela molaetsa. – I receive the message. (Ek ontvang die boodskap.)

6. **arola** – divide (verdeel)

   Ha o arola leshome ka pedi o fumana hlano – When you divide ten by two you get five. (Wanneer jy tien deur twee deel kry jy vyf.)

7. **apesa** (v) – clothe, dress (klee)

   Apesa ngwana hobane ho a bata. – Dress the child because it is cold. (Klee die kind want dit is koud.)

8. **bua** (v) – talk, tell, speak (praat)

   Bua nnete. – Tell the truth. (Praat die waarheid.)

9. **bua** (v) – skin (die vel afstroop)

   Banna ba bua kgomo. – The men are skinning the cow. (Die mans stroop die vel van 'n koei af.)

10. **bana** – children (kinders)

    Bana ba kena sekolo. – Children are entering school, i.e. they are at school. (Kinders gaan skool toe.)

11. **bona** (verb) – see (sien)

    Ke bona ka mahlo. – I see with my eyes. (Ek sien met my oë.)

12. **bona** (adverb) – this

    Jwala bona bo monate. – Liquor this is delicious, i.e. this liquour is delicious. (Hierdie sterk drank is lekker.)

13. **bona** (pronoun) – they, them (hulle)

    Ke tla botsa bona. – I will ask them. (Ek sal hulle vra.)

14. **besa** – make fire, roast (vuur maak)

    Ke besa mollo. – I make fire. (Ek maak vuur.)

    Banna ba besa nama. – The men are roasting meat. (Die mans braai vleis.)

15. **botsa** (v) – ask (vra)

    Ke o botsa potso e boima. – I am asking you a difficult question. (Ek vra jou 'n moeilike vraag.)

16. **bobebe** (adjective) – easy, light (maklik, lig)

    Ngwana o botsa potso e bobebe. – A child is asking an easy question. ('n Kind vra 'n maklike vraag.)

17. **bala** (v) – read (lees)

    Mosuwe o bala buka. – A teacher is reading a book. ('n Onderwyser lees 'n boek.)

18. **bula** (v) – open (maak oop)

    Ke bula monyako. – I open the door. (Ek maak die deur oop.)

19. **bela** (v) – boil (kook)

    Etsa teye, metsi a a bela. – Make tea, the water is boiling. (Maak tee, die water kook.)

20. **bola** (v) – rot, decay, go off (verrot, word sleg)

Dijo di a bola. – The food is going off, rotting. (Die kos verrot, bederf.)

21. **dula** (v) – sit, stay (sit, bly)

Monnamoholo o dula setulong. – The old man sits on a chair. (Die ou man sit op 'n stoel.)

22. **dila** (v) – smear, apply (smeer)

Banna ba dila tsela ka sekontiri. – The men smear the road with tar. (Die mans smeer die pad met teer.)

23. **fiela** (v) – sweep (vee)

Moshemane o thusa ngwanana ho fiela. – The boy helps the girl to sweep. (Die seun help die meisie om te vee.)

24. **fala** (v) – scrape (krap)

Mosadi o fala pitsa. – The woman scrapes a pot. (Die vrou krap 'n pot.)

25. **fola** (v) – heal, become well, (gesond word)

Mokudi o se a fola. – The patient is now becoming well. (Die pasiënt word gesond.)

Batshwaruwa ba a fola hore ba balwe. – The prisoners queue so that they can be counted. (Die gevangenes staan tou sodat hulle getel kan word.)

26. **fula** (v) – graze (wei)

Dikgomo di a fula. – The cattle are grazing. (Die koeie wei.)

27. **fela** (v) – get finished, wane (klaar raak)

Mollo o a fela. – The fire is getting finished/waning. (Die vuur raak klaar of die vuur gaan dood.)

28. **hapa** (v) – capture (vang, aangryp)

Mmino o hapa maikutlo. – Music captures feelings. (Musiek gryp die gevoelens aan.)

29. **hula** (v) – pull (trek)

Dipere di hula kariki. – The horses pull a cart. (Die perde trek 'n wa.)

30. **hola** (v) – grow (groei)

Lesea le a hola. – The baby is growing. (Die baba groei.)

31. **haufi** (adverb) – near, soon (naby, binnekort)

O se ke wa ema haufi le terene. – Do not stand near the train. (Moenie naby die trein staan nie.)

32. **hana** (v) – refuse (weier)

Ngwana o hana ho robala. – The child refuses to sleep. (Die kind wil nie slaap nie, d.w.s. hy/sy weier om te slaap.)

33. **hama** (v) – milk (melk)

Modisa o hama kgomo. – A shepherd milks the cow. (Die herder melk die koei.)

34. **hata** (v) – trample, step (trap)

O se ke wa hata noha mohatleng. – Do not trample a snake on the tail. (Moenie op 'n slang se stert trap nie.)

35. **hasa** (v) – sprinkle, spread (sprei)

Moruti o hasa evangedi. – A minister spreads the gospel. ('n Predikant verkondig die evangelie.)

36. **hema** (v) – breathe (asemhaal)

Nko e thibane, ke hema ka molomo. – My nose is blocked, I breathe through my mouth. (My neus is toe, ek haal deur my mond asem.)

37. **hampe** (adverb) – badly, seriously (sleg, ernstig)

Nkgono o kula hampe. – Grandmother is ill seriously, i.e. she is seriously ill. (Ouma is ernstig siek.)

38. **hara** (adverb) – among, inside, in the middle of (tussen, binne, in die middel van)

Esele e eme hara tsela. – A donkey is standing in the middle of the road. ('n Donkie staan in die middel van die pad.)

39. **hora** (n) – hour (uur)

Ke hora ya bosupa. – It is the hour of seven, i.e. it is seven o'clock. (Dit is seweuur.)

40. **hore** (adverb) – that, so that, in order that (sodat, omdat)

Ke batla hore ngwana a robale. – I want the child to fall asleep. (Ek wil hê die kind moet slaap.)

41. **hira** (v) – hire (huur)

Ke ilo hira koloi. – I am going to hire a car. (Ek gaan 'n motor huur.)

42. **ja** (v) – eat (eet)

Mmutla o ja sehwete. – A hare eats a carrot. ('n Haas eet 'n wortel.)

43. **jala** (v) – plant (plant, kweek)

Ba jala dipalesa. – They plant flowers. (Hulle kweek blomme.)

44. **jo!** (interjection) – oh! (o!)

Jo! ke tshaba lefu. – Oh! I am afraid of death. (O! ek is bang vir die dood.)

45. **kena** (v) – enter (kom, stap in)

Phutheho e a kena kerekeng. – The congregation enters the church. (Die gemeente kom die kerk binne.)

46. **kuta** (v) – cut, shave (kap, sny)

Ke kuta jwang. – I cut grass. (Ek sny gras.)

47. **lapa** (v) – starve (honger wees)

Bana ba Ntswaki ba a lapa. – Ntswaki's children are starving. (Ntswaki se kinders ly honger.)

48. **lakatsa** (v) – desire, wish, long for (begeer)

Ke lakatsa seno se phodileng. – I desire a cool drink. (Ek begeer 'n koue drankie.)

49. **lata** (v) – fetch (haal)

O ilo lata tjhelete. – He/she has gone to fetch money. (Hy/sy het gaan geld haal.)

50. **lala** (v) – sleep, abide by, spend a night at (bly, vertoef)

Lala ho nna. – Stay with me. (Bly by my.)

51. **lebala** – forget (vergeet)

O se ke wa lebala. – Do not forget. (Moenie vergeet nie.)

52. **lemala** (v) – get hurt (beseer word)

O tla lemala ha o bapala hampe. – You will get hurt if you play roughly. (Jy sal seerkry as jy rof speel.)

53. **lesela** (n) – cloth (lap)

lesela le lesweu – a white cloth ('n wit lap)

54. **lefielo** (n) – broom (besem)

Lefielo le lekgutshwane. – A broom is short. ('n Besem is kort.)

55. **lemati** (n) – door (deur)

Kwala lemati, ho a bata. – Close the door, it is cold. (Maak asseblief die deur toe, dit is koud.)

56. **lehlafi** (n) – door (deur)

Ke penta lehlafi. – I paint the door. (Ek verf die deur.)

57. **lerapo** (n) – thong, piece of leather string (riem)

Ntja e kgaotse lerapo. – A dog bit off the thong/piece of leather string. ('n Hond het die riem afgebyt.)

58. **lesapo** (n) – bone (been)

Ke kokona lesapo. – I suck a bone. (Ek suig 'n been.)

59. **loma** (v) – bite (byt)

ntja e bohale, e lomang – a ferocious dog, a dog that bites ('n kwaai hond, 'n hond wat byt)

Domestic issues and relations (Huislike sake en familiebetrekkinge)

1. **hae/haeso** – home (huis, tuis)

   Ke hae mona. – It is home here. (Dit is my tuiste hier.)

   Ke ya heso. – I am going to my home. (Ek gaan na my huis toe.)

2. **heno/haeno** – your home (jou huis)

   O tla robala heno (haeno). – You will sleep at your home. (Jy sal by jou huis slaap.)

3. **habo** – at his/her home/place (by sy/haar huis)

   Habo ke Kapa. – His/her home or place is the Cape. (Sy/haar huis/plek is die Kaap.)

4. **ha bona** – at their home or place (by hulle huis/plek)

   Ba ile ha bona. – They have gone to their home/place. (Hulle het na hul huis gegaan.)

5. **lelapa** – home/place (woning, huis, tuis)

   Monna o sebeletsa lelapa la hae. – A man works for home of his, i.e. a man works for his home. ('n Man werk vir sy woning/huis.)

6. **motse** – village/home (dorp)

   Motse wa Tshwane o moholo. – The city of Pretoria is big. (Die stad van Pretoria is groot.)

7. **phaposi** – room (kamer)

   Ntlo e na le diphaposi tse hlano. – A house has rooms which are five, i.e. it has five rooms. ('n Huis het vyf kamers, 'n vyfvertrekhuis.)

8. **kamore** – bedroom (slaapkamer)

   Kgantsha kamore ya baeti. – Light up the room of the visitors. (Verlig die kamer van die besoekers, skakel die ligte van die besoekers se kamer aan.)

9. **kitjhine** – kitchen (kombuis)

   Dijo di phehwa kitjheneng. – Food is cooked in the kitchen. (Kos word in die kombuis gekook.)

10. **sekotlolo** – dish (skottel)

    Ha o qeta ho ja, o hlatswe sekotlolo. – When you finish eating, you should wash the dish/plate. (Wanneer jy klaar geëet het, moet jy die bord was.)

11. **sejana** – plate (bord)

    Ke jela sejaneng. – I eat from a plate. (Ek eet uit die bord.)

12. **mme** – mother (moeder, ma)

    Ke rata mme wa ka. – I love mother of mine, i.e. I love my mother. (Ek is lief vir my ma.)

13. **ntate** – father

    Ntate o moholo ho malome. – My father is older than my uncle. (My vader is ouer as my oom.)

14. **kgaitsedi** – sister, i.e. brother referring to sister (suster, d.w.s. broer verwys na suster)

    Mmaletsatsi ke kgaitsedi ya ka. – Mmaletsatsi is sister of mine. (Mmaletsatsi is my suster.)

15. **kgaitsedi** – brother, i.e. sister referring to brother (suster verwys na broer)

    Tshepo ke kgaitsedi ya ka. – Tshepo is brother of mine, i.e. he is my brother. (Tshepo is my broer.)

16. **moholwane** – elder brother (ouer broer)

    Molepo ke moholwane wa Mohapi. – Molepo is elder brother to Mohapi. (Molapo is Mohapi se ouer/oudste broer.)

17. **monyane** – junior brother (kleiner/jonger broer)

    Mohapi ke monyane wa Molepo. – Mohapi is junior brother to Molepo. (Mohapi is Molepo se jonger broer.)

18. **ausi** – elder sister (ouer suster)

    Nnuku ke ausi wa rona. – Nnuku is elder sister of ours, i.e. she is our elder sister. (Nnuku is ons ouer suster.)

19. **aubuti** – elder brother (ouer broer)

    Mpho ke aubuti wa lona. – Mpho is elder brother of yours. (Mpho is julle ouer broer.)

20. **malome** – uncle, i.e. mother's brother (oom)

    Thabo ke malome. – Thabo is my uncle. (Thabo is my oom.)

21. **rangwane** – uncle, i.e. father's younger brother (oom, d.w.s. pa se jonger broer)

    Morake ke rangwane. – Morake is (my) uncle. (Morake is my oom.)

22. **ntatemoholo** – grandfather/father's elder brother (oupa)

    Ntatemoholo o se a tsofetse. – Grandfather is already old. (Oupa is al oud.)

23. **nkgono** – grandmother or mother's elder sister (ouma)

    Nkgono o sa le motjha. – Grandmother is still young. (Ouma is nog jonk.)

24. **motswala** – cousin (kleinneef, kleinniggie)

    Motho a ka nyala motswala wa hae. – A person may marry his/her cousin. ('n Persoon kan met sy kleinniggie trou.)

25. **moahelani** – neighbour (buurman)

    Re phedisana ha monate le moahelani wa rona. – We live well with neighbour of ours. (Ons lewe gesellig met ons buurman.)

26. **mmangwane** – aunt, i.e. mother's younger sister (ma se jonger suster)

27. **rakgadi** – aunt, i.e. father's sister

    Nthato ke rakgadi. – Nthato is my aunt. (Nthato is my tante.)

28. **batswadi** – parents (ouers)

    Ho monate ho ba le batswadi. – It is fine (enjoyable) to have parents. (Dit is lekker om ouers te hê.)

29. **bana** – children (kinders)

    Bana ba bapala ka ntle. – The children play outside. (Die kinders speel buitekant.)

30. **lesea** – baby (baba(tjie))

    Lesea le lla bosiu bohle. – A baby cries night whole, i.e. a baby cries the whole night. (Die babatjie huil die hele nag.)

31. **raka** – cupboard (kas)

    Bula raka. – Open the cupboard. (Maak die kas oop.)

32. **kopi** – cup (koppie)

    Kopi e tletse kofi. – The cup is full of coffee. (Die koppie is vol koffie.)

33. **lebekere** – mug (beker)

    Ntatemoholo o nwa kofi ka lebekere. – Grandfather drinks coffee from a mug. (Oupa drink koffie uit 'n beker.)

34. **kgalase** – glass (glas)

    Kgalase e tjhwatlehile. – The glass is broken/smashed. (Die glas is stukkend.)

35. **thipa** – knife (mes)

    Tlisa thipa e bohale. – Bring a sharp knife. (Bring 'n skerp mes.)

36. **foroko** – fork (vurk)

    foroko e hlabang – a sharp fork ('n skerp vurk)

37. **pane** – pan (pan)

    Rakgadi o hadika mahe ka pane. – Aunt fries eggs in a pan. (Tante braai die eiers in 'n pan.)

38. **pitsa** – pot (pot)

Pitsa e maoto a mararo e bitswa mmadikotwana. – A pot with legs that are three is called mmadikotwana. ('n Pot met drie pote word mmadikotwana genoem.)

39. **setofo** – stove (stoof)

Setofo se a tjhesa. – A stove is hot. ('n Stoof is warm.)

40. **paola** – brazier (konka)

Mosi wa paola o matla. – The smoke of a brazier is strong. (Die rook van 'n konka is sterk.)

41. **bethe** – bed (bed)

Ke paqame betheng. – I am lying on a bed. (Ek lê op 'n bed.)

42. **lakane** – sheet (laken)

Kgaitsedi o hlatswa lakane. – Sister is washing a sheet. (Suster was 'n laken.)

43. **kobo** – blanket (kombers)

A re hlatsweng dikobo. – Let us wash the blankets. (Laat ons die komberse was.)

44. **mosamo** – pillow (kussing)

Mosamo ona o matofotofo. – Pillow this is cosy, i.e. this pillow is cosy. (Hierdie kussing is sag.)

45. **diphate** – blankets (komberse)

Diphate di futhumetse. – The blankets are warm. (Die komberse is warm.)

46. **mealo** – bedding (beddegoed)

O lokisitse mealo? – Have you prepared the bedding? (Het jy die beddegoed reggemaak? Het jy die bed opgemaak?)

47. **otsela** – become drowsy (vaak word)

Le se ke la otsela sekolong. – Do not be drowsy at school. (Julle moenie by die skool vaak word nie.)

48. **robala** (v) – sleep (slaap)

Ke batla ho robala. – I want to sleep. (Ek wil slaap.)

49. **tsoha** – rise (opstaan)

Kgarebe e tsoha hoseng. – A lass rises early in the morning. ('n Meisie staan vroeg in die môre op.)

50. **phaphama** (v) – wake up (wakker word)

Ke ile ka phaphama ka hora ya pele hoseng. – I woke up at the hour of one in the morning, i.e. at one o' clock. (Ek het eenuur in die oggend wakker geword.)

51. **hlapa** (v) – wash (was)

    Hlapa maoto. – Wash the feet. (Was die voete.)

52. **tola** (v) – bathe (afspoel, bad)

    Ke tola ka metsi a foofo. – I bathe with water that is lukewarm. (Ek spoel af met louwarm water, ek bad in louwarm water.)

53. **kama** (v) – comb (kam)

    Malome o kama moriri. – Uncle combs his hair. (Oom kam sy hare.)

54. **otlolla** (v) – stretch (strek)

    Ke otlolla mesifa. – I stretch the muscles. (Ek oefen die spiere.)

55. **sidila/silla** (v) – iron, stretch, massage (stryk)

    Mme o sidila hempe ya mora. – Mother irons the shirt of a son, i.e. she irons the son's shirt. (Moeder stryk die seun se hemp.)

56. **tshasa/tlola** (v) – apply ointment (salf (aan) smeer)

    Mooki o tshasa mokudi ka moriana. – A nurse applies ointment on the patient. (Die verpleegster smeer die salf aan die pasiënt.)

57. **hlwekisa** (v) – clean (skoonmaak)

    Banana ba hlwekisa ntlo. – The girls are cleaning the house. (Die meisies maak die huis skoon.)

58. **silafatsa** (v) – dirty, soil (vuilmaak)

    Bashemane ba silafatsa ntlo. – The boys are dirtying the house. (Die seuns maak die huis vuil.)

59. **kwala** – close (toemaak)

    Kwala monyako hle! – Close the door, please! (Maak asseblief die deur toe!)

60. **bula** (v) – open (oopmaak)

    Bula monyako ka pele! – Open the door quickly! (Maak asseblief die deur gou oop!)

61. **fonane** – good night (goeienaand)

    Fonaneng bahaeso. – Good night, colleagues. (Goeienaand, kollegas.)

62. **sala** – remain, stay (bly, agterbly)

    Sala hantle. – Stay well, i.e. one person.

    Salang hantle. – Stay well, i.e. more than one person because of -ng. (Laat dit goed gaan.)

63. **tsamaya** – go (loop, gaan)

    Tsamaya hantle. – Go well, i.e. one person. (Mooi loop.)

Tsamayang hantle. – Go well, i.e. more than one person because of -ng. (Mooi loop.)

64. **lora** (v) – dream (droom)

    Ke lora ha monate. – I dream well. (Ek droom lekker.)

65. **motho** – person (persoon, 'n mens)

    Motho ke sebopuwa sa Modimo. – Man is a creature of God. (Die mens is 'n skepsel van God.)

    Motho o lokela ho hlonepha setjhaba. – A person is obliged to respect the nation. ('n Mens moet die volk eer.)

66. **monna** – man, husband (man)

    Monna ha a boi. – A man is not cowardly. ('n Man is nie lafhartig nie.)

    Tshediso ke monna wa Matshediso. – Tshediso is a husband to Matshediso. (Tshediso is Matshediso se man.)

67. **mosadi** – woman, wife (vrou)

    Mosadi wa ka o motle. – My wife is beautiful. (My vrou is mooi.)

    Moleboheng ke mosadi wa nnete. – Moleboheng is a true woman. (Moleboheng is 'n opregte vrou.)

68. **mora** – son (seun)

    Molefi ke mora wa ka. – Molefi is a son of mine, i.e. he is my son. (Molefi is my seun.)

69. **moradi** – daughter (dogter)

    Pontsho ke moradi wa Nkatlo. – Pontsho is Nkatlo's daughter. (Pontsho is Nkatlo se dogter.)

70. **morwetsana** – young woman, lass (nooi)

    Seipone ke morwetsana ya makgethe. – Seipone is a young woman who is decent. (Seipone is 'n ordentlike nooi.)

71. **ngwanana** – girl (meisie)

    Ngwanana o kgola dipalesa. – A girl picks flowers. ('n Meisie pluk blomme.)

72. **Moshemane** – boy (seun)

    Moshemane o raha bolo. – A boy kicks the ball. ('n Seun skop die bal.)

73. **mohlankana** – young man, lad (seun, knaap)

    Mohlankana o mafolofolo. – A young man is energetic. ('n Knaap is energiek.)

74. **nako** – time (tyd)

    Ke nako mang? – What time is it? (Hoe laat is dit?)

75. **naha** – country, land (land)

Naha yohle e tala. – Land whole is green, i.e. the whole land is green. (Die hele land is groen.)

Afrika Borwa ke naha e ntle. – Africa South is country which is beautiful, i.e. South Africa is a beautiful country. (Suid-Afrika is 'n mooi land.)

76. **noka** – river (rivier)

Senqu ke noka e telele. – The Orange River is a river which is long. (Die Oranjerivier is 'n lang rivier.)

77. **noha** – snake (slang)

Ke tshaba noha. – I am afraid of the snake. (Ek is bang vir die slang.)

78. **nyoloha** (v) – go up, climb (opklim)

Re nyoloha thaba. – We go up the mountain. (Ons klim teen die berg, ons klim die berg uit of op.)

79. **ngola** (v) – write (skryf)

Bana ba ngola moqoqo. – The children are writing an essay. (Die kinders skryf 'n opstel.)

80. **ngaka** – doctor (dokter, geneesheer)

Ngaka e hlahloba mokudi. – A doctor examines a patient. (Die dokter ondersoek 'n pasiënt.)

81. **ngata** (enumerative) – many (baie)

O na le dieta tse ngata. – You have shoes which are many, i.e. you have many shoes. (Jy het baie skoene.)

82. **opa** – be painful (om seer te hê)

Hlooho ya ka e a opa. – Head of mine is painful, i.e. I have a headache. (Ek het 'n hoofpyn.)

83. **oma** (v) – dry up, get dry (droog word)

Diaparo di a oma. – The clothes are getting dry. (Die klere word droog.)

84. **otla** (v) – thrash, beat (slaan)

Ke tla o otla. – I will you thrash, i.e. I will thrash you. (Ek sal jou slaan.)

85. **ola** – pick up waste, rubbish (die vuilgoed verwyder of optel)

Ke ola molora. – I pick up ash. (Ek tel die as op.)

86. **oka** (v) – nurse (verpleeg)

Mme o oka mokudi. – Mother nurses the patient. (Ma verpleeg die pasiënt.)

87. **ora** (v) – bask, enjoy heat of fire (koester, bak)

Bana ba ora letsatsi mariha. – Children bask in the sun in winter. (Kinders bak in die son in die winter.)

88. **onto** – oven (oond)

    Onto e a tjhesa. – An oven is hot. ('n Oond is warm.)

89. **pono** – vision, sight (gesig, gesigsvermoë)

    Pono ya ka e hlakile. – Vision of mine clear, i.e. my vision is clear. (Ek kan goed sien.)

90. **palo** – figure, number (nommer)

    Palo ena e fosahetse. – Figure this one is wrong, i.e. this figure is wrong. (Hierdie nommer is verkeerd.)

91. **palo** – pole (paal)

    Palo ya motlakase e robehile. – An electricity pole is broken. (Die elektrisiteitspaal is gebreek.)

92. **pina** – song (lied, sang)

    Pina ya Tshepo e monate. – A song of Tshepo is lovely. (Tshepo se lied is mooi.)

93. **pene** – pen (pen)

    Pene ena ha e ngole. – A pen this one does not write, i.e. this pen does not write. (Hierdie pen skryf nie.)

Time, duration and seasonal concepts (Tydsduur- en seisoenale konsepte)

1. **nako** – time (tyd)

   Ke nako ya ho tsamaya. – It is time to go. (Dit is tyd om te loop.)

2. **hora** – hour (uur)

   Ke hora o ntse o bua. – You have been talking for an hour. (Jy praat al 'n uur lank.)

3. **motsotso** – minute (minuut)

   Semathi se nkile motsotso ho beisa. – A runner (athlete) took a minute to race. (Die hardloper het `n minuut gevat om te hardloop.)

4. **motsotswana** – second (sekonde)

   Motsotswana o feta ka pele. – A second passes quickly. ('n Sekonde gaan gou verby.)

5. **letsatsi** – day (dag)

   Re tla o emela letsatsi lohle. – We shall wait for you day long, i.e. the whole day. (Ons sal die hele dag vir jou wag.)

6. **hoseng** –in the morning (in die môre)

   Baeti ba fihlile hoseng. – The visitors they arrived in the morning, i.e. the visitors arrived in the morning. (Die besoekers het in die môre aangekom.)

7. **motsheare** – daytime, during the day (gedurende die dag)

   Motsheare ho a tjhesa. – During the day it is hot. (Gedurende die dag is dit warm.)

8. **mantsiboya** – in the evening (in die aand)

   Ho phodile mantsiboya. – It is cool in the evening. (Dit is koel in die aand.)

9. **thapama** – sunset, twilight, dusk (sonsondergang)

   Letsatsi le a dikela thapama. – The sun sets. (Die son gaan onder.)

10. **shwalane** – twilight, dusk (sonsondergang)

    Shwalane e wele. – Dusk has fallen, i.e. it is dusk. (Die son het onder gegaan.)

11. **bosiu** – night, at night (nag)

    Ho hotsho bosiu. – It is dark at night. (Dit is donker in die nag.)

12. **beke** – week (week)

    Beke e na le matsatsi a supileng. – A week has days which are seven, i.e. a week consists of seven days. ('n Week het sewe dae.)

13. **mafelo-a-beke** – weekend (naweek)

    mafelo-a-beke a malelele – a weekend which is long ('n langnaweek)

14. **Sontaha** – Sunday (Sondag)

15. **Mantaha** – Monday (Maandag)

16. **Labobedi** – Tuesday (Dinsdag)

17. **Laboraro** – Wednesday (Woensdag)

18. **Labone** – Thursday (Donderdag)

19. **Labohlano** – Friday (Vrydag)

20. **Moqebelo** – Saturday (Saterdag)

21. **kgwedi** – month (maand)

    Ke fumana moputso ha kgwedi e fela. – I receive a salary when the month ends. (Ek kry 'n salaris aan die einde van die maand.)

22. **kgweditharo** – a three-month period, a quarter of a year ('n kwart van die jaar)

Re ngola tlhahlobo ya kgweditharo. – We write a quarterly examination. (Ons skryf 'n kwartaallikse eksamen.)

23. **selemo** (1) – year (jaar)

    Selemo se fedile. – A year has ended. ('n Jaar het geëindig.)

24. **sehla** – season (seisoen)

    Mariha ke sehla se batang. – Winter is a season that is cold. (Winter is 'n koue seisoen.)

25. **selemo** (2) – spring/season (lente)

    Selemo dimela di a palesa. – In spring plants they blossom, i.e. plants blossom. (In die lente blom die plante.)

26. **lehlabula** – summer (somer)

    Lehlabula re ja ditholwana. – In summer we eat fruit. (In die somer eet ons vrugte.)

27. **hwetla** – autumn (herfs)

    Hwetla ke nako ya ho kotula. – Autumn is the time of reaping. (Herfs is die tyd om te oes.)

28. **mariha** – winter (winter)

    Mariha ho a bata. – In winter it is cold. (In die winter is dit koud.)

29. **Pherekgong** – January (Januarie)

    Pherekgong ke kgwedi ya pele. – January is the first month. (Januarie is die eerste maand.)

30. **Hlakola** – February (Februarie)

    Kgwedi ya bobedi ke Hlakola. – The month of second is February, i.e. the second month is February. (Die tweede maand is Februarie.)

31. **Hlakubele** – March (Maart)

    Hlakubele ke kgwedi ya boraro. – March is the month of third, i.e. March is the third month. (Maart is die derde maand.)

32. **Mmesa** – April (April)

    Mmesa ke kgwedi ya bone. – April is the month of fourth, i.e. April is the fourth month. (April is die vierde maand.)

33. **Motsheanong** – May (Mei)

    Kgwedi ya bohlano ke Motsheanong. – The month of fifth is May, i.e. the fifth month is May. (Die vyfde maand is Mei.)

34. **Phupjane** – June (Junie)

Phupjane ke kgwedi ya botshelela. – June is the month of the sixth, i.e. June is the sixth month. (Junie is die sesde maand.)

35. **Phupu** – July (Julie)

    Kgwedi ya bosupa ke Phupu. – The month of the seventh is July, i.e. the seventh month is July. (Die sewende maand is Julie.)

36. **Phato** – August (Augustus)

    Phato ke kgwedi ya borobedi. – August is the month of the eighth, i.e. the eighth month is August. (Augustus is die agste maand.)

37. **Loetse** – September (September)

    Kgwedi ya borobong ke Loetse. – The month of the ninth is September, i.e. September is the ninth month. (Die negende maand is September.)

38. **Mphalane** – October (Oktober)

    Mphalane ke kgwedi ya boleshome. – October is the month of the tenth, i.e. October is the tenth month. (Oktober is die tiende maand.)

39. **Pudungwane** – November (November)

    Kgwedi ya boleshome le motso o mong ke Pudungwane. – The eleventh month is November, i.e. November is the eleventh month. (Die elfde maand is November.)

40. **Tshitwe** – December (Desember)

    Tshitwe ke kgwedi ya boleshome le metso e mmedi. – December is the month of the twelfth, i.e. December is the twelfth month. (Desember is die twaalfde maand.)

41. **kajeno** – today (vandag)

    Kajeno ke letsatsi la ho amohela. – Today is the day of to pay, i.e. today is pay-day. (Vandag is betaaldag.)

42. **maobane** – yesterday (gister)

    Ke lorile ha bohloko maobane. – I dreamed badly yesterday. (Ek het gister sleg gedroom.)

43. **maoba** – the day before yesterday (eergister)

    Ba fihlile maoba. – They arrived the day before yesterday. (Hulle het eergister gekom.)

44. **ngwahola** – last year (verlede jaar)

    Ngwahola pula e ile ya na. – Last year the rain fell. (Verlede jaar het die reën geval.)

45. **ngwahola-kola** – the year before last (voorverlede jaar)

Komello e ne e le kgolo ngwahola-kola. – The drought was great the year before last. (Die droogte was kwaai voorverlede jaar.)

46. **hosane/hosasa** – tomorrow (môre)

    Ke tla penta lebota hosane. – I will paint the wall tomorrow. (Ek sal die muur môre verf.)

47. **isao** – in future or next year (in die toekoms)

    Bothata bona re tla bo rarolla isao. – This difficulty we will solve in future. (Hierdie probleem sal ons in die toekoms oplos.)

48. **monongwaha** – this year (vanjaar)

    Monongwaha pula e ngata. – This year the rain is abundant. (Vanjaar is die reën oorvloedig.)

49. **sejwale-jwale** – of modern times, fashionable (modern)

    Nkgono ha a rate motjeko wa sejwale-jwale. – Grandmother does not like the jive of modern times, i.e. she does not like modern jiving. (Ouma hou nie baie van die moderne dans nie.)

5

The noun

(Die selfstandige naamwoord)

Orientation (Oriëntering)

In our everyday life, we see things, we meet people, we touch objects, and go to places. In language, the word that is given to name things is a noun.

Definition (Definisie)

A noun is the name of a place, person or a thing. This means that a noun is a word that signifies names of anything one can imagine.

Look at the following examples of nouns

motho – person (persoon)
Gauteng – place (plek)
sediba – thing (ding)

There are four types of nouns:

1. Proper noun: It names a particular person, place or thing, e.g. Mokoena, Gauteng. All proper nouns always begin with a capital letter.
2. A common noun: It is the name that refers to one thing, e.g. koloi (car), pula (rain).
3. A collective noun: It refers to a set or group of people or things, e.g. sehlopha (class or team), phutheho (congregation).
4. An abstract noun: It refers to those things that cannot be recognised by the five senses, i.e sight, smell, hearing, taste and touch, e.g. bohlale (cleverness, intelligence), mohau (grace, mercy).

Exposition (Uitleg)

Let us now look at the 15 noun classes in the following table:

Table 2

Class	Prefix	Noun	English equivalent
1	**mo-**	**motho**	person
2	**ba-**	**batho**	people
3	**mo-**	**motse**	village
4	**me-**	**metse**	villages
5	**le-**	**lerako**	wall
6	**ma-**	**marako**	walls
7	**se-**	**selepe**	axe
8	**di-**	**dilepe**	axes
9	**n-**	**ntja**	dog
10	**din-**	**dintja**	dogs
Classes 11,12 & 13 are non-existent in Sesotho. These noun classes occur in other African languages such as isiZulu, isiXhosa, etc.			
14	**bo-**	**bohobe**	bread
15	**ho-**	**ho ja**	to eat
16	**fa-**	**fatshe**	down
17	**ho-**	**hodimo**	up
18	**mo-**	**mose**	abroad

N.B. Classes 16, 17, & 18 indicate space or place

Let us look at some important aspects of noun class 1: This is a noun class of names of persons only. This indicates personal names.

Examples of people:

motho – person (persoon)
monna – man or person (man)
mosadi – wife or female person (vrou)
molekane – partner or spouse (vennoot)
moruti – minister (predikant)
molebedi – guard (wag)
monghadi – sir (meneer)
mofumahadi – lady (dame)
mofu – the deceased or dead person (die dooie persoon)
moeti – visitor (besoeker)

N.B. The following nouns belong to class 1 in that they refer to persons. However, because of their form, they do not take the common prefix of class 1, i.e. ***mo-***. They are referred to as belonging to class 1 (a).

Here are a few examples:

rangwane – uncle (oom)
rakgadi – aunt, i.e. father's sister (tante)
mangwane – aunt, i.e. mother's younger sister (tante)

Classes 16, 17 and 18 are actually locatives, i.e. they indicate location or place.

The plural prefix ***ma*** which is meant for class 14, corresponds to the prefix ***ma-*** of class 6. Hence the classes are not duplicated.

Class 14 ***bo*** contains the majority of abstract nouns, e.g.

boloi – witchcraft (toordery)
boshodu – theft (diefstal)
boima – heaviness (swaarheid)
boikaketsi – hypocrisy (skynheiligheid)
bokgonatha – greediness (gulsigheid)

Please note that it is advisable to know the above table because it reflects the outline of Sesotho. You do not have to memorise the table but you should understand and familiarise yourself with it because it will feature frequently throughout this book, especially where we deal with those parts of Sesotho that have a bearing on the noun.

In our definition, we said that the noun also refers to places. Here are a few examples:

Gauteng (Province)
Maseru (Commercial Capital of Lesotho)
Tshwane (Pretoria)
Lekwa (the Vaal area)
Mangaung (Bloemfontein)
Maokeng (Kroonstad)
Lesotho
Qwa-Qwa
Leribe

We also said that the noun refers to things or objects. Here are a few examples:

sefate – tree (boom)
thaba – mountain (berg)
selepe – axe (byl)
thupa – stick (stok)
mollo – fire (vuur)
buka – book (boek)
pene – pen (pen)
ntlo – house (huis)
seretse – mud (modder)
komello – drought (droogte)

We now give you the original classification of the Sesotho nouns with a comparative view of the singular and plural noun classes in table 3 below.

However, please note that this is no longer in use. The revised and acceptable noun classification is what is reflected at the beginning of this chapter.

Table 3

Class	Prefix	Singular	Plural	English singular	English plural
1	***mo/ba***	**motho**	**batho**	person	people
2	***mo/me***	**motse**	**metse**	village	villages
3	***le/ma***	**lesole**	**masole**	soldier	soldiers

Table 3 (continued)

Class	Prefix	Singular	Plural	English singular	English plural
4	*se/di*	**selepe**	**dilepe**	axe	axes
5	*n/di*	**ntlo**	**dintlo**	house	houses
6	*bo/ma*	**bohobe**	**mahobe**	bread	"breads", many loaves of bread
7	*ho/ho*	**ho**	**ho**	to be	to be

Further examples of the noun class.

Class 1 **morena** – king, chief (koning)
Class 1 **moahi** – civilian, resident (inwoner)
Class 5 **letshwao** – mark (merk)
Class 5 **lehlatsipa** – casualty (verlies)
Class 7 **sesosa** – cause (oorsaak)
Class 9 **sente** – cent (sent)
Class 14 **boko** – brain brein)
Class 9 **tsuonyana** – chicken, i.e. baby fowl not meat (kuiken)
Class 9 **kotsi** – accident (ongeluk)
Class 9 **kopano** – meeting (vergadering)

Below are more examples of current singular noun classes with their plural counterparts.

Table 4

Class	Prefix	Noun	English equivalent	Afrikaanse ekwivalent
1	*mo-*	**motho**	person	persoon
2	*ba-*	**batho**	people	mense
3	*mo-*	**molomo**	mouth	mond
4	*me-*	**molomo**	mouths	monde
5	*le-*	**lehapu**	watermelon	waatlemoen
6	*ma-*	**mahapu**	watermelons	waatlemoene
7	*se-*	**seledu**	chin	ken
8	*di-*	**diledu**	chins	kenne
9	*n-*	**nkwe**	tiger	tier
10	*din-*	**dinkwe**	tigers	tiere
Classes 11, 12 & 13 do not exist in Sesotho. The noun classes occur in other African languages such as isiZulu, isiXhosa, etc.				
14	*bo-*	**borokgo**	bridge	brug
15	*ho-*	**ho nwa**	to drink	om te drink

Table 4 (continued)

Class	Prefix	Noun	English equivalent	Afrikaanse ekwivalent
16	***fa-***	**fatshe**	down	onder
17	***ho-***	**hodimo**	up	op
18	***mo-***	**morao**	back	rug

Exercises on the noun (Oefeninge)

To which classes do the following nouns belong?

serope – thigh (dybeen)
morao – back (rug)
mofumahadi – lady (dame)
nta – louse (luis)
ketlele – kettle (ketel)

Increase your vocabulary (Verbreed u woordeskat)

Learn the following nouns:

noto – note (nota)
lerata – noise (geraas)
letlowa – net (net)
naledi – star (ster)
nalete – needle (naald)
letata – netting (sifdraad)
tlhoko – need (nood)
mmasepala – municipality (munisipaliteit)
moqoqo – essay, narrative (opstel)
sekepe – ship (skip)

6

The prefix

(Die voorvoegsel)

Orientation (Oriëntering)

In the study of language, a root is a basic morpheme from which other words are derived. These additional morphemes are called affixes because they are affixed to the basic morpheme. There are two types of affixes, namely prefixes and suffixes.

Definition (Definisie)

The prefix is a little word form which is attached in front of a root. Put differently, a prefix is a morpheme composed of letters with a definite meaning which is placed in front of a root. The prefix is the element that governs the sentence in that the form of the noun prefix determines all other forms of words in a sentence such as the pronoun, verb, adjective, adverb, etc. Prefixes indicate the class to which a particular noun belongs. Accordingly, the prefix takes the same class as the noun, as the following examples will illustrate:

mo-tho – person (persoon), i.e. where ***mo-*** is a prefix and ***-tho*** a root.

n-tho – thing (ding), i.e. where ***n-*** is a prefix and ***-tho*** a root

se-tulo – chair (stoel), i.e. where ***se-*** is a prefix and ***-tulo*** a root

Exposition (Uitleg)

You will note that affixes, in this case prefixes, play a major role in the formation of many words and also convey different meanings when attached to a root. Prefixes are used in creating nouns, verbs, adjectives, adverbs, etc.

Let us look at more examples, using new nouns (according to the new and acceptable system of classifying nouns).

Table 5

Class	Prefix	Noun	English equivalent
1	*mo-*	**motho**	person
2	*ba-*	**batho**	people
3	*mo-*	**molomo**	mouth
4	*me-*	**melomo**	mouths
5	*le-*	**lehapu**	watermelon
6	*ma-*	**mahapu**	watermelons
7	*se-*	**seledu**	chin
8	*di-*	**diledu**	chins
9	*n-*	**nkwe**	tiger
10	*din*	**dinkwe**	tiger
Classes 11, 12 & 13 are non-existent in Sesotho. These noun classes occur in other African languages such as isiZulu, isiXhosa, etc.			
14	*bo-*	**borokgo**	bridge
15	*ho-*	**ho nwa**	to drink
16	*fa-*	**fatshe**	down
17	*ho-*	**hodimo**	up
18	*mo-*	**morao**	back

NB: Class 15, the infinitive **ho,** "to do", also conforms to the noun categorisation.

A prefix plays an important part in a Sesotho sentence in that it effects concordial agreement or harmony among words in the construction of a sentence. We shall learn more about the concord in Chapter 11. However, a few examples are in order here:

sefate se setala – a green tree ('n groen boom)

lebala le leholo – a big field ('n groot terrein)

bohobe bo bosweu – white bread (wit brood)

As may be seen from these examples, the Sesotho prefix is monosyllabic, i.e. it is a single little word form that is uttered once.

Further examples of the prefix (Verdere voorbeelde van die voorvoegsel)

Class 1 **mo-nna** – man (man)

Class 2 **ba-nna** – men (mans)

Class 3 **mo-ropa** – drum (tamboer)

Class 4 **me-ropa** – drums (tamboere)

Class 5 **le-hapu** – watermelon (waatlemoen)

Class 6 **ma-hapu** – watermelons (waatlemoene)

Class 7 **se-ledu** – chin (ken)
Class 8 **di-ledu** – chins (kenne)
Class 9 **n-twa** – war (oorlog)
Class 10 **din-twa** – wars (oorloë)
Class 14 **bo-hobe** – bread (brood)
Class 15 **ho-busa** – to govern (om te regeer)
Class 16 **fa-tshe** – down (af)
Class 17 **ho-dimo** – up (op)
Class 18 **mo-se** – abroad (buitelands)

Exercises on the prefix (Oefeninge)

To which noun classes do the following prefixes belong (the order is mixed up to test the learner):

le-	*mo-*
se-	*bo-*
n-	*fa-*

Increase your vocabulary (Verbreed u woordeskat)

moya – air (lug)
leru – cloud (wolk)
monono – wealth, riches (rykdom)
mmutla – hare (haas)
noka – river (rivier)
puo – talk, speech (spraak)
papadi – game, match (spel, wedstryd)
mokgwa – habit (gewoonte)
seatla – palm, hand (palm, hand)

7

The root

(Die wortel)

Orientation (Oriëntering)

Like the root of a tree, from which the rest of the tree is derived, a word also has a root which gives it its meaning. The stem is an outer cover that clothes the word, as will be explained further under Exposition.

Definition (Definisie)

The root is the main or primary form of the word structure. A root is the core of a word. A root cannot be changed without altering the meaning of the word. It is onto this basic word structure that other word forms are added. Such additions may either be in front or at the end of the root. In chapters 6 and 8, these word additions have been called affixes which, in turn, are broken up into prefixes (in front of the root) and suffixes (at the end of the root). The following are examples of a root or basic word form.

-tho-

-holo-

-fu-

As can be seen from these examples, a root may be said to be in a naked or neutral form because it does not stand for any class on its own without affixes.

Exposition (Uitleg)

We must say something briefly about another element of a word structure, called the stem. The stem encompasses the root, i.e. it is more than the root in that it is formed by the root together with its suffixes. At times a stem is a complete word that can stand on its own, e.g.

ja – eat (eet)

tadima – look (kyk)

jara – carry (dra)

Words can be built by affixes, specifically prefixes and suffixes, in various combinations. We will give simple examples and avoid being too technical at this stage of learning Sesotho.

prefix + root

root + suffix

1. We can add the prefix ***mo*** to **-tho** to form **motho** (person).
   Similarly, we can add the suffix **-nyana** at the end to form **mothonyana.**
2. We can add the prefix ***bo*** to root **-holo** to form **boholo** (size).
   However, we can duplicate **boholo** to **boholoholo** to produce a different meaning, i.e. a long time ago.
3. We can add the prefix ***le*** to the root **-fu**, to form **lefu** (death or disease) or prefix ***mo*** to form **mofu** which means a corpse or dead person.
4. An interesting example of how the root may be formed is: **-sotho**
   From the stem **-sotho** the following words may be derived:

Mo + **sotho** = **Mosotho** (a native speaker of **Sesotho)**

Se + **sotho** = **Sesotho** (the language of the Basotho or their culture)

Bo + **sotho** = **bosotho** (the act of being **Mosotho**)

Le + **sotho** = **Lesotho** (the country of **Lesotho)**

Further examples of the root (Verdere voorbeelde van die wortel)

We will provide the examples according to the noun classes:

Table 11

Class	Prefix	Root	Word
1	mo-	-fu	**mofu** – a dead person (oorledene)
2	ba-	-fu	**bafu** – dead people (oorledenes)
3	mo-	-leko	**moleko** – temptation (versoeking)
4	me-	-leko	**meleko** – temptations (versoekings)
5	le-	-bone	**lebone** – light (lig)
6	ma-	-bone	**mabone** – lights (ligte)
7	se-	-ipone	**seipone** – mirror (spieël)
8	di-	-ipone	**diipone** – mirrors (spieëls)
9	n-	-kgo	**nkgo** – clay pot (kleipot)
10	din-	-kgo	**dinkgo** – clay pots (kleipotte)
14	bo-	-hobe	**bohobe** – bread (brood)
15	ho-	-kgetha	**ho kgetha** – to choose (om te kies)
16	fa-	-tshe	**fatshe** – down (af)
17	ho-	-dimo	**hodimo** – up (op)
18	mo-	-theo	**motheo** – foundation (fondament)

The above treatment of the prefix and the suffix in relation to the root shows that prefixes and suffixes can modify the original idea contained in the root, change the grammatical form of the root, as well as bring about a change to another part of speech.

Exercises (Oefeninge)

Identify the root in the following words:

morui – a rich person ('n ryk persoon)

ithuta – teach oneself (jouself onderrig, leer)

leleme – tongue (tong)

banna – men (mans)

bongata – majority (meerderheid)

lefika – rock (rots)

morao – at the back (agter)

mabaka – reasons (redes)

setulo – chair (stoel)

semumu – a dumb person ('n spraaklose persoon)

Increase your vocabulary (Verbreed u woordeskat)

thuso – relief (hulp)

kopo – request (versoek)

dula – to sit, stay, reside (sit, bly)

araba – to answer, respond (antwoord)

fiela – sweep (vee)

duma – to sound (klink)

bontsha – to show (wys)

boholo – size (grootte)

letlalo – skin (vel)

lehata – skull (skedel, kopbeen)

mpa – stomach (maag)

nko – nose (neus)

hempe – shirt (hemp)

tswekere – sugar (suiker)

nama – meat (vleis)

8

The suffix

(Agtervoegsel)

Orientation (Oriëntering)

As we stated in Chapter 7, a root is the basic morpheme upon which other words are formed. These added forms are called affixes because they are affixed or attached to the root of the word. Affixes may be divided into prefixes and suffixes. In chapter 6 we dealt with prefixes. Here we shall treat the suffix.

Definition (Definisie)

The suffix is a morpheme that is attached onto the end of the noun or an adverb. Whereas we said, in Chapter 6, that the prefix came in front, the suffix occupies an opposite position and performs a definite function with a specific meaning. The following examples will illustrate this point:

(i) **ntlohadi** – house (huis):

ntlo + **hadi** – house + big (groot huis)
i.e. where ***-tlo-*** is a root and ***-hadi*** the suffix

(ii) **mothonyana** – person (persoon):

motho + **nyana** – person + small ('n klein persoon)
i.e. where ***-tho-*** is a root and ***-nyana*** the suffix

(iii) **tauhadi** – lion (leeu):

tau + **hadi** – lioness (leeuwyfie)
i.e. where ***tau-*** is a root and ***-hadi*** the suffix

Exposition (Uitleg)

The major contribution of suffixes when attached to roots is to form different types of words that convey different meanings. Suffixes make nouns, verbs, adjectives, adverbs, etc. In (i) we attach **-hadi** at the end of **ntlo** (house) to form **ntlohadi,** which means big house. In this case **-hadi** adds value to **ntlo** and makes it big – a big house.

In (ii) **motho** (person), the suffix **-nyana** is added to the end of **motho**, to form **mothonyana,** which means small person. The suffix **-nyana** thus reduces the value of motho.

In the case of (iii), where **-hadi** is added to the end of **tau, tauhadi** is formed and this means a female lion, i.e. lioness, and not a big lion as is the case in (i).

Further examples of the suffix (Verdere voorbeelde van die agtervoegsel)

1 Using the suffix **-hadi** (Die gebruik van die agtervoegsel **-hadi**)

motho + hadi = mothohadi – a big person ('n groot persoon)
ntho + hadi = nthohadi – a huge thing ('n groot ding)
thaba + hadi = thabahadi – a colossal mountain ('n groot berg)

2 Using the suffix **-nyana** (Die gebruik van die agtervoegsel **-nyana**)

koloi + nyana = koloinyana – a small car ('n klein motor)
pina + nyana = pinanyana – a small/short musical piece ('n klein/kort musiekstuk)
lebanta + nyana = lebantanyana – a small belt ('n gordeltjie)

Exercises (Oefeninge)

1 Which suffix do you use to form the following words?
sefefohadi – a huge thunderstorm ('n groot donderstorm)
sekepehadi – a huge ship ('n groot skip)
bohobehadi – large bread (groot brood)

2 Use the suffix **-nyana** to complete the following words:
tau – lion (leeu)
lebala – open piece of ground or foreground ('n oop stuk grond)
lejwe – stone (klip)
monyako – door (deur)
molomo – mouth (mond)

Increase your vocabulary (Verbreed u woordeskat)

bana – children (kinders)
terene – train (trein)
lesale – ear-ring (oorring)
lentswe – voice, word (stem)
ho ngola – to write (om te skryf)
ho sheba – to see, look (om te kyk)
thuto – education (opvoeding)

kgubedu – red (rooi)
tala – green (groen)
tshweu – white (wit)
putswa –grey (grou, grys)
lesedi – light (lig)
lefifi – darkness (donker)

9

The pronoun

(Die voornaamwoord)

Orientation (Oriëntering)

It would be repetitive to always use a noun in constructing a sentence. Language has provided a relief by creating another word called a pronoun.

Definition (Definisie)

The pronoun is a word that substitutes a noun. This means that a pronoun stands for a noun. We may use a pronoun without using a noun and the meaning of the sentence will be understood. As the noun in Sesotho is grouped according to classes, so is the pronoun. A few examples of the pronoun are: **ke, o, le,** as in:

***ke* ja nama** – I am eating meat (Ek eet vleis)
***o* lefa rente** – He is paying rent (Hy betaal huur)
***le* bohloko** – It is painful (Dit is seer)

Exposition (Uitleg)

In these examples, the pronouns, **ke, o** and **le** stand in the place of

nna – I, the speaker (Ek, die spreker)
tshepo – or anybody else (of iemand anders)
letsoho – hand (hand)

This means that each pronoun is a word on its own and can stand in the place of a noun or may be used in opposition to it. Learners are, however, advised not to confuse nouns with concords that are used with verbs.

Table 6

Class	Prefix	Noun/pronoun	English equivalent
1	*mo-*	**motho/yena**	person
2	*ba-*	**batho/bona**	people
3	*mo-*	**motse/wona**	village
4	*me-*	**metse/yona**	villages
5	*le-*	**lerako/lona**	wall
6	*ma-*	**marako/ona**	walls
7	*se-*	**selepe/sona**	axe
8	*di-*	**dilepe/tsona**	axes
9	*n-*	**ntja/yona**	dog
10	*din*	**dintja/tsona**	dogs
Classes 11, 12 & 13 are non-existent in Sesotho. These noun classes occur in other African languages such as isiZulu, isiXhosa, etc.			
14	*bo-*	**bohobe/bona**	bread
15	*ho-*	**ho ja/hona**	to eat
16	*fa-*	**fatshe/hona**	down
17	*ho-*	**hodimo/hona**	up
18	*mo-*	**mose/hona**	abroad

In Sesotho, there are four types of pronouns, namely:

the absolute pronoun,
the qualificative pronoun,
the quantitative pronoun,
the demonstrative pronoun.

We shall treat each one of them briefly:

The absolute pronoun

This pronoun indicates a noun and is used in the place of a noun. It does not describe or limit it. It simply indicates it.

Let us look at the following table of the absolute pronoun:

Table 7

	Singular (enkelvoud)	Plural (meervoud)
1st person (eerste persoon)	**nna** – I (ek)	**rona** – we (ons)
2nd person (tweede persoon)	**wena** – you (jy)	**lona** – you (julle)
3rd person (derde persoon)	**yena** – he/she (hy/sy)	**bona** – them (hulle)

Table 7 (continued)

Class	Noun	Absolute pronoun
1	**moruti** – minister (predikant)	**yena** – he/she (hy/sy)
2	**baruti** – ministers (predikante)	**bona** – they (hulle)
3	**molala** – neck (nek)	**wona** – it (dit)
4	**melala** – necks (nekke)	**yona** – they (hulle)
5	**leru** – cloud (wolk)	**lona** – it (dit)
6	**maru** – clouds (wolke)	**ona** – they (hulle)
7	**sephadi** – whip (sweep)	**sona** – it (dit)
8	**diphadi** – whips (swepe)	**tsona** – they (hulle)
9	**ntho** – thing (ding)	**yona** – it (dit)
10	**dintho** – things (dinge)	**tsona** – they (hulle)
Classes 11, 12, & 13 do not exist in Sesotho.		
14	**borokgo** – bridge (brug)	**bona** – it (dit)
15	**ho bona** – to see (om te sien)	**hona** – it (dit)
16	**fatshe** – down (af)	**hona** – it (dit)
17	**hodimo** – up (op)	**hona** – it (dit)
18	**motsheo** – yonder (daar (gunter))	**hona** – it (dit)

The qualificative pronoun (Betreklike voornaamwoord)

A qualificative pronoun is a word that adds quality to or qualifies the noun. The qualificative pronoun is used instead of the noun it qualifies. Please note that all qualificatives can be used as pronouns. The qualificative pronoun encompasses the adjective (which is separately dealt with in Chapter 14), the possessive (which is dealt with in Chapter 20) and the enumerative (which is dealt with in Chapter 23).

Let us consider the following examples:

Using the adjectival concord: ba, tse, le

(barutuwa) ba batle
students who are beautiful (studente wat mooi is)

(dikepe) tse kgolo
ships that are big (groot skepe)

(lentswe) le leholo
a voice that is big ('n stem wat groot is)

Using the possessive concord: ya, tsa, ha

(buka) ya ka
a book of mine ('n boek van my)

(dintho) tsa hae
things of his; hers (dinge van haar)

(ho shwa) ha hae
the death of his/her (die dood van hom/haar)

Using the enumerative concord: tse/e, ya

Tse pedi di ile.
The two have gone. (Die twee het gegaan.)

E le nngwe e setse.
The one is left. (Die een bly agter.)

Ya bone e jelwe.
The fourth one is eaten. (Die vierde een is geëet.)

The demonstrative pronoun (Aanwysende voornaamwoorde)

This pronoun is dealt with in detail in Chapter 18, where we treat the demonstrative as a significant part of speech. However, for the sake of a systematic presentation, we will give a brief outline of the demonstrative pronoun. As its name suggests, the demonstrative pronoun shows a position. There are three positions that a particular noun may occupy at any given time, namely the position "here" (**mona**), the position "there" (**mono**) and the position "yonder" (**mane**). An interesting feature in Sesotho is that each of these positions has two forms. This means there is an alternative for each of the positions. These alternatives will be dealt with in Chapter 18. Below is a simple table of the demonstrative pronoun.

Table 8 The demonstrative pronoun (Aanwysende voornaamwoorde)

1st person	**enwa**	this one	(hierdie een)
2nd person	**enwa**	this one	(hierdie een)
3rd person	**enwa**	this one	(hierdie een)

Class	Noun	Demonstrative
1	**mosadi** – woman (vrou)	**enwa** – this (hierdie) (*ook* dié)
2	**basadi** – women (vrouens)	**bana** – this (hierdie)
3	**mosifa** – muscle (spier)	**ona** – this (hierdie)
4	**mesifa** – muscles (spiere)	**ena** – these (hierdie)
5	**lefika** – rock (rots)	**lena** – this (hierdie)
6	**mafika** – rocks (rotse)	**ana** – these (hierdie)
7	**seboko** – worm (wurm)	**sena** – this (hierdie)
8	**diboko** – worms (wurms)	**tsena** – these (hierdie)

Table 8 (continued)

Class	Noun	Demonstrative
9	**nkwe** – tiger (tier)	**ena** – this (hierdie)
10	**dinkwe** – tigers (tiere)	**tsena** – these (hierdie)
Remember that classes 11, 12 & 13 do not exist in Sesotho		
14	**bohobe** – bread (brood)	**bona** – this (hierdie)
15	**ho kganna** – to drive (bestuur)	**hona** – this (hierdie)
16	**fatshe** – down (af)	**hona** – this (hierdie)
17	**hodimo** – up (op)	**hona** – this (hierdie)
18	**morao** – back (terug)	**ona** – this (hierdie)

The quantitative pronoun

This pronoun simply indicates a measure of the noun or its quantity. In Sesotho, the quantitative pronoun is chiefly characterised by the stem **-hle,** meaning "all". You will notice that not all noun classes in Sesotho have the quantitative pronoun. This is illustrated in the following table.

Table 9

Class	Noun	Quantitative pronoun
1	**motho** – person (persoon, mens)	**wohle** – all (die hele mens)
2	**batho** – people (mense)	**bohle** – all (al die mense)
3	**motse** – village (dorp)	**wohle** – all (die hele dorp)
4	**metse** – villages (dorpe)	**yohle** – all (al die dorpe)
5	**lelapa** – family (familie)	**lohle** – all (die hele familie)
6	**malapa** – families (families)	**ohle** – all (al die families)
7	**sefate** – tree (boom)	**sohle** – all (die hele boom)
8	**difate** – trees (bome)	**tsohle** – all (al die bome)
9	**ntwa** – war, fight (oorlog)	**yohle** – all (die hele oorlog)
10	**dintwa** – wars (oorloë)	**tsohle** – all (al die oorloë)
Remember that noun classes 11, 12, & 13 do not exist in Sesotho		
14	**bohobe** – bread (brood)	**bohle** – all (die hele brood)
15	**ho dula** – to sit (om te sit)	**hohle** – all (orals)
16	**fatshe** – down (af)	**hohle** – all (orals af)
17	**hodimo** – up (op)	**hohle** – all (orals op)
18	**motsheo** – yonder (daar (gunter))	**wohle** – all (orals daarso)

Further examples of the pronoun (Verdere voorbeelde van die voornaamwoord)

Please note that concords may also be used pronominally, i.e. as pronouns:

Table 10

Class	Noun	Pronoun
1	**moruti** – minister (predikant)	**o**
2	**baruti** – ministers (predikante)	**ba**
3	**monwang** – mosquito (muskiet)	**o**
4	**menwang** – mosquitos (muskiete)	**e**
5	**leoto** – foot (voet)	**le**
6	**maoto** – feet (voete)	**a**
7	**seboko** – worm (wurm)	**se**
8	**diboko** – worms (wurms)	**di**
9	**ntja** – dog (hond)	**e**
10	**dintja** – dogs (honde)	**di**
14	**borokgo** – bridge (brug)	**bo**
15	**ho ema** – to stand (om te staan)	**ho**
16	**fatshe** – down (af)	**ho**
17	**hodimo** – up (op)	**ho**
18	**morao** – at the back (agter)	**o**

Exercises (Oefeninge)

Group the following pronouns according to their noun classes: (The order is mixed up to test the learner):

le
o
a
se
bo
di

Increase your vocabulary (Verbreed u woordeskat)

malome – uncle (oom)
molato – debt (skuld)
peke – pick (pik)
phoka – dew (dou)
kgomo – cow (koei)
tsebe – ear (oor)
ketso – action, act (aksie)
sebini – singer (sanger)
sesenyi – wrongdoer (kwaaddoener)
ho tsheha – to laugh (om te lag)
ho roka – to sew (om naaldwerk te doen)
ho tsamaya – to walk (om te loop)
ho ja – to eat (om te eet)
ho botsa – to ask (om te vra)
ho bua – to talk (om te praat)

10

The verb

(Die werkwoord)

Orientation (Oriëntasie)

We all engage in one action or another in our everyday lives. We walk **(tsamaya),** sleep **(robala)**, talk **(bua)**, listen **(mamela)**, kick **(raha)**, etc. These words are called verbs.

Definition (Definisie)

The verb is a doing word. The following examples illustrate this:

ja, bua, tsamaya, dula, bula

Ke ja nama. – I eat meat. (Ek eet vleis.)

Ke bua le wena. – I am talking to you. (Ek praat met jou.)

Tsamaya hantle. – Go well. (Mooi loop.)

Dula fatshe. – Sit down. (Sit.)

Bula monyako. – Open the door. (Maak die deur oop.)

A verb denotes an action performed by a noun/pronoun, e.g.

Koloi e eme. – The car stopped. (Die motor het gestop.)

A verb can also denote a state of being, e.g.

Ha a batle. – She is unwilling. (Sy is onwillig.)

Exposition (Uitleg)

As can be seen from the above five examples, in Sesotho, the verb may come between the pronoun **ke** and the noun **nama.** The verb may also start a sentence, e.g. in **Dula fatshe.**

There are three kinds of verbs:

1. Transitive verb. This verb is followed by an object, e.g.

Subject	Verb	Object
Leshodu	**le robile**	**monyako**
The chief	broke	the door

2. Intransitive verb. This verb has no object, e.g.

Subject	Verb	Object
Moruti	**o rapetse**	–
The preacher	prayed	–

3. Linkage verb or copulative. This requires a broad discussion but may be briefly stated as follows: The linkage verb indicates a connection between a noun and another noun, or a noun and a qualificative.

   Sebapadi seo ke sethoto.
   That player is a fool.
   (i.e. noun + linking verb + qualificative)

   Dipalesa tseo di ntle.
   Those flowers are beautiful.
   (i.e. noun + linking verb + adjective)

In Sesotho, the verb has many applications, derivations and extensions. We shall treat them systematically for the sake of simplicity.

1. The verb may be used in various tenses, i.e. past, present, future or perfect. These are treated separately in chapter 12 for the sake of detailed attention.
2. The verb may also be used in various moods. Again, for the sake of a detailed treatment, moods are dealt with separately in chapter 21.
3. The verb may also be used in the positive and negative forms or conjugations. This is dealt with in chapter 25.
4. It is very important to note that, in Sesotho, the verb is mostly prefaced by the infinitive **ho**, the English equivalent of which is "to", e.g.

   ho bala – to read (om te lees)
   ho rata – to love (om lief te hê)
   ho bona – to see (om te sien)
   ho nosetsa – to water (om nat te maak)
   ho atleha – to succeed/pass (om te slaag)

5. The verb may be used in an instrumental sense, i.e. **ka** (with), **le** (with) or **ho** (towards, to), e.g.

bua: **Ke bua ka molomo.**
I speak with my mouth. (Ek praat met my mond.)

kgasa: **Ngwana o kgasa ka mpa.**
A baby crawls on the stomach. ('n Baba kruip op sy maag.)

tsamaya: **Ba tsamaya le yena.**
They walk with him/her. (Hulle loop saam met hom/haar.)

ya: **Re ya ho malome.**
We are going to uncle. (Ons gaan na oom toe.)

6. However, it must be noted that apart from functioning in a verbal capacity, the infinitive **ho** also functions in a nominal capacity, e.g.

Ho shwa ho tletse lefatsheng.

Dying is prevalent on earth. (Die dood is algemeen op aarde.)

This usage is different from the verbal one:

O shwa ha bohloko.

He/she dies painfully. (Hy/sy sterf pynlik.)

7. In Sesotho, a verb is formed with a monosyllabic word form, i.e. a verb formed with a single sound, e.g.

(i) **ja,** i.e. **ho ja** – **Ke ja sehwete.**
to eat – I eat a carrot.
(om te eet – Ek eet 'n wortel.)

(ii) **na,** i.e. **ho na** – **Pula e na bosiu.**
to rain – The rain falls (rains) at night.
(om te reën – Dit reën in die nag.)

(iii) **fa, i.e. ho fa** – **Ke fa ngwana.**
to give – I give a child.
(om te gee – Ek gee die kind.)

(iv) **re,** i.e. **ho re** – **Ke re tloo mona.**
to say – I say come here.
(om te sê – Ek sê kom hier.)

(v) **wa,** i.e. **ho wa** – **Sefofu se wa ha bohloko.**
to fall – A blind person falls terribly painfully.
(om te val – 'n Blinde persoon val baie seer.)

8. Verbs are also found in two or more syllables:

(i) **bua,** i.e. **ho bua** – **O rata ho bua.**
to speak – You like to talk.
(om te praat – Jy hou daarvan om te praat.)

(ii) **bona,** i.e. **ho bona** – **Ho molemo ho bona.**
to see – It is better to see.
(om te sien – Dit is beter om te sien.)

(iii) **dula,** i.e. **ho dula** – **Ke dula fatshe.**
to sit – I sit down.
(om te sit – Ek sit.)

(iv) **mema,** i.e. **ho mema** – **Ke mema baeti.**
to invite – I invite visitors.
(om te nooi – Ek nooi gaste.)

(v) **qala,** i.e. **ho qala** – **ke qala ho bala.**
to start, begin – I start to read.
(om te begin – ek begin lees.)

9. Verbs also occur as an instruction:

(i) **Thola!** – Keep quiet, be silent! (Bly stil!)
(ii) **Matha!** – Run! (Hardloop!)
(iii) **Tsoha!** – Wake up! (Word wakker!)
(iv) **Ema!** – Stand up! (Staan op!)
(v) **Nka!** – Take! (Vat!)

10. In Sesotho a verb may be doubled to express emphasis, doubt, disrespect or irritability.

(i) **betsabetsa** – to beat effortlessly (om sonder moeite te verslaan, wen)

Sehlopha sa bolo sa betsabetsa se seng.
A soccer team beat another one.
('n Sokkerspan het 'n ander span gewen.)

(ii) **kenakena** – to involve oneself in matters that do not concern one (om jou te bemoei met iets wat jou nie aangaan nie)

O kenakena ditaba tsa baditjhaba.
You involve yourself in affairs of strangers.
(Jy bemoei jou met vreemdelinge se sake.)

(iii) **duladula** – to sit for a short while (om vir 'n kort rukkie te sit)
Ka duladula, ka tsamaya.
I sat for a while and left.
(Ek het 'n rukkie gesit en toe vertrek.)

(iv) **shebasheba** – to look casually (om terloops rond te kyk)

Mosadi o a shebasheba empa ha a reke.

A woman looks casually but does not buy.
('n Vrou kyk terloops rond, maar koop niks nie.)

(v) **tsamatsamaya** – to walk about (om rond te loop, stap)
(note not **tsamayatsamaya**)

Modisa a tsamatsamaya mme a fumana nku ya hae.

A shepherd walked about and then found his sheep.
('n Skaapwagter het rondgestap en toe sy skape gevind.)

11. The verb has a **passive** form. The passive form of the verb is when some action is done to the noun and the ending of the verb changes to **wa**, e.g.

(i) **ja** – eat (eet); **jewa** – being eaten (word geëet)

Nama e a jewa.

The meat is being eaten.
(Die vleis word geëet.)

(ii) **nwa** – drink (drink); **nowa** – being drunk (word gedrink)

Lebese le nowa ke ngwana.

The milk is being drunk by the child.
(Die melk word deur die kind gedrink.)

(iii) **fa** – give (gee); **fuwa** – being given (word gegee)

Sefofu se fuwa tjhelete.

A blind person is being given money.
('n Blinde persoon word geld gegee.)

(iv) **bitsa** – call (roep); **bitswa** – being called (word geroep)

Seipone o bitswa ke malome.

Seipone is being called by uncle.
(Seipone word deur oom geroep.)

(v) **loma** – bite (byt); **longwa** – being bitten (word gebyt)

Mmutla o longwa ke ntja.

A hare is being bitten by a dog.
('n Haas word deur 'n hond gebyt).

12. The verb has a neutral form called the **neuter.** This form of the verb expresses the noun in a transformative manner. When the neuter is created, the ending part of the verb changes to **-ahala** or **-leh**, e.g.

(i) **bona** – see (sien); **bonahala** – be visible (sigbaar wees)

Hlooho e a bonahala.

The head is visible.
(Die kop is sigbaar.)

(ii) **tseba** – know (ken); **tsebahala** – be known (bekend wees)

Dimakatso o a tsebahala.

Dimakatso is (well) known.
(Dimakatso is bekend.)

(iii) **utlwa** – hear (hoor); **utlwahala** – be audible (hoorbaar wees)

Lentswe le a utlwahala.

The voice is audible. (Die stem is hoorbaar.)

(iv) **bula** – open (oop); **buleha** – become open (oopgaan)

Monyako o a buleha.

The door opens.
(Die deur gaan oop.)

(v) **roba** – break (breek); **robeha** – get broken (gebreek word)

Sefate se a robeha.

A tree gets broken.
('n Boom word gebreek.)

13. The verb has an **applied** form. When the applied form of the verb is created, the ending part of the verb changes to **etsa** or **ela**, e.g.

(i) **botsa** – ask (vra); **botsetsa** – ask for (vra namens)

Ke botsetsa wena.

I am asking for you, i.e. on your behalf.
(Ek vra namens jou.)

(ii) **sheba** – watch, look (dophou, kyk); **shebela** – watch for, look for (dophou, kyk na)

Ke tla o shebela ngwana.

I will watch the child for you.
(Ek sal namens jou na die kind kyk.)

(iii) **kganna** – drive (bestuur); **kgannela** – drive for (bestuur namens)

Ke kgannela sefofu.

I am driving for a blind person.
(Ek bestuur namens 'n blinde persoon.)

(iv) **hlatswa** – wash (was); **hlatswetsa** – wash for (was namens)

Rakgadi o hlatswetsa mme.

Aunt is doing the washing for mother.
(Tante doen die wasgoed namens moeder.)

(v) **sebetsa** – work (werk); **sebeletsa** – work for (werk vir)

Lepantiti le sebeletsa mahala.

A convict works for nothing.
('n Gevangene werk vir niks nie.)

14. The verb has a **causative** form. The causative form of the verb is when something is caused to happen to the noun. When the causative form of the verb is created, the ending part of the verb changes to **-ntsha** or **-nya** or **-tsa**, e.g.

(i) **bona** – see (sien); **bontsha** – cause to see (om te laat sien)

Ke tla o bontsha.

I will show you.
(Ek sal jou wys.)

(ii) **benya** – shine (blink); **bentsha** – to cause to shine (om te laat blink)

Oli e bentsha letlalo.

Oil causes the skin to shine.
(Olie laat die vel blink.)

(iii) **hlanya** – mad (mal); **hlantsha** – make mad (mal maak)

Lerato le hlantsha baratani.

Love maddens lovers.
(Liefde maak geliefdes mal.)

(iv) **makala** – surprise (verrassing); **makatsa** – to cause to be surprised (verras)

Sebapadi se makatsa setjhaba.

A player surprises the nation.
('n Speler verras die volk.)

15. The verb has the **intensive** form. The intensive form of the verb is when an act is done thoroughly or properly. When the intensive form of the verb is created, the ending part of the verb is changed to **-isisa**, e.g.

(i) **utlwa** – hear (hoor) ; **utlwisisa** – hear properly, understand (hoor duidelik, verstaan)

Jwale ke a utlwisisa.

Now I understand/hear properly.
(Nou verstaan ek/hoor ek duidelik.)

(ii) **hlahloba** – examine (ondersoek); **hlahlobisisa** – examine thoroughly (ondersoek deeglik)

Ngaka e hlahlobisisa mokudi.

The doctor examines the patient thoroughly.
(Die dokter ondersoek die pasiënt deeglik.)

(iii) **suha** – rub clothing (vryf wasgoed); **suhisisa** – rub clothing thoroughly (vryf wasgoed deeglik)

Mosadi o suhisisa kobo.

A woman rubs clothing thoroughly.
('n Vrou vryf die wasgoed deeglik.)

(iv) **sotha** – wring (omdraai); **sothisisa** – wring thoroughly (deeglik omdraai)

Monna o sothisisa molala wa tau.

A man wrings the neck of a lion thoroughly.
('n Man draai die leeu se nek deeglik om.)

(v) **omisa** – dry (afdroog); **omisisa** – dry thoroughly (deeglik afdroog)

Nkgono o omisisa matokomane.

Grandmother dries the nuts thoroughly.
(Ouma droog die neute deeglik af.)

16. The verb has a **reciprocal** form. The reciprocal form of the verb is when the action is naturally carried out among parties involved almost in a sense of retaliation. When the reciprocal form of the verb is created, the ending part of the verb is changed to **-ana**, e.g.

(i) **fa** – give (gee); **fana** – give each other, one another (aan mekaar gee)

Ba fana dimpho.

They give each other presents.
(Hulle gee geskenke aan mekaar.)

(ii) **bona** – see (sien); **bonana** – see each other (mekaar sien)

Metswalle ya kgale e a bonana hape.

Old friends see each other again.
(Ou vriende sien mekaar weer.)

(iii) **moma**– join (saamvoeg); **momahana** – become joined together (saamgevoeg word)

Mahlahahlela a a momahana.

Chains are becoming joined together.
(Kettings word saamgevoeg.)

(iv) **tseba** – know (ken); **tsebana** – know each other (mekaar ken)

Re a tsebana.

We know each other.
(Ons ken mekaar.)

(v) **nka** – take (aanpak); **nkana** – tackle, engage each other (mekaar aanpak)

Mabotho a nkana.

The armies engaged each other.
(Die vyande het mekaar gepak.)

17. The verb has a **reversive** form. The reversive form of the verb expresses the idea that the action is being reversed or undone. When the reversive form of the verb is created, the ending part of the verb is changed to **-olla** or **-oloha**, e.g.

(i) **epela** – bury (begrawe); **epolla** – dig out or up, exhume (opgrawe)

Ntja e epolla lesapo.

A dog digs out the bone.
('n Hond grawe die been uit.)

(ii) **tlama** – tie (vasknoop); **tlamolla** – untie (losknoop)

Lepolesa le tlamolla motshwaruwa.

The policeman unties the convict.
(Die polisieman knoop die gevangene los.)

(iii) **koba** – bend (buig); **kobolla** – straighten (reguit maak)

Ke kobolla tshepe ka mollo.

I straighten the iron with fire.
(Ek maak die yster met vuur reguit.)

(iv) **kgathala** – get tired (moeg word); **kgatholoha** – become refreshed (verfris word)

Ka robala mme ka kgatholoha.

I slept and became refreshed.
(Ek het geslaap en verfris gevoel.)

(v) **hlompha** – respect (respekteer); **hlompholla** – disrespect (minag)

O se ke wa hlompholla motho e moholo.

Do not disrespect (dishonour) an adult person.
(Moenie 'n volwasse persoon minag nie.)

18. The verb has a **reflexive** form. The reflexive form of the verb expresses the idea that the action is being done by the actor, i.e. the subject or object, to itself. When the reflexive form of the verb is created, the letter **i** is attached to the front of the verb, if the action is directed at the subject.

Where action is directed at the subject: **i** is used

rata love (liefde) – **irata** becomes **ithata** love oneself (jouself liefhê)

ruta teach (leer) – **iruta** becomes **ithuta** teach oneself (jouself leer)

roba break (breek) – **iroba** becomes **ithoba** break oneself (jouself breek)

loma bite (byt) – **iloma** becomes **itoma** bite oneself (jouself byt)

leboha thank (bedank) – **ileboha** becomes **iteboha** thank oneself (jouself bedank)

bona see (sien) – **ibona** becomes **ipona** see oneself or to be conceited (om verwaand te wees)

bontsha show (wys) – **ibontsha** becomes **ipontsha** show oneself (jouself wys)

sebetsa work (werk) – **isebetsa** becomes **itshebetsa** work oneself, i.e. to be self-employed (vir jouself werk)

Further examples of the verb (Verdere voorbeelde van die werkwoord)

palama – climb (klim)
tlosa – remove (verwyder)
bona – see (sien)
fepa – feed (voer)
haha – build (bou)
rapela – pray (bid)
bina – sing (sing)
ema – stand (staan)
nahana – think (dink)
tshosa – surprise, shock (verrassing, skok)
sireletsa – protect (verdedig)
omanya – scold, reprimand (uitskel, berispe)

Exercises (Oefeninge)

1. Differentiate between nouns and verbs. The following words are nouns and verbs. You are asked to indicate which are the nouns and which are the verbs:

setulo – chair (stoel)
tafole – table (tafel)
bua – talk (praat)
ja – eat (eet)
tadima – look (kyk)
ngola – write (skryf)
thabisa – make happy (bly maak)
thabo – happiness (blydskap)
ruta – teach (leer)
thuto – education (opvoeding)
hlatswa – wash (was)
lengolo – letter (brief)

2. Create the **passive** form of the following verbs:
   (i) **nka** – take (vat)
   (ii) **loma** – bite (byt)
   (iii) **ruta** – teach (onderrig)

3. Create the **neuter** form of the following verbs:
   (i) **tseba** – know (weet)
   (ii) **dula** – sit (sit)
   (iii) **ja** – eat (eet)

4. Create the **applied** form of the following verbs:
   (i) **bitsa** – call (roep)
   (ii) **ngola** – write (skryf)
   (iii) **tshwara** – hold (hou)

5. Create the **causative** form of the following verbs:
   (i) **utlwa** – hear, feel (hoor, voel)
   (ii) **kganna** – drive (dryf)
   (iii) **pheha** – cook (kook)

6. Create the **intensive** form of the following verbs:
   (i) **sheba** – look (kyk)
   (ii) **hlatswa** – wash (was)
   (iii) **tseka** – contest (betwis)

7. Create the **reciprocal** form of the following verbs:
   (i) **batla** – want (hê)
   (ii) **roba** – break (breek)
   (iii) **otla** – beat (slaan)

8. Create the **reversive** form of the following verbs:
   (i) **ina** – immerse (insteek)

(ii) **tjhekela** – dig, bury (grawe, begrawe)
(iii) **nyala** – marry (trou)

9. Create the **reflexive** form of the following verbs (using the letter i)
   (i) **tsamaisa** –take away, send away (wegneem, wegstuur)
   (ii) **emisa** – cause to stand (laat staan)
   (iii) **buisa** – cause to talk (laat praat)

Increase your vocabulary (Verbreed u woordeskat)

kopa – beg (smeek)
amohela – receive (ontvang)
qeta – finish (klaarmaak)
phetha – complete (voltooi)
tsamaya – go, walk (gaan, loop)
bolaya – kill (doodmaak)
reka – buy (koop)
tseka – contest (bestry, betwis)
sebetsa – work (werk)
kopana – meet (ontmoet)
botsa – ask (vra)
bala – read (lees)
leleka – chase (wegjaag)
kganna – drive (bestuur)
fofa – fly (vlieg)

11

The concord

(Kongruensie)

Orientation (Oriëntering)

In our daily speech, it is absolutely important that the elements or parts of speech that we use are compatible or agree with each other. For instance, a verb must always agree with its subject or object either in singular or plural forms. In Sesotho, use is made of a concord to realise this agreement. Hence we speak of a concordial agreement.

Definition (Bepaling)

The concord is a word that links words in a sentence. In Sesotho, a concord is a little word that links, refers to or agrees with either the subject or the object in a sentence.

(i) **Ke a ja.**
I am eating. (Ek eet.)

(ii) **Le a bua.**
You are talking. (Julle praat.)

(iii) **Di a fela.**
They are finishing. (Hulle maak klaar.)

Exposition (Uitleg)

In the above examples, the concord **a** performs the function of linking the subject **ke, le** and **di** with the verbs, **ja, bua** and **fela** respectively. In this case, the concord is called a subjectival concord. However, the concord can also link the verb with an object, and is called the objectival concord, e.g.

(i) **Ke mo romme.**
I have sent him/her. (Ek het hom gestuur.)

The object here is **mo** – him (hom).

(ii) **Re ba bone.** – We saw them. (Ons het hulle gesien.)

The object here is **ba** – them (hulle).

(iii) **Se di tshwere.** – It has caught them. (Dit het hulle gevang.)

The object here is **di** – them (hulle).

Further examples (Verdere voorbeelde)

1. The subjectival concord, i.e. the concord that refers to and agrees with the subject (according to noun classes):

Person	Singular	Plural
1st person:	**ke**	**re**
2nd person:	**o**	**le**
3rd person:	**o**	**ba**

Table 12

Class	Concord	Sentence usage	English
1	**o**	**o batla dijo**	he wants food
2	**ba**	**ba batla dijo**	they want food
3	**o**	**o batla dijo**	it wants food
4	**e**	**e batla dijo**	they want food
5	**le**	**le batla dijo**	it wants food
6	**a**	**a batla dijo**	they want food
7	**se**	**se batla dijo**	it wants food
8	**di**	**di batla dijo**	they want food
9	**e**	**e batla dijo**	it wants food
10	**di**	**di batla dijo**	they want food
Classes 11, 12 & 13 do not exist in Sesotho			
14	**bo**	**bo batla dijo**	it wants food
15	**ho**	**ho batla dijo**	it wants food
16	**ho**	**ho hotle**	it is beautiful
17	**ho**	**ho hotle**	it is beautiful
18	**ho**	**hop hotle**	it is beautiful

2. The concord that refers to and agrees with the object (according to noun classes):

Person concord	Subjectival concord	Objectival
1st person	**ke**	**mo**
2nd person	**o**	**mo**
3rd person	**o**	**mo**

Table 13

Class	Subjectival concord	Objectival concord	Sentence usage	English
1	**ke**	**mo**	**ke mo shapile**	I have thrashed him/her
2	**ke**	**ba**	**ke ba shapile**	I have thrashed them
3	**ke**	**o**	**ke o shapile**	I have thrashed it
4	**ke**	**e**	**ke e shapile**	I have thrashed them
5	**ke**	**le**	**ke le shapile**	I have thrashed it
6	**ke**	**a**	**ke a shapile**	I have thrashed them
7	**ke**	**se**	**ke se shapile**	I have thrashed it
8	**ke**	**di**	**ke di shapile**	I have thrashed them
9	**ke**	**e**	**ke e shapile**	I have thrashed it
10	**ke**	**di**	**ke di shapile**	I have thrashed them
Classes 11, 12 & 13 do not exist in Sesotho				
14	**ke**	**bo**	**ke bo shapile**	I have thrashed it
15	**ke**	**ho**	**ke ho shapile**	I have thrashed it
16	**ke**	**ho**	**ke ho bone**	I have seen it
17	**ke**	**ho**	**ke ho bone**	I have seen it
18	**ke**	**ho**	**ke ho bone**	I have seen it

Exercises (Oefeninge)

1. Supply the subjectival concords for the following noun classes:

1st person	singular and plural
2nd person	singular and plural
3rd person	singular and plural

Classes:

1	4
2	9
3	10

2. Supply the objectival concords for the following noun classes:

Classes:

1	5
2	14
3	
4	15

Increase your vocabulary (Verbreed u woordeskat)

Objectival formations

mo + bitse = mmitse – call him/her (roep hom/haar)

mo + bone = mmone – see him/her (sien hom/haar)

nna + fa = mphe – give me (gee my)

nna + nke = nkuke – pick me up (tel my op)

nna + tshepa = ntshepa – trust me (vertrou my)

nna + oka = nkoka – nurse me (verpleeg my)

nna + suna = ntshuna – kiss me (soen my)

nna + baballa = mpaballa – preserve, protect me (beskerm my)

nna + amohele = nkamohele – welcome, receive me (verwelkom, ontvang my)

nna + tlohele = ntlohele – leave me (los my)

Subjectival formations

Monna *o* ja nama. – A man eats some meat. ('n Man eet vleis.)

Banna *ba* ja nama. – Men eat meat. (Mans eet vleis.)

Moriana *o* molemo. – Medicine is good. (Die geneesmiddel is goed.)

Meriana *e* molemo. – Medicines are good. (Die geneesmiddels is goed.)

Lelapa *le* letjha. – The home is new. (Die huis is nuut.)

Malapa *a* matjha. – Homes are new. (Die huise is nuut.)

Setulo *se* seholo. – The chair is big. (Die stoel is groot.)

Ditulo *di* kgolo. – The chairs are big. (Die stoele is groot.)

12

The tenses

(Die tye)

Orientation (Oriëntering)

All our actions happen at a particular time, either yesterday, today or tomorrow. Earlier on we said that a verb was a "doing word". In the study of language, the timing of a verb is called a tense. The tense, therefore, indicates when the action happened, is happening or will happen.

Definition (Definisie)

A tense is a grammatical indication of time. It shows when a particular act or deed happens,, i.e. whether in the past, present or future. The verb is, therefore, the heart of the tense. There are four broad categorisations of a tense. We want to restrict you to those four at this stage of learning Sesotho. Look at the following brief examples:

The verb used here is **"tsamaya"**, walk (loop)

Present tense:	**Ngwana o a tsamaya.** The child walks. (Die kind loop.)
Past tense:	**Ngwana o ile a tsamaya.** The child walked. (Die kind het geloop.)
Future tense:	**Ngwana o tla tsamaya.** The child will walk. (Die kind sal loop.)
Perfect tense:	**Ngwana o tsamaile.** The child has walked. (Die kind het al geloop.)

We should also mention that a tense is said to be continuous when the action has been going on for some time.

Exposition (Uitleg)

We shall now treat each category of a tense, using 10 different verbs. We shall use the same 10 verbs in the past and future tenses. Note how some verbs change in structure as they assume different tenses:

The present tense (Die teenwoordige tyd)

The present tense indicates that the action takes place now

1. Verb: **reka** – buy (koop)

   Ke reka nama.
   I buy meat. (Ek koop vleis.)

2. Verb: **bua** – talk (praat)

   O bua nnete.
   You tell the truth. (Jy praat die waarheid.)

3. Verb: **loma** – bite (byt)

   Ntja e loma leshodu.
   the dog bites the thief. (Die hond byt die dief.)

4. Verb: **bina** – sing (sing)

   Ba bina sefela.
   They sing a hymn. (Hulle sing 'n gesang.)

5. Verb: **roka** – sew (naai)

   Mosadi o roka mose.
   The woman sews a dress. (Die vrou maak 'n rok.)

6. Verb: **ja** – eat (eet)

   Ke ja dijo
   I eat food. (Ek eet kos.)

7. Verb: **bala** – read (lees)

   Ngwana o bala buka
   The child reads a book. (Die kind lees 'n boek.)

8. Verb: **dula** – sit (sit)

   Mme o dula setulong
   Mother sits on a chair. (Moeder sit op 'n stoel.)

9. Verb: **robala** – sleep (slaap)

   Ntate o a robala.
   Father sleeps. (Pa slaap.)

10. Verb: **kganna** – drive (bestuur)

    Monna o kganna koloi.
    The man drives a car. (Die man bestuur 'n kar.)

The past tense (Die verlede tyd)

The past tense indicates that the action has already taken place. We shall use the examples in a corresponding order:

1. Verb: **reka**

   The present tense changes to **ile ka reka** (bought) in the past tense., i.e.

   Ke ile ka reka nama.

   I bought meat. (Ek het vleis gekoop.)

2. Verb: **bua**

   O ile wa bua nnete.

   You told the truth. (Jy het die waarheid gepraat.)

3. Verb: **loma**

   Ntja e ile ya loma leshodu.

   The dog bit the thief. (Die hond het die dief gebyt.)

4. Verb: **bina**

   Ba ile ba bina sefela

   They sang a hymn. (Hulle het 'n gesang gesing.)

5. Verb: **roka**

   Mosadi o ile a roka mose.

   The woman sewed a dress. (Die vrou het 'n rok gemaak.)

6. Verb: **ja**

   Ke ile ka ja dijo.

   I ate food. (Ek het kos geëet.)

7. Verb: **bala**

   Ngwana o ile a bala buka.
   The child read a book. (Die kind het 'n boek gelees.)

8. Verb: **dula**

   Mme o ile a dula setulong.
   Mother sat on a chair. (Moeder het op 'n stoel gesit.)

9. Verb: **robala**

   Ntate o ile o robala.
   Father slept. (Pa het geslaap.)

   Note the change of form, **robala** and not **robadile.**

10. Verb: **kganna**

    Monna o ile a kganna koloi.
    The man drove a car. (Die man het 'n kar bestuur.)

The future tense (Die toekomende tyd)

The future tense indicates that the action is about to take place. We shall use the above examples in a corresponding order:

1. Verb: **reka**

   In order to form the future tense of **reka**, we add **tla** (will) before this verb, i.e.

   Ke tla reka nama.
   I will buy meat. (Ek sal vleis koop.)

2. Verb: **bua**

   O tla bua nnete.
   You will tell the truth. (Jy sal die waarheid praat.)

3. Verb: **loma**

   Ntja e tla loma leshodu.
   The dog will bite the thief. (Die hond sal die dief byt.)

4. Verb: **bina**

   Ba tla bina sefela.
   They will sing a hymn. (Hulle sal 'n gesang sing.)

5. Verb: **roka**

Mosadi o tla roka mose.

The woman will sew a dress. (Die vrou sal 'n rok maak.)

The perfect tense (Die voltooide tyd)

The perfect tense indicates that the action is over and complete. This tense expresses the fact that the action has been accomplished or completed. In Sesotho the perfect tense is formed by adding three common formatives **-ile**, **-ele**, **-etse** at the end of the verb. We shall take each of the these formatives to form the perfect tense:

1. **-ile**

	Present tense	Perfect tense
(i)	**Ke a bua.** I speak. (Ek praat.)	**Ke buile.** I have spoken (Ek het gepraat.)
(ii)	**Bana ba a tsamaya** The children go (Die kinders gaan.)	**Bana ba tsamaile** The children have gone (Die kinders het gegaan.)
(iii)	**Mosadi o a pheha** The woman cooks (Die vrou kook.)	**Mosadi o phehile** The woman has cooked (Die vrou het gekook.)
(iv)	**Sehahi se diha lejwe** The builder drops a stone (Die bouer laat 'n klip val.)	**Sehahi se dihile lejwe** The builder has dropped a stone (Die bouer het 'n klip laat val.)
(v)	**Mosuwe o shapa ngwana** The teacher thrashes a child (Die onderwyser slaan 'n kind.)	**Mosuwe o shapile ngwana** The teacher has thrashed the child (Die onderwyser het die kind geslaan.)

2. **-ele**

	Present tense	Perfect tense
(i)	**Ke ja nama.** I eat meat. (Ek eet vleis.)	**Ke jele nama.** I have eaten meat. (Ek het vleis geëet.)
(ii)	**Lehlanya le a wa.** The lunatic falls. (Die kranksinnige val.)	**Lehlanya le wele.** The lunatic has fallen. (Die kranksinnige het geval.)
(iii)	**Katse e nwa lebese.** The cat drinks milk. (Die kat drink melk.)	**Katse e nwele lebese.** The cat has drunk milk. (Die kat het melk gedrink.)

(iv)	**Lesea le kgwa lesapo.** The baby spits out a bone. (Die babatjie spoeg 'n been uit.)	**Lesea le kgwele lesapo.** The baby spat out a bone. (Die babatjie het 'n been uitgespoeg.)
(v)	**Ntja e a shwa.** The dog dies. (Die hond vrek.)	**Ntja e shwele.** The dog has died. (Die hond het gevrek.)
3. **-etse**	**Present tense**	**Perfect tense**
(i)	**Ke rwala patsi.** I carry (on my head) wood. (Ek dra hout.)	**Ke rwetse patsi.** I have carried (on my head) wood. (Ek het hout gedra.)
(ii)	**Phoofolo e a hatsela.** The animal feels cold. (Die dier kry koud.)	**Phoofolo e hatsetse.** the animal has felt cold. (Die dier het koud gekry.)
(iii)	**Mokudi o a kgathala.** The patient gets tired. (Die pasiënt word moeg.)	**Mokudi o kgathetse.** The patient has got tired. (Die pasiënt het moeg geword.)
(iv)	**Metsi a a bela.** The water boils. (Die water kook.)	**Metsi a betse.** The water has boiled. (Die water het gekook.)
(v)	**Dijo di a futhumala.** The food gets warm. (Die kos word warm.)	**Dijo di futhumetse.** the food has got warm. (Die kos het warm geword.)

Further examples of the tenses (Verdere voorbeelde)

In order to help you understand tenses better, we will group the following sentences in tenses:

Present tense

(i) **Mosadi o fepa ngwana.**

The woman feeds the child. (Die vrou voed die kind.)

(ii) **Katse e palama sefate.**

A cat climbs a tree. ('n Kat klim in die boom.)

(iii) **Pula e na haholo.**

The rain falls heavily, i.e. It rains heavily. (Dit reën hard.)

(iv) **Ke bua nnete.**

I tell the truth. (Ek praat die waarheid.)

(v) **Ntate o tjho jwalo.**
Father says so. (Pa sê so.)

(vi) **Mme o re jwalo.**
Mother says so. (Ma sê so.)

(vii) **Nkgono o robala motsheare.**
Grandmother sleeps during the day. (Ouma slaap gedurende die dag.)

(viii) **Tau e tsoma bosiu.**
A lion hunts at night. ('n Leeu jag in die nag.)

(ix) **Letsatsi le dikela mantsiboya.**
The sun sets in the evening. (Die son gaan onder in die aand.)

Perfect tense

(i) **Mosadi o fepile ngwana.**
The woman has fed the child. (Die vrou het die kind gevoed.)

(ii) **Katse e palame sefate.**
A cat has climbed a tree. ('n Kat het in die boom geklim.)

(iii) **Pula e nele haholo.**
The rain has fallen heavily, i.e. It has rained heavily. (Dit het hard gereën.)

(iv) **Ke buile nnete.**
I have told the truth. (Ek het die waarheid gepraat.)

(v) **Ntate o tjhelo jwalo.**
Father has said so. (Pa het so gesê.)

(vi) **Mme o itse jwalo.**
Mother has said so. (Ma het so gesê.)

(vii) **Nkgono o robetse motsheare.**
Grandmother has slept during the day. (Ouma het gedurende die dag geslaap.)

(viii) **Tau e tsomme bosiu.**
A lion has hunted at night. ('n Leeu het in die nag gejag.)

(ix) **Letsatsi le diketse mantsiboya.**
The sun has set in the evening. (Die son het in die aand ondergegaan.)

Future tense

(i) **Mosadi o tla fepa ngwana.**
The woman will feed the child. (Die vrou sal die kind voed.)

(ii) **Katse e tla palama sefate.**
A cat will climb a tree. ('n Kat sal in die boom klim.)

(iii) **Pula e tla na haholo.**
The rain will fall heavily, i.e. It will rain heavily. (Dit sal hard reën.)

(iv) **Ke tla bua nnete.**
I will tell the truth. (Ek sal die waarheid praat.)

(v) **Ntate o tla tjho jwalo.**
Father will say so. (Pa sal so sê.)

(vi) **Mme o tla re jwalo.**
Mother will say so. (Ma sal so sê.)

(vii) **Nkgono o tla robala motsheare.**
Grandmother will sleep during the day. (Ouma sal gedurende die dag slaap.)

(viii) **Tau e tla tsoma bosiu.**
A lion will hunt at night. ('n Leeu sal in die nag jag.)

(ix) **Letsatsi le tla dikela mantsiboya.**
The sun will set in the evening. (Die son sal in die aand ondergaan.)

Past tense

(i) **Mosadi o ile a fepa ngwana.**
The woman fed the child. (Die vrou het die kind gevoed.)

(ii) **Katse e ile ya palama sefate.**
A cat climbed a tree. ('n Kat het in die boom geklim.)

(iii) **Pula e ile ya na haholo.**
The rain fell heavily, i.e. It rained heavily. (Dit het hard gereën.)

(iv) **Ke ile ka bua nnete.**
I told the truth. (Ek het die waarheid gepraat.)

(v) **Ntate o ile a tjho jwalo.**
Father said so. (Pa het so gesê.)

(vi) **Mme o ile a re jwalo.**
Mother said so. (Ma het so gesê.)

(vii) **Nkgono o ile a robala motsheare.**
Grandmother slept during the day. (Ouma het gedurende die dag geslaap.)

(viii) **Tau e ile ya tsoma bosiu.**
A lion hunted during the night. ('n Leeu het gedurende die nag gejag.)

(ix) **Letsatsi le ile la dikela mantsiboya.**
The sun set in the evening. (Die son het in die aand ondergegaan.)

Exercises (Oefeninge)

Write the following sentences in the past tense:

1. **Ke sheba dipalesa.**
I look at the flowers. (Ek kyk na die blomme.)

2. **Ngwana o anya letswele.**
The child sucks the breast. (Die kind suig aan die ma se bors.)

3. **Podi e tlola fentshe**
A goat jumps the fence. ('n Bok spring oor die draad.)

4. **Bana ba ngola tlhahlobo.**
Children write examination. (Kinders skryf eksamen.)

5. **Malome o besa mollo.**
Uncle makes fire. (Oom maak vuur.)

Write the following sentences in the future tense:

1. **Ke jele bohobe.**
I ate bread. (Ek het brood geëet.)

2. **Rakgadi o hlatswitse mose.**
Aunt washed a dress. (Tante het 'n rok gewas.)

3. **Sello o robile setulo.**
Sello broke the chair. (Sello het die stoel gebreek.)

4. **Kamele e jere merwalo.**
A camel carried a load. ('n Kameel het 'n vrag gedra.)

5. **Nnuku o phehile masutsa.**
Nnuku cooked delicious food. (Nnuku het lekker kos gekook.)

Write the following sentences in the perfect tense:

1. **Moruti o tla rera.**
   The minister will preach. (Die predikant sal preek.)
2. **Sekolo se tla kwalwa.**
   The school will close or will be closed. (Die skool sal sluit.)
3. **Dipere di tla matha.**
   The horses will run. (Die perde sal hardloop.)
4. **Tjhelete e tla fihla.**
   Money will come/arrive. (Geld sal kom.)
5. **Leqeba le tla fola.**
   A wound will heal. ('n Wond sal gesond word.)

Increase your vocabulary (Verbreed u woordeskat)

bola – to rot, decay (om vrot te word)
fufulelwa – to perspire, sweat (om te sweet)
apara – to dress, wear (om aan te trek)
bolaya – to kill, murder (om dood te maak)
nwa – to drink (drink)
seno – a drink ('n drankie)
kobo – a blanket ('n kombers)
koloi – a car ('n kar)
seboko – a worm ('n wurm)
seboko – a surname ('n van)
seboko – a loud cry ('n harde gil)
tapole – a potato (aartappel)
tafole – a table (tafel)
leru – a cloud ('n wolk)
maru – clouds (wolke)
moru – a forest ('n bos)
leoto – a foot ('n voet)
nyaroha – to be scared (om bang te wees)
nyamela – to disappear, vanish (om te verdwyn)
fumana – to find (om te vind)

13

The singular and the plural forms

(Die enkelvoud en die meervoud)

Orientation (Oriëntering)

We all know that objects, places and names of things do not only occur in singular form. They also occur in plural form. However, there are exceptions, i.e. a noun may have the same form for the singular and the plural or may only exist in the one form and not in the other, e.g. metsi (water) and madi (blood). In Sesotho, the prefix that is dealt with in chapter 6, plays a crucial role in the determination of the plural.

Definition (Definisie)

The singular refers to the conceptualisation of counting objects in being one, i.e. in expressing them in single form. The plural form, on the other hand, expresses the idea of majority. It is, therefore, the opposite of the singular.

Exposition (Uitleg)

Below we give you a table that indicates the singular and plural forms. Please do not confuse this table with the one of the noun classes. It is only drawn like this to show you how the singular forms correspond to their plural counterparts.

Table 14

Noun	Singular form	Plural form
motho	**motho** – person (persoon, mens)	**batho** – people (mense)
motse	**motse** – village (dorp)	**metse** – villages (dorpe)
lehapu	**lehapu** – watermelon (waatlemoen)	**mahapu** – watermelons (waatlemoene)
selepe	**selepe** – axe (byl)	**dilepe** – axes (byle)
ntlo	**ntlo** – house (huis)	**matlo** – houses (huise)

Table 14 (Continued)

Noun	Singular form	Plural form
borokgo	**borokgo** – bridge (brug)	**marokgo** – bridges (brûe)
ho ja	**ho ja** – to eat (eet)	**ho ja** – to eat (eet)

Further examples of the singular and the plural forms

	Singular	Plural
(i)	**Moruti o tlile.** The minister has come. (Die predikant het gekom.)	**Baruti ba tlile.** The ministers have come. (Die predikante het gekom.)
(ii)	**Moleko o a qala.** Temptation is beginning. (Versoeking begin.)	**Meleko e a qala.** Temptations are beginning. (Versoekings begin.)
(iii)	**Lefielo le robehile.** A broom is broken. ('n Besem is gebreek.)	**Mafielo a robehile.** Brooms are broken. (Besems is gebreek.)
(iv)	**Sekepe se setle.** A ship is beautiful. ('n Skip is mooi.)	**Dikepe di ntle.** Ships are beautiful. (Skepe is mooi.)
(v)	**Ntwa e fedile.** A war/fight has ended. ('n Oorlog is beëindig.)	**Dintwa di fedile.** Wars/fights have ended. (Oorloë is beëindig.)
(vi)	**Bohobe bo butswite.** Bread is cooked. (Brood is gekook/gebak.)	**Mahobe a butswitse.** Bread is cooked. (Brode is gekook/gebak.)

Exercises

The following words (nouns) are in the singular form, supply their corresponding plural forms:

moeti – visitor (besoeker)

mokopu – pumpkin (pampoen)

lehlanya – mahlanya (mal mens, kranksinnige)

setulo – chair (stoel)

ntho – thing (ding)

borokgo – bridge (brug)

ho kotula – to reap (om te oes)

Increase your vocabulary (Verbreed u woordeskat)

Singular	Plural
mofu – dead person (dooie persoon, oorledene)	**bafu** – dead people (oorledenes)
morena – king, chief (koning)	**morena** – kings (konings)
mofumahadi – madam (mevrou)	**mafumahadi** – mesdames (mevroue)
rakgadi – aunt (tante)	**borakgadi** – aunts (tantes)
malome – uncle (oom)	**bomalome** – uncles (ooms)
mangwane – aunt (words denoting blood relationship) (tante)	**bomangwane** – aunts (tantes)
nkgono – grandmother (ouma)	**bonkgono** – grandmothers (oumas)
ntatemoholo – grandfather (oupa)	**bontatemoholo** – grandfathers (oupas)
moropa – drum (tamboer)	**meropa** – drums (tamboere)
monyako – door (deur)	**menyako** – doors (deure)
mobu – soil (grond)	**mebu** – soils (gronde)
mohobelo – dance (dans)	**mehobelo** – dances (danse)
mohato – step (tree)	**mehato** – steps (treë)
molomo – mouth (mond)	**melomo** – mouths (monde)
leoto – foot (voet)	**maoto** – feet (voete)
letswele – breast (bors)	**matswele** – breasts (borste)
lefu – illness, death (siekte, dood)	**mafu** – ilnesses, diseases (siektes, dood)
letamo – dam (dam)	**matamo** – dams (damme)
leshala – coal (kool)	**mashala** – coals (kole)
leqeba – wound (wond)	**maqeba** – wounds (wonde)
seboka – congregation (gemeente)	**diboka** – congregations (gemeentes)
seboko – worm (wurm)	**diboko** – worms (wurms)
seboko – surname (van)	**diboko** – surnames (vanne)
seipone – mirror (spieël)	**diipone** – mirrors (spieëls)
sejana – dish (bord)	**dijana** – dishes (borde)
ntja – dog (hond)	**dintja** – dogs (honde)
nta – louse (luis)	**dinta** – lice (luise)
nko – nose (neus)	**dinko** – noses (neuse)
ntlo – house (huis)	**matlo** – houses, many houses (huise)
nkwe – tiger (tier)	**dinkwe** – tigers (tiers)
bohobe – bread (brood)	**mahobe** – much bread (brode)

borokgo – bridge (brug)
ho ja – to eat (om te eet)
ho nwa – to drink (om te drink)
ho sheba – to look (om te kyk)
ho reka – to buy (om te koop)
ho kena – to enter (om in te gaan)

marokgo – bridges (brûe)
ho ja – to eat (om te eet)
ho nwa – to drink (om te drink)
ho sheba – to look (om te kyk)
ho reka – to buy (om te koop)
ho kena – to enter (om in te gaan)

14

The adjective

(Die byvoeglike naamwoord)

Orientation

In our daily lives, we observe beautiful things and ugly ones; tall objects and short ones; come across good people and bad ones; experience a pleasant smell and an unpleasant one, etc. All these words give us more information about nouns or pronouns and they make their meaning more accurate. These words are called adjectives.

Definition (Definisie)

An adjective is a word that qualifies the noun. This means that the adjective explains the nature or function of the noun in a sentence, e.g.

sefahleho (face) **se setle** – a beautiful face ('n mooi gesig)

sefapano se selelele – a cross which is long, i.e. a long cross ('n lang kruis)

ntlo e kgolo – house which is big, i.e. a big house ('n groot huis)

mose o mosweu – a dress which is white, i.e. a white dress ('n wit rok)

lejwe le leholo – a stone which is huge, i.e. a big stone ('n groot klip)

borokgo bo boholo – a bridge which is huge, i.e. a huge bridge ('n groot brug)

In these six sentences, the following words qualify the noun in each sentence. Those qualifying words or adjectives are:

setle, kgolo, leholo

selelele

mosweu, boholo

Because the adjective qualifies the noun, the adjective conforms to concordial agreement, i.e. the adjective must take the prefix of the noun it is describing (in this case **se**) as well as the linking word or concord **se** to ensure the harmony or concordial agreement referred to in Chapter 10.

Exposition (Uitleg)

Since the adjective has to do with the noun, in Sesotho, it has to assume the prefix of the noun it is describing. In the following table we present the adjective and its concord according to the noun classes.

Table 15

Class	Prefix	Noun		Concord (English)	Adjective
1	**mo-**	**motho**	person	**e** (who is)	**motle** (beautiful)
2	**ba-**	**batho**	people	**ba** (who are)	**batle** (beautiful)
3	**mo-**	**morara**	grape	**o** (which is)	**motala** (green, unripe)
4	**me-**	**merara**	grapes	**e** (which are)	**metala** (green, unripe)
5	**le-**	**lesapo**	bone	**le** (which is)	**lesweu** (white)
6	**ma-**	**masapo**	bones	**a** (which are)	**masweu** (white)
7	**se-**	**seboko**	worm	**se** (which is)	**selelele** (long)
8	**di-**	**diboko**	worms	**tse** (which are)	**telele** (long)
9	**n-**	**ntwa**	war/battle	**e** (which is)	**boima** (heavy)
10	**din-**	**dintwa**	wars/battles	**tse** (which are)	**boima** (heavy)
Classes 11, 12 & 13 are non-existent in Sesotho. These noun classes occur in other African languages such as isiZulu, isiXhosa, etc.					
14	**bo-**	**bohobe**	bread	**bo** (which is)	**boholo** (big)
15	**ho-**	**ho kula**	to be sick	**ho** (which is)	**hobe** (bad)
16	**fa-**	**fatshe**	down	**ho** (which is)	**hotle** (beautiful)
17	**ho-**	**hodimo**	up	**ho** (which is)	**tshabehang** (awesome)
18	**mo-**	**mose**	abroad	**o** (which is)	**hole** (far)

Further examples of the adjective (Verdere voorbeelde)

1. **monna e molelele**
   a man who is tall, i.e. a tall man ('n lang man)

2. **banna ba balelele**
   men who are tall, i.e. tall men (lang mans)

3. **motse o moholo**
   a village which is big, i.e. a big village ('n groot dorp)

4. **metse e meholo**
   villages which are big, i.e. big villages (groot dorpe)

5. **lebanta le letle**
   a belt which is beautiful ('n mooi gordel)

6. **mabanta a matle**
   belts which are beautiful, i.e. beautiful belts (mooi gordels)

7. **sekolo se sebe**
   a school which is bad, i.e. a bad school ('n slegte skool)

8. **dikolo tse mpe**
   schools which are bad, i.e. bad schools (slegte skole)

9. **nkwe e ntle**
   a tiger which is beautiful, i.e. a beautiful tiger ('n mooi tier)

10. **dinkwe tse ntle**
    tigers which are beautiful, i.e. beautiful tigers (mooi tiere)

N.B. Remember, noun classes 11, 12 & 13 do not exist in Sesotho.

14. **borikgwe bo botle**
    a pair of trousers which is beautiful, i.e. a beautiful pair of trousers ('n mooi broek).

15. **ho tjhaka ho monate**
    a visit which is pleasant, i.e. a pleasant visit ('n aangename besoek)

16. **fatshe ho tshosang**
    down which is scaring, i.e. scaring depth ('n vreeslike diepte)

17. **hodimo ho makatsang**
    up which is amazing, i.e. amazing height (wonderbaarlike hoogte)

18. **morao o tebileng**
    back which is deep, i.e. far back (ver agter)

Positive degree

happy: **Pitso o thabile.**
Pitso is happy. (Pitso is gelukkig.)

Comparative degree

happier: **Pitso o thabile haholo.**
Pitso is happier. (Pitso is gelukkiger.)

N.B. We use **haholo**, meaning "more".

Superlative degree

happiest: **Pitso o thabile haholo-holo.**
Pitso is the happiest. (Pitso is die gelukkigste.)

N.B. We use **"haholo-holo"** as a duplicate to indicate the superlative or highest form of happiness.

To indicate the comparative and superlative degrees in Sesotho, use is also made of a word **hampe**, which does not literally mean "badly" but "terribly" in an intense but positive manner, e.g.

Positive degree

happy: **Pitso o thabile.**
Pitso is happy. (Pitso is gelukkig.)

Comparative degree

happier: **Pitso o thabile hampe**, i.e. terribly happy.
Pitso is happier. (Pitso is gelukkiger.)

Superlative degree

happiest: **Pitso o thabile hampe-mpe** (he is happy to a very great degree).
Pitso is happiest. (Pitso is die gelukkigste.)

Exercises on the adjective (Oefeninge)

Add the correct prefix to complete the following adjectives:

Class 1 **mosadi e -tle** – a beautiful woman ('n mooi vrou)
2 **basadi ba -tle** – beautiful women (mooi vrouens)
3 **mokopu o -nate** – a delicious pumpkin ('n lekker pampoen)
4 **mekopu e -nate** – delicious pumpkins (lekker pampoene)
5 **lebota le -lelele** – a high wall ('n hoë muur)
6 **mabota a -lelele** – high walls (hoë mure)
7 **setlama se -tala** – a green plant ('n groen plant)
8 **ditlama tse -tala** – green plants (groen plante)
9 **ntja e -kgolo** – a big dog ('n groot hond)
10 **dintja tse -kgolo** – big dogs (groot honde)

N.B. Remember noun classes 11, 12, & 13 do not exist in Sesotho.

14 **borokgo bo -holo** – a big bridge ('n hoë brug)

15 **ho robala ho -nate** – pleasant sleep (aangename slaap)

Increase your vocabulary (Verbreed u woordeskat)

mobe – ugly (lelik)

monate – delicious (lekker)

meharo – greedy (gulsig)

mona – jealous (jaloers)

mona – here (hier)

lebitla – grave (graf)

lebollo – traditional initiation school (tradisionele bergskool)

lehae – home (huis, tuis)

lebitso – name (naam)

lepolanka – plank (plank)

sediba – fountain (fontein)

seso – wound (wond)

sepoko – ghost (spook)

sephooko – owl (uil)

senqanqane – frog (padda)

serurubele – butterfly (skoenlapper)

nkgo – clay calabash, vase (klei blompot)

ntwa – fight, war (oorlog)

mpa – stomach (maag)

paola – brazier (konka)

15

The adverb

(Die bywoord)

Orientation (Oriëntering)

We speak in a particular manner; we sleep in a certain way; we understand situations in a particular manner; we see things in a certain fashion. All these doing words, called verbs as explained in chapter 10, are described by words called adverbs.

Definition (Definisie)

An adverb describes a verb. It is a word that gives us more information about a verb, adjective, phrases or whole sentences in order to make their meaning more accurate. Remember, we said that the verb is a doing word. Thus the adverb sheds more light on the action that is done.

Consider the following examples:

(i) **Ke ja haholo.**
I eat too much. (Ek eet te veel.)

(ii) **Pere e raha ha bohloko.**
A horse kicks painfully. ('n Perd skop seer.)

(iii) **Lesea le bososela ha monate.**
A baby smiles pleasantly. ('n Babatjie glimlag mooi.)

Exposition (Uitleg)

There are five types of adjectives:

1. The adverb of manner which answers the question: how? = how the action is done (hoe die aksie gedoen word).
2. The adverb of time which answers the question: when? = when is the action done (wanneer word die aksie gedoen).

3. The adverb of place which answers the question: where? = where the action is being done (waar die aksie gedoen word).

4. The adverb of logic which asks the question: what? = what is being done (wat gedoen word).

5. The adverb of degree which answers the question: to what extent? = to what extent is action being done (tot watter mate word aksie uitgevoer).

We shall treat each adverb:

The adverb of manner (how?)

This adverb "how?" in Sesotho has the equivalent, **jwang?**

Let us consider the following examples:

(i) **O phela jwang?** How are you? (Hoe gaan dit?)

(ii) **Ngwana o robala jwang?** How does the child sleep? (Hoe slaap die kind?)

(iii) **Mpho ke motho ya jwang?** What type of a person is Mpho? (Watter soort persoon is Mpho?)

The adverb of time (when?)

This adverb concerns itself with when a particular action happens. In Sesotho we use **neng?**

Let us look at the following examples:

(i) **Moeti o fihla neng?** – When does the visitor arrive? (Wanneer kom die besoeker?)

(ii) **Dikolo di tlo kwalwa neng?** – When will the schools close? (Wanneer sal die skole sluit?)

(iii) **Mosebetsi o tla fela hosasa.** – The work will be completed tomorrow. (Die werk sal môre klaar wees.)

The adverb of place (where?)

This adverb concerns itself with where a particular action takes place. In Sesotho we use **kae?**

Consider the following examples:

(i) **O dula kae?** – Where do you stay? (Waar bly jy?)

(ii) **Ba ile kae?** – Where have they gone to? (Waarheen het hulle gegaan?)

(iii) **Gauteng ke kae?** – Gauteng is where? i.e. Where is Gauteng? (Waar is Gauteng?)

The adverb of logic (what? and who?)

This adverb asks the basic question "what is being done?" In Sesotho we use **eng?** and **mang?**

Consider the following examples:

(i) **Ke eng eo?** What is that? (Wat is dit?)
(ii) **O rata eng?** What do you like? (Waarvan hou jy?)
(iii) **Ba bua eng?** What are they talking? (Waaroor praat hulle?)

The use of who? **mang?**

(i) **Ke mang eo?** Who is that one? (Wie is daardie een?)
(ii) **O rata mang?** Who do you like? (Van wie hou jy?)
(iii) **Ba bua le mang?** With whom are they talking? (Met wie praat hulle?)

The adverb of degree

This adverb refers to the extent to which something is happening. In Sesotho we use the following words:

Haholo, meaning to a great extent (te veel)

(i) **Mosadi o bua haholo.** A woman talks too much. ('n Vrou praat te veel.)
(ii) **Sebapadi se raha bolo haholo.** A player kicks the ball hard. ('n Speler skop die bal hard.)
(iii) **Mme o tshola haholo.** Mother dishes out too much, i.e. food. (Moeder deel te veel kos uit.)

Hanyenyane, meaning to a small degree (in 'n klein mate)

(i) **Seapehi se tshola hanyenyane.** A cook dishes out little, i.e. food. ('n Kok deel min kos uit.)
(ii) **Ngwana o kula hanyenyane.** Baby is sick to a little extent. (Die babatjie is siekerig.)
(iii) **Pula e na hanyenyane.** The rain falls softly. (Die reën val sag.)

Further examples of the adverb

Adverb of manner (how?), i.e. jwang?

(i) **O bona jwang?**
You see how? i.e. How do you see? (Hoe sien jy?)

(ii) **O mpone jwang?**

You saw me how? i.e. How did you see me? (Hoe het jy my gesien?)

(iii) **Ke tla tsamaya jwang?**

I will travel, walk how? i.e. How will I travel? (Hoe sal ek reis, loop?)

The adverb of time (when?), i.e. neng?

(i) **Ba tla kgutla neng?**

They will return when? i.e. When will they return? (Wanneer sal hulle terugkom?)

(ii) **Pula e nele neng?**

The rain fell when? i.e. When did it rain? (Wanneer het dit gereën?)

(iii) **Dijo di tla butswa neng?**

Food will be cooked when? i.e. When will food be ready for eating? (Wanneer sal die kos reg wees?)

The adverb of place (where?), i.e. kae?

(i) **Ke motho wa ho kae?**

He/she is a person of where? i.e. Where does he/she belong? (Waar (be)hoort hy/sy?)

(ii) **Ba tla hlaha le ka kae?**

They will appear from where? i.e. From where will they appear? (Waarvandaan sal hulle verskyn?)

(iii) **O ya kae?**

You are going where? i.e. Where are you going? (Waarheen gaan jy?)

The adverb of logic (what?, i.e. eng, and who?, i.e. mang?)

(i) **Dikeledi o jele eng?**

Dikeledi has eaten what? i.e. What has Dikeledi eaten? (Wat het Dikeledi geëet?)

(ii) **O bala eng?**

You are reading what? i.e. What are you reading? (Wat lees jy?)

(iii) **Na ke bomang?**

They are who? i.e. Who are they? (Wie is hulle?)

(iv) **O bua le mang?**

You are talking to whom? i.e. Whom are you talking to? (Met wie praat jy?)

The adverb of degree (the extent to which something is happening)

(i) **O ja haholo.**
You eat too much. (Jy eet te veel.)

(ii) **Akgela bolo haufinyane.**
Throw the ball nearby. (Gooi die bal naby.)

(iii) **O hatela hodimo.**
He/she walks fast, i.e. literally up (Hy/sy loop vinnig.)

(iv) **Molemi o kotutse hanyenyane.**
The farmer reaped a little bit. (Die boer het bietjie geoes.)

Exercises on the adverb (Oefeninge)

1. Write your own two sentences using the adverb of manner **jwang?** (how?)
2. Write your own two sentences using the adverb of time **neng?** (when?)
3. Write your own two sentences using the adverb of place **kae?** (where?)
4. Write your own two sentences using the adverb that concerns itself with logic **eng?** (what?) **mang?** (who?)
5. Write your own two sentences using the adverb of degree **ha kae?** (to what extent?)

Increase your vocabulary (Verbreed u woordeskat)

botsa – ask (vra)
mamela – listen (luister)
thupa – stick (kierie)
thaba – mountain (berg)
thabo – happiness (blydskap)
jwang – grass (gras)
molora – ash (as)
lehlabathe – sand (sand)
majwe – stones (klippe)
tshepe – iron, steel (yster, staal)

kgauta – gold (goud)
taemane – diamond (diamand)
koporo – copper (koper)
silivera – silver (silwer)
kgalase – glass (glas)
lehlwa – snow (sneeu)
leqhwa – ice (ys)
sefako – hail (hael)
phoka – dew (dou)
serame – cold (koud)

16

The diminutive

(Die verkleinwoord)

Orientation (Oriëntering)

In language, there are big words and small words. There are also full words and reduced words. Big and fuller words convey bigger and fuller meaning. In the same way, reduced words convey smaller meaning. In the study of language, reduced words are called diminutives.

Definition (Definisie)

A diminutive is a word or word form that reduces another word. The diminutive is used in order to lessen or weaken the meaning of a word. This is done by means of the suffix. Several suffixes are used. Typical examples of suffixes in the creation of the diminutive are, **-nyana, -ana** and **-tsana.** It may also be used to undermine or ridicule. In certain instances, the diminutive is used to express admiration. It is also used to denote genders and even pity.

Exposition (Uitleg)

Let us look at the various categories of the usage of the diminutive in Sesotho:

1. To express diminutive

(i) **ntja** – dog (hond); **ntjanyana** – puppy (hondjie); **-nyana**

(ii) **pere** – horse (perd); **petsana** – foal (vul); **-tsana**

(iii) **palo** – pole (paal); **palwana** – small pole (paaltjie) **-ana**

2. To express contempt

(i) **motho** – person (persoon); **mothwana** – small person (klein persoon)

(ii) **moruti** – minister (predikant); **morutinyana** – little minister (predikantjie)

(iii) **borikgwe** a pair of trousers (broek); **borikgwana** – small trousers (broekie)

3. To express admiration or love

ntle – beautiful (mooi); **ntlenyana** – pretty (mooi)

4. To denote gender

tshweu – white (wit) = **tshowana**

thehla – yellow (geel) = **tshehlana**

5. To express pity

lerantha – tattered piece of clothing ('n verflenterde kledingstuk) = **leranthana**

Further examples of the diminutive

1. Using the suffix -ana:

Noun	**Dimunitive**
thaba mountain (berg)	**thabana** small mountain (bergie)
seeta shoe (skoen)	**seetana** small shoe (skoentjie)
lenala nail (nael)	**lenalana** small nail (naeltjie)
buka book (boek)	**bukana** small book (boekie)
sabole sword (swaard)	**sabolana** small sword (swaardjie)

2. Using the suffix -ane

Noun	**Diminutive**
koto knobkerrie (knopkierie)	**kotjane** small knobkerrie (knopkierietjie)
mma, mme mother (moeder)	**mangwane** aunt, i.e. mother's younger sister (tante)
ra, ntate dad, father (vader)	**rangwane** uncle, i.e. father's younger brother (oom)
podi goat (bok)	**potsane** or **potsanyane** kid, i.e. baby goat (bokkie)

3. Using the suffix -nyana

Noun	Diminutive
sekolo school (skool)	**sekolonyana** little school (skooltjie)
thipa knife (mes)	**thipanyana** small knife (messie)
nama meat (vleis)	**namanyana** little meat (vleisie)
monna man (man)	**monnanyana** little man (mannetjie)
lesedi light (lig)	**lesedinyana** little light (also a newspaper) (liggie)

4. Using the suffix -nyane

Noun	Diminutive
lenong vulture (aasvoël)	**lenonyane** small vulture (aasvoëltjie)
podi goat (bok)	**potsanyane** kid (bokkie)

5. Using the suffix -tsane/-tsana

Noun	Diminutive
naledi star (ster)	**naletsana** little star (sterretjie)
pere horse (perd)	**petsana** colt or filly (vulletjie)
koloi car (kar)	**kolotsana** small car (karretjie)

6. Using the suffix -tjana

Noun	Diminutive
sefate tree (boom)	**sefatjana** small tree (boompie)
koto knobkerrie (knopkierie)	**kotjana or kotjane** small knobkerrie (knopkierietjie)
lemati door (deur)	**lematjana** small door (deurtjie)
seriti shadow (skaduwee)	**seritjana** small shadow (skaduweetjie)

7. Using the suffix -tshana

Noun	Diminutive
phiri hyena (hiëna)	**phitshana** small hyena (hiënatjie)
moriri hair (hare)	**moritshana** little hair (haartjie)
nare buffalo (buffel)	**natshana** calf of a buffalo (buffelkalfie)
sehlare medicine (medisyne)	**sehlatshana** little medicine (bietjie medisyne)

Exercises on the diminutive

1. Give the diminutive of the following nouns, using the suffix **-ana**:

    (i) **monna** – man (man)
    (ii) **lejwe** – stone (klip)

2. Give the diminutive of the following nouns, using the suffix **-ane**:

    (i) **koto** – knobkerrie (knopkierie)
    (ii) **podi** – goat (bok)

3. Give the diminutive of the following nouns, using the suffix **-nyana**

    (i) **tsela** – road (pad)
    (ii) **mpho** – gift (geskenk)

4. Give the diminutive of the following nouns, using the suffix **-nyane**

    (i) **lenong** – vulture (aasvoël)

5. Give the diminutive of the following nouns, using the suffix **-tsane/-tsana**

    (i) **podi** – goat (bok)
    (ii) **koloi** – car (kar)

6. Give the diminutive of the following nouns, using the suffix **-tjana**

    (i) **lemati** – door (deur)
    (ii) **lebota** – wall (muur)

7. Give the diminutive of the following nouns, using the suffix **-tshana**

    (i) **moriri** – hair (hare)
    (ii) **phiri** – hyena (hiëna)

Increase your vocabulary (Verbreed u woordeskat)

tau – lion (leeu)
phoofolo – animal (dier)
bere – bear (beer)
leleme – tongue (tong)
molomo – mouth (mond)
selemo – year (jaar)
lerumo – spear (spies)
molamu – stick (stok)
lengope – ditch (gat)
lesapo – bone (been)
lerapo – thong, piece of leather string (riem)
selepe – axe (byl)
mabele – sorghum (graansorghum)
makgethe – decency, purity (ordentlikheid)
kgoho – fowl (hoender)
fariki – pig (vark)
moeti – visitor (besoeker)
lengeloi – angel (engel)
lehodimo – heaven (hemel)
dihele – hell (hel)

17

The augmentative

(Die vergrotingswoord)

Orientation (Oriëntering)

Language uses big words and small words to convey big meaning and little meaning respectively. For the expression of big ideas we use words that are called augmentatives.

Definition (Definisie)

The augmentative is a morpheme that is used to add value to the meaning of another word. It indicates an enlargement. An augmentative is an extension of the verb. In Sesotho, the augmentative is a little word form attached to the end of the word whose meaning is being enhanced, e.g. **-hadi** such as **thaba** (mountain) – **thabahadi** (big mountain). Other suffixes used in the formation of the augmentative are discussed under exposition.

Exposition (Uitleg)

1. Although there are several suffixes that may be used in the formation of the augmentative, the common one that is generally used is **-hadi.** Look at the following examples using the suffix **-hadi.**

Table 16

Class	Prefix	Noun	Augmentative suffix	Augmentative word
1	mo-	motho	+ hadi	mothohadi
2	ba-	batho	+ hadi	bathohadi
3	mo-	morara	+ hadi	morarahadi
4	me-	merara	+ hadi	merarahadi
5	le-	lerako	+ hadi	lerakohadi

Table 16 (continued)

Class	Prefix	Noun	Augmentative suffix	Augmentative word
6	ma-	marako	+ hadi	marakohadi
7	se-	serope	+ hadi	seropehadi
8	di-	dirope	+ hadi	diropehadi
9	n-	ntja	+ hadi	ntjahadi
10	din-	dintja	+ hadi	dintjahadi
Classes 11, 12 & 13 do not exist in Sesotho. These noun classes occur in other African languages such as Zulu, Xhosa etc.				
14	bo-	bohobe	+ hadi	bohobehadi
15	ho-	ho robala	—	—
16	fa-	fatshe	—	—
17	ho-	hodimo	—	—
18	mo-	morao	—	—

2. Classes 15, 16, 17 and 18 do not have an augmentative. Other words are used such as the following to denote the augmentative for these classes:

   (i) **haholo** for class 15

   (ii) **tebileng** or **fatshefatshe** (duplicated) for class 16.

   (ii) **phahameng** or **hodimodimo** (duplicated) for class 17.

   (iv) **moraorao** for class 18, e.g.

   Class 15: **ho robala ho hoholo** – a deep or big sleep ('n diep slaap)

   Class 16: **motheo o fatshefatshe** – a deep foundation ('n diep fondament)

   Class 17: **mahodimo a hodimodimo** – high heavens (hoë hemel)

   Class 18: **morao kwana** – far back or behind (ver agter)

3. The augmentative is also formed by separate words and **kaalo, kana-kana** or **kaa ka** as in the following sentences:

   (i) **kaalo:** This means "as big as" or "as much as" and implies bigness

   Matona o nonne; o kaalo ka thaba.

   Matona is fat, he is as big as a mountain.
   (Matoma is vet, hy is so groot soos 'n berg.)

   Bohale ba hae bo kaalo ka ba tau.

   Anger of his/hers is as much as that of a lion, i.e.
   his/her anger is as much as that of a lion (too much).
   (Sy/haar kwaadheid is meer as die van 'n leeu.)

(ii) **kana-kana**: This means "as big as" or "as much as"

Ntswaki o dirope tse kana-kana.

Ntswaki is the thighs that are as big as, i.e. Ntswaki's thighs are very big. (Ntswaki se dybene is baie groot.)

Lentswe la hae le lekana-kana.

The voice of his/hers is as much as this, i.e. his/her voice is very gruff or deep. (Sy/haar stem is baie dik of diep.)

(iii) **kaa ka**: This means "as many as" or "as big as":

Dinku tsa Thipe di kaa ka lehlabathe la lewatle.

The goats of Thipe are as many as the grains of the sand of the sea, i.e. Thipe's goats are as many as the sand of the sea. (Thipe se bokke is so baie soos die sand van die see.)

Ntho ena e kaa ka tlou.

Thing this is as big as an elephant, i.e. this thing is as big as an elephant. (Hierdie ding is so groot soos 'n olifant.)

4. The augmentative is also formed by other suffixes such as the following:

from **dika** + **oloha**, e.g. **dikoloha** – encircle or go round, i.e. in a wider sense

(i) **Masole a dikoloha motsheare wohle.**
The soldiers walk around the whole day.
(Die soldate loop die hele dag rond.)

from **ahlama** + **olla,** e.g. **ahlamolla** (to make wider)

(ii) **Kwena ya ahlamolla molomo.**
The crocodile opened its mouth widely.
(Die krokodil maak sy mond wyd oop.)

from **olosa** (to pour out sticky or gluey liquid or grain in an elaborate manner)

(iii) **Mme o olosa motoho ho o fodisa.**
Mother pours out soft porridge in order to cool it.
(Moeder gooi sagte pap uit om dit te laat afkoel.)

5. Another independent word that is used in the formation of the augmentative is **tonanahadi**, meaning "very very huge" often using **"ya"** as the possessive prefix, e.g.

(i) **ntlo ya tonanahadi**
a house of bigness, i.e. a very, very big house ('n baie baie groot huis)

(ii) **thaba ya tonanahadi**
a mountain of bigness, i.e. an enormous mountain ('n baie groot berg)

(iii) **lehlahahlela la letonanahadi**
a chain which is very large ('n baie lang ketting)

(iv) **mosamo wa motonanahadi**
a pillow which is very big ('n baie groot kussing)

6. The augmentative is also formed by the repetition or duplication of nouns. The simple example is **kgolo** to become **kgolo-kgolo,** meaning literally big-big, i.e. "very, very huge" or "the real or main thing" as in the following examples:

(i) **tshimo e kgolo-kgolo**
a farm which is big-big, i.e. a very large farm ('n baie groot plaas)

(ii) **Taba-taba ya ntwa ena ke tjhelete.**
The main issue or cause of this fight is money. (Die hoofoorsaak van hierdie geveg, is geld.)

Further examples of the augmentative (Verdere voorbeelde)

(i) **Kubu e na le molomohadi o tshabehang.**
A hippopotamus has a big mouth which is frightening.
('n Seekoei het 'n vreeslike groot mond.)

(ii) **Senqu ke nokahadi e telele Afrika Borwa.**
The Orange river is the longest river in South Africa.
(Die Oranjerivier is die langste rivier in Suid-Afrika.)

(iii) **Seapehi se atolosa dijo ka dinawa.**
The cook multiplies or increases the food by adding beans.
(Die kok vermeerder die kos deur boontjies by te voeg.)

(iv) **Nnuku o otlolla moriri ka kama.**
Nnuku stretches her hair with a comb.
(Nnuku stryk haar hare met 'n kam.)

Exercises (Oefeninge)

1. Form the augmentative from the following words

mpa – stomach (maag)
hlooho – head (kop)
nko – nose (neus)
bethe – bed (bed)

ntlo – house (huis)

ata – multiply (vermenigvuldig)

ngata – many, more (baie, meer)

Increase your vocabulary (Verbreed u woordeskat)

kotsihadi – big danger (groot gevaar)

mosa – mercy (genade)

leratahadi – big noise (groot bohaai)

leshanohadi – big lies (groot leuens)

bosiu – night (nag)

motsheare – daytime (dag)

letsatsi – day (dag)

kgwedi – month or moon (maand of maan)

pente – paint (verf)

setofo – stove (stoof)

lebenkele – shop (winkel)

sephadi – whip (sweep)

kerekehadi – big church (groot kerk)

holohadi – big hall (groot saal)

koloi – car (kar)

lebidi – wheel (wiel)

rekere – rubber (uitveër)

lephela – a cockroach (kokkerot)

tshepe – iron (yster)

terata – wire, fence (draad)

taba-taba – main issue (hoofsaak)

sepheo-pheo – major objective (hoofdoel)

18

The demonstrative

(Die aanwysende voornaamwoord)

Orientation (Oriëntering)

When we speak, we address ourselves to things in relation to where they are situated. In the study of language, the word that is used, for this purpose, is called the demonstrative.

Definition (Definisie)

The demonstrative is simply a word that indicates a position or location. In English, examples of the demonstrative are here, there and yonder. In Sesotho, equivalent examples are **mona, mono** and **mane**. However, it must be noted that languages do differ in their structures. In Sesotho, there are two forms for each positional type, the first one usually for emphasis. This will be illustrated later.

Exposition (Uitleg)

The Sesotho demonstrative, like all other parts of the Sesotho grammar, conforms to the class system:

The table below shows the three positions or locations of the demonstrative.

Table 17

Class	Noun	Position Here/Hier	Position There/Daar	Position Yonder/Daar gunter
1	**motho** (person)	**enwa** (this person)	**eno** (that person)	**yane** (that person)
2	**batho** (people)	**bana** (these people)	**bano** (those people)	**bane** (those people)
3	**mose** (dress)	**ona** (this dress)	**ono** (that dress)	**wane** (that dress)
4	**mese** (dresses)	**ena** (those dresses)	**eno** (those dresses)	**yane** (those dresses)
5	**lesela** (cloth)	**lena** (this cloth)	**leno** (that cloth)	**lane** (that dress)
6	**masela** (cloths)	**ana** (these cloths)	**ano** (those cloths)	**ane** (those cloths)

Table 17 (continued)

Class	Noun	Position here/hier	Position there/daar	Position yonder/daar gunter
7	**senwelo** (cup)	**sena** (this cup)	**seno** (that cup)	**sane** (that cup)
8	**dinwelo** (cups)	**tsena** (these cups)	**tseno** (those cups)	**tsane** (those cups)
9	**nku** (sheep)	**ena** (this sheep)	**eno** (that sheep)	**yane** (that sheep)
10	**dinku** (many sheep)	**tsena** (these sheep)	**tseno** (those sheep)	**tsane** (those sheep)
Classes 11, 12 & 13 do not exist in Sesotho. These noun classes occur in other African languages such as isiZulu, isiXhosa, etc.				
14	**bohobe** (bread)	**bona** (this bread)	**bono** (that bread)	**bane** (that bread)
15	**ho nwa** (to drink)	**hona** (this drinking)	**hono** (that drinking)	**hwane** (that drinking)
16	**fatshe** (down)	**mona** (this down)	**mono** (that down)	**mane** (that down)
17	**hodimo** (up)	**hona** (this up)	**hono** (that up)	**hwane** (that up)
18	**morao** (back)	**ona** (this back)	**ono** (that back)	**wane** (that back)

Further examples of the demonstrative (Verdere voorbeelde)

Sesotho has an alternative for each of the three demonstratives here, there and yonder:

Table 18

Class	Noun	Position here/hier	Position there/daar	Position yonder/daar gunter
1	**motho** (person)	**enwa, eo**	**eno, eo**	**yane, elwa**
2	**batho** (people)	**bana, baa**	**bane, bao**	**bane, bala/bale**
3	**mose** (dress)	**ona, oo**	**ono, oo**	**wane, ola**
4	**mese** (dresses)	**ena, ee**	**eno, eo**	**yane, ela**
5	**lesela** (cloth)	**lena, lee**	**leno, leo**	**lane, lela**
6	**masela** (cloths)	**ana, aa**	**ano, ao**	**ane, ala**
7	**senwelo** (cup)	**sena, see**	**seno, seo**	**sane, sela**
8	**dinwelo** (cups)	**tsena, tsee**	**tseno, tseo**	**tsane, tsela**
9	**nku** (sheep)	**ena, ee**	**eno, eo**	**yane, ela**
10	**dinku** (many sheep)	**tsena, tsee**	**tseno, tseo**	**tsane, tsela**
Classes 11, 12 & 13 do not exist in Sesotho. These noun classes occur in other African languages such as isiZulu, isiXhosa, etc.				
14	**bohobe** (bread)	**bona, boo**	**bono, boo**	**bane, bola**
15	**ho nwa** (to drink)	**hona, hoo**	**hono, hoo**	**hwane, hola**
16	**fatshe** (down)	**mona, moo**	**mono, moo**	**mane, mola**
17	**hodimo** (up)	**hona, hoo**	**hono, hoo**	**hwane, hola**
18	**morao** (back)	**mona, moo**	**mono, moo**	**mane, mola**

It is also worth letting you know that in the position "yonder" there is another variant position which is the duplicate or repetition of the first alternative in the "yonder" position, e.g. (according to the noun classes).

1. **yane – yanene** that one
2. **bane – banene** those ones
3. **wane – wanene** that one
4. **yane – yanene** those ones
5. **lane – lanene** that one
6. **ane – anene** those ones
7. **sane – sanene** that one
8. **tsane – tsanene** those ones
9. **yane – yanene** that one
10. **tsane – tsanene** those ones

(Remember classes 11, 12 & 13 do not exist)

14. **bane – banene** that one
15. **hwane – hwanene** that one
16. **mane – manene** there (over there)
17. **hwane – hwanene** there (over there)
18. **mane – manene** there (over there)

Exercises on the demonstrative (Oefeninge)

Supply the demonstrative of the nouns in the following noun classes, for the first position, "here":

Table 19

Class	Noun	Demonstrative for position "here"
1	**monna** – man (man)	
2	**banna** – men (mans)	
3	**moseme** – grass mat (grasmat)	
4	**meseme** – grass mats (grasmatte)	
5	**lenala** – nail (nael)	
6	**manala** – nails (naels)	
7	**sehwapa** – biltong (biltong)	
8	**dihwapa** – biltongs (biltong)	
9	**nta** – louse (luis)	
10	**dinta** – lice (luise)	
Classes 11, 12 & 13 do not exist in Sesotho		

Table 19 (continued)

Class	Noun	Demonstrative for position "here"
14	**borokgo** – bridge (brug)	
15	**ho kula** – to be ill (om siek te wees)	
16	**fatshe** – down (af)	
17	**hodimo** – up (op)	
18	**motsheo** – back (terug)	

Increase your vocabulary (Verbreed u woordeskat)

katiba – hat (hoed)
thupa – stick (stok)
noha – snake (slang)
neta – smear (smeer)
nnete – truth (waarheid)
maka – lies (leuens)
mariha – winter (winter)
seporo – railway (treinspoor)
boka – tar (teer)
lengolo – letter (brief)
lengole – knee (knie)
madi – blood (bloed)
mathe – saliva (spuug, speeksel)
mofufutso – sweat, perspiration (sweet)
enke – ink (ink)
ente – vaccination (inenting)
tlama – bind, tie (verbind, vasmaak)
kadima – to lend, to borrow from (om te leen)
fantisi – auction (vendusie)
thapelo – prayer (gebed)
metsi – water (water)
jeresi – jersey (trui)
baki – jacket (baadjie)
jase – overcoat (oorjas)

19

The interrogative

(Die vraende voornaamwoord)

Orientation (Oriëntering)

In our daily lives, we ask questions. We enquire into and about certain things. In the study of language, it is called the interrogative.

Definition (Definisie)

The interrogative is the word that asks a question. It interrogates the listeners in order to obtain an explanation for a state of affairs. The interrogative is always followed by a question mark (?).

Examples of the interrogative in Sesotho are **mang?** (who), **kae?** (where), **neng?** (when) as in the following sentences:

(i) **O tlile ho mang?**

You have come to whom? i.e. Whom have you come to? (Na wie toe het jy gekom?)

(ii) **Ba tswa kae?**

They come from where? i.e. Where do they come from? (Waarvandaan kom hulle?)

(iii) **Le tla kgutla neng?**

You will return when? i.e. When will you (plural) return? (Wanneer sal julle terugkeer?)

Exposition (Uitleg)

Let us see how the interrogative relates to the noun classes in Sesotho. We shall use the following table for illustration:

Table 20

Class	Noun	Interrogative
1	**motho**	**ofe?** – which person?
2	**batho**	**bafe?** – which people?
3	**morara**	**ofe?** – which grape?
4	**merara**	**efe?** – which grapes?
5	**lehapu**	**lefe?** – which watermelon?
6	**mahapu**	**afe?** – which watermelons?
7	**seboko**	**sefe?** – which worm?
8	**diboko**	**dife?** – which worms?
9	**nko**	**efe?** – which nose?
10	**dinko**	**dife?** – which noses?
Classes 11, 12, & 13 do not exist in Sesotho. These noun classes occur in other African languages such as isiZulu, isiXhosa, etc.		
14	**borokgo**	**bofe?** – which bridge?
15	**ho kula**	**hofe?** – which illness?
16	**fatshe**	**lefe?** – which down?
17	**hodimo**	**hofe?** – which up?
18	**morao**	**ofe?** – which back?

Further examples of the interrogative (Verdere voorbeelde)

In Sesotho, the interrogative is very versatile. It may be formed in different ways and may perform various functions.

1. Using **mang?** – who? (wie?)

   O batla mang?

   You want whom? i.e. Whom do you want? (Wie wil jy hê?)

   Ke mang ya buang?

   It is who who is talking? i.e. Who is talking? (Wie praat?)

2. Using **kae?** – where? (waar?)

   O ya kae?

   You are going where? i.e. Where are you going? (Waarheen gaan jy?)

   Ba dula kae?

   They live where? i.e. Where do they live? (Waar bly hulle?)

3. Using **neng?** – when? (wanneer?)

   Ba fihlile neng?

   They arrived when? i.e. When did they arrive? (Wanneer het hulle gekom?)

Feme e tla bulwa neng?
The firm will be opened when? i.e. When will the firm be opened?
(Wanneer sal die firma oopgemaak word?)

4. By adding **mo** to **kae** to indicate nationality

Wena o mokae?
You are which nationality? i.e. What nationality are you?
(Watter nasionaliteit is jy?)

Menejara ke mokae?
The manager is of what nationality? i.e. What is the manager's nationality?
(Wat is die nasionaliteit van die bestuurder?)

5. By adding **se** to **kae** to indicate language

Ntswaki o bua sekae?
Ntswaki speaks which language? i.e. Which language does Ntswaki speak?
(Watter taal praat Ntswaki?)

O bua sekae?
You speak which language? i.e. Which language do you speak?
(Watter taal praat jy?)

6. By adding **bo** to **kae** to indicate amount

Ke bokae buka ena?
It is how much book this one? i.e. How much is this book?
(Hoeveel kos hierdie boek?)

Dieta tsee di bitsa bokae?
The shoes these ones they cost how much? i.e. How much do these shoes cost?
(Hoeveel kos hierdie skoene?)

7. By adding **ba** to **kae** to indicate quantity or numbers. (This is applied according to noun classes.)

Baeti ba bakae?
The visitors they are how many? i.e. How many visitors are there?
(Hoeveel besoekers is daar?)

Ba batla ba bakae?
They want how many? i.e. How many do they want? (Hoeveel wil hulle hê?)

8. By using the exclusive **-ng** (what?)

Lesea ke mong?
The baby is which sex? i.e. Which sex is the baby? (Watter geslag is die baba?)

O jewa keng?
You are eaten by what? i.e. What is troubling you? (Wat pla jou?)

Exercises on the interrogative (Oefeninge)

1. Give the interrogative of the following noun classes:

7	**sekolo**	**-fe?**	school (skool)
9	**ntlo**	**-fe?**	house (huis)
14	**bohobe**	**-fe?**	bread (brood)
4	**metse**	**-fe?**	villages (wonings)
2	**banna**	**-fe?**	men (mans)

2. Identify the correct interrogative in each of the following sentences with **mang?, kae, neng, eng?**

O tla fihla __________ ?
You will arrive __________ ?
Ba tlile le __________ ?
They came with __________ ?

O tshwere __________ letsohong?
You are carrying __________ in your hand?

Tshepo o robetse __________ ?
Tshepo has slept __________ ?

Increase your vocabulary (Verbreed u woordeskat)

mmutla – hare (haas)
kolobe – pig (vark)
lehe – egg (eier)
lebete – pancreas (pankreas)
sebete – liver or bravery (lewer, dapperheid)
mollo – fire (vuur)
ifo – fireplace (vuurherd)
moifo – elders of the nation (bejaardes van die nasie)
leino – tooth (tand)
leihlo – eye (oog)
ina – to immerse (indompel)
empa – but, however (maar)
athe – whereas (aangesien)
kapa – or (of)
ka – with (met)
ho – to (na)
hore – in order that, so that (sodat)
tla – come (kom)
ile – gone (gegaan)
ila – mourn, fast (treur)

20

The possessive

(Die besitlike voornaamwoord)

Orientation (Oriëntering)

People own one thing or another in life. In the study of language, the word that is used to indicate ownership or possession is called the possessive.

Definition (Definisie)

The possessive is a word which qualifies a noun. The pronoun shows the relationship that the noun has with the object. In Sesotho, the possessive is a little word that conforms to concordial agreement, i.e. the prefix of the noun class determines the form that the possessive assumes. Let us consider the following examples:

(i) **lefielo la ka**
broom of mine (my besem)

(ii) **sekepe sa Mmuso**
a ship of the Government ('n skip van die regering)

(iii) **lelapa la Thabiso**
Thabiso's family (Thabiso se familie)

Exposition (Uitleg)

As we have said the possessive relates to the noun, i.e. something that is possessed to that which possesses it. We will now treat the possessive according to the various noun classes:

Table 21

Class	Noun	Possessive concord	Subject/object
1	**mosadi** (wife)	**wa** (of)	**ka** (mine)
2	**basadi** (wives)	**ba** (of)	**ka** (mine)
3	**motse** (village)	**wa** (of)	**hao** (yours)
4	**metse** (villages)	**ya** (of)	**lona** (yours)
5	**lesiba** (feather)	**la** (of)	**hao** (yours)
6	**masiba** (feathers)	**a** (of)	**lona** (yours)
7	**seboko** (worm)	**sa** (of)	**poone** (mealies)
8	**diboko** (worms)	**tsa** (of)	**poone** (mealies)
9	**nkwe** (tiger)	**ya** (of)	**moru** (forest)
10	**dinkwe** (tigers)	**tsa** (of)	**moru** (forests)
Classes 11, 12 & 13 do not exist in Sesotho. These noun classes occur in other African languages such as isiZulu, isiXhosa, etc.			
14	**boko** (brain)	**ba** (of)	**nku** (sheep)
15	**ho shwa** (to die)	**ha** (of)	**morena** (king)
16	**fatshe** (down)	**ha** (of)	**thaba** (mountain)
17	**hodimo** (up)	**ha** (of)	**thaba** (mountain)
18	**morao** (back)	**ha** (of)	**ntlo** (house)

The possessive also uses personal pronouns as in the following examples, both in the singular and plural forms according to the noun class system as shown in table 22:

Table 22

Class	Noun	Possessive	Personal pronoun
1	**moruti** (minister)	**wa** (of)	**ka** (mine)
2	**baruti** (ministers)	**ba** (of)	**rona** (ours)
3	**morabe** (racial group)	**wa** (of)	**ka** (mine)
4	**merabe** (races)	**ya** (of)	**rona** (ours)
5	**letswele** (breast)	**la** (of)	**ka** (mine)
6	**matswele** (breasts)	**a** (of)	**rona** (ours)
7	**serope** (thigh)	**sa** (of)	**ka** (mine)
8	**dirope** (thighs)	**tsa** (of)	**rona** (ours)
9	**ntho** (thing)	**ya** (of)	**ka** (mine)
10	**dintho** (things)	**tsa** (of)	**rona** (ours)
Classes 11, 12 & 13 do not exist in Sesotho. These noun classes occur in other African languages such as isiZulu, isiXhosa, etc.			
14	**borokgo** (bridge)	**ba** (of)	**ka** (mine)
15	**ho kula** (to get ill)	**ha** (of)	**ka** (mine)

Table 22 (continued)

Class	Noun	Possessive	Personal pronoun
16	**fatshe** (down)	**la** (of)	**ka/rona** (mine/our)
17	**hodimo** (up)	**ha** (of)	**ka/rona** (mine/ours)
18	**morao** (behind)	**ha** (of)	**ka/rona** (mine/ours)

In Sesotho, we have two types of possessives, namely the direct possessive and the indirect possessive. The three sentences on p. 147 are an example of a direct possessive, i.e. reference of possession is expressed. Consider the following examples where indirect possession is indicated:

(i) **ntlo ya jwang**
house of grass – grass house (grashuis)

(ii) **letsatsi la mariha**
day of winter – a winter's day ('n winterdag)

(iii) **sello sa bosiu**
cry of night – a night cry ('n (ge)roep in die nag)

In the above examples, only a relationship is shown:

(i) the grass does not own the house

(ii) the winter does not own the day

(iii) the night does not own the cry

Because the possessive qualifies the noun or pronoun, it conforms to the noun classes and is subject to concordial agreement.

Further examples of the possessive (Verdere voorbeelde)

In Sesotho possessives may be formed by using various parts of speech, as will be illustrated in the following examples:

1. Using nouns: **(moruti, ngwana, kubu, kgoho)**

(i) **ntlo ya moruti**
a house of a minister ('n huis van 'n predikant)

(ii) **Sello sa ngwana**
cry of a child ('n (ge)roep van 'n kind)

(iii) **mokorotlo wa kubu**
the roar of a hippopotamus (die gebrul van 'n seekoei)

(iv) **nama ya kgoho**
the meat of a fowl (die vleis van 'n hoender)

2. Using the conjunctive (here, such and such)

(i) **ntho ya hore**
an issue of such and such, i.e. such and such an issue (so en so 'n ding)

(ii) **tulo ya hore**
a place of such and such, i.e. such and such a place (so en so 'n plek)

3. Using the infinitive (**ho** : to)

(i) **sebaka sa ho phomola**
a place of to rest, i.e. place of rest ('n plek om te rus)

(ii) **monyetla wa ho utswa**
an opportunity to steal ('n geleentheid om te steel)

Exercises (Oefeninge)

1. Supply the possessive concord for each of the following noun classes:

(i) **lebitso – nkgono**
the name (die naam) – grandmother (ouma)

(ii) **mabitso – bonkgono**
names (die name) – grandmothers (oumas)

(iii) **setjhaba – Basotho**
the nation (die nasie) – the Basotho (die Basotho)

(iv) **ditjhaba – Lefatshe**
the nations (die nasies) – the world (die wêreld)

(v) **nku – ntate**
the sheep (die skaap) – father's (pa s'n)

(vi) **dinku – ntate**
the sheep (die skape) – father's (pa s'n)

2. Supply the relevant possessive concord in each of the following sentences:

(i) **monna – Dineo**
the husband – Dineo's (die man – Dineo)

(ii) **leleme – kgomo**
the tongue – a cow (die tong – 'n koei)

(iii) **moriri – tshwene**
the hair – a monkey (die hare – 'n aap)

(iv) **mosadi – enwa**
the wife – this one (die vrou – hierdie een)

(v) **ke baki – mang?**
It is the jacket – who? – whose jacket is it? (wie se baadjie is dit?)

(vi) **morena – Lesotho**
the king – Lesotho (die koning – Lesotho)

(vii) **sejana – ho jela**
a dish – to eat, i.e. a dish of eating ('n bord – te eet)

Increase your vocabulary (Verbreed u woordeskat)

leta – to wait (om te wag)
lelapi – cloth (lap)
lelwapi – membrane (vlies)
kobo – blanket (kombers)
sesepa – soap (seep)
leleka – to chase away (om weg te jaag)
rohaka – to swear at people (om te vloek)
lemoha – to notice (om op te merk)
qabola – to amuse (om te vermaak)
wena – you (jy)
loma – bite (byt)
ditshila – dirt, filth (vuiligheid)
dithole – dust (stof)
lerole – dust (stof)

21

The moods

(Die wyses)

Orientation (Oriëntering)

We all have moods. We feel happy, sad, worried, are in high spirits, low spirits, etc. In the study of language, there are also moods. The mood of a verb reflects the exact sense of the verb. It indicates the state of mind of the person speaking.

Definition (Definisie)

Moods are forms of a verb that express a particular condition, e.g. a statement, command, appeal, wish, etc.

Exposition (Uitleg)

There are six main moods in the study of language. Look at the following examples:

(i) **Ke a dula.**

A simple statement meaning "I am sitting" (Ek sit). This mood is called the **indicative mood** (aantonende wyse).

(ii) **Dula!**

This is a command meaning "Sit!" (Sit). This mood is called the **imperative mood** (gebiedende wyse).

(iii) **A ka dula.**

This is a verbal expression of an ability, meaning "He/she may sit" (Hy/sy mag sit). This mood is called the **potential mood** (potensiële wyse).

(iv) **Ba dule.**

This is a subdued verbal expression of appeal, meaning "May they sit" (Mag hulle sit). This mood is called the **subjunctive mood** (aanvoegende wyse).

(v) **Re tsamaya re bina.**

This is an expression of two verbal forms, meaning "We walk while we sing" (Ons loop terwyl ons sing). This mood is called the **participial mood** (deelwoordelike wyse).

(vi) **Ha ba dule hle.**

This is an appealing verbal expression meaning, "Let them sit, please" (Laat hulle sit asseblief). This mood is called the **hortative mood** (vermanende wyse).

Below we give more examples of each category of moods.

The indicative mood (Aantonende wyse)

This is a mood that indicates. It is a simple statement of a fact or which asks a question for a factual answer, as in the following examples:

(i) **Pula e a na.** – It is raining. (Dit reën.)

(ii) **Bana ba a bala.** – Children are reading. (Kinders lees.)

(iii) **Letsatsi le a tjhesa.** – The sun is hot. (Die son is warm.)

(iv) **Dijo di monate.** – The food is delicious. (Die kos is lekker.)

(iv) **Ho a bata.** – It is cold. (Dit is koud.)

The imperative mood (Gebiedende wyse)

This mood expresses an instruction, command or a politely strong request as illustrated below:

(i) **Bua!** – Talk! (Praat!)

(ii) **Tloha mona!** – Go away from here! (Gaan weg van hier af!)

(iii) **Kwalang monyako!** – Close the door! (Maak die deur toe!)

(iv) **Epang mokoti!** – Dig a hole! (Grawe 'n gat!)

(v) **Mo shapeng!** – Beat him/her up! (Slaan hom/haar!)

The potential mood (Potensiële wyse)

This mood express the ability or potential that is there. Consider the following examples:

(i) **Mokudi a ka fola.** – The patient can get healed. (Die pasiënt kan gesond word.)

(ii) **Mollo o ka tuka.** – The fire can burn. (Die vuur kan brand.)

(iii) **Diaparo di ka koloba.** – The clothes can get wet. (Die klere kan nat word.)

(iv) **A ka atleha.** – He/she can succeed. (Hy/sy kan slaag.)

(v) **Ba ka fihla.** – They can arrive. (Hulle kan arriveer.)

The subjunctive mood (Aanvoegende wyse)

This mood is used in a subdued or subordinate sense. It is used to express doubt, uncertainty, impossibility or an imaginary thing as is shown below:

(i) **Ba bue?** – May they speak? (Mag hulle praat?)

(ii) **Re bone le rona.** – We may also see. (Ons mag ook sien.)

(iii) **Ba je le bona.** – They too may eat. (Hulle mag ook eet.)

(iv) **Re be batho le rona.** – We too should be people, i.e. we should be well off or dignified. (Ons moet ook soos ander mense wees; gerespekteerd.)

(v) **Ba utlwe.** – Let them feel or hear. (Laat hulle hoor of voel.)

The participial mood (Deelwoordelike wyse)

This mood expresses actions that happen simultaneously. Consider the following examples:

(i) **Ba tsamaya ba bua.** – They walk whilst they talk. (Hulle loop terwyl hulle praat.)

(ii) **O bina a tlola.** – He/she sings whilst he/she jumps. (Hy/sy sing terwyl hy/sy spring.)

(iii) **O hlafuna a tsheha.** – He/she chews whilst he/she laughs. (Hy/sy kou terwyl hy/sy lag.)

(iv) **Di ja di nona.** – They eat whilst they get fat. (Hulle eet terwyl hulle vet word.)

(v) **O lora a bina.** – He/she dreams whilst he/she sings. (Hy/sy droom terwyl hy/sy sing.)

The hortative mood (Vermanende wyse)

This mood expresses a wish or appeal. Consider the following sentences:

(i) **Ha ba kene hle.** – Let them come inside, please. (Laat hulle asseblief inkom.)

(ii) **Mo dumelleng hle.** – Please allow him/her. (Laat hom/haar asseblief toe.)

(iii) **Ha re mo thuseng.** – Let us help him/her. (Laat ons hom/haar help.)

(iv) **Ha ba mo jare.** – Let them carry him/her. (Laat hulle hom/haar dra.)

(v) **Ha ba nyalane.** – Let them marry each other. (Laat hulle met mekaar trou.)

Further examples of the moods (Verdere voorbeelde)

1. **Ke rata dijo** – indicative mood
   I like food. (Ek hou van kos.)

2. **Re a bua** – indicative mood
   We are talking. (Ons praat.)

3. **Tsoha!** – imperative mood
   Wake up! (Word wakker!)

4. **Nka!** – imperative mood
   Take! (Vat!)

5. **Ba ka mo thusa** – potential mood
   They could help him/her. (Hulle kon hom/haar help.)

6. **Pula e ka na** – potential mood
   The rain might fall. (Die reën mag val.)

7. **Ha ba ke ba utlwe** – subjunctive mood
   Let them too feel. (Laat hulle ook voel.)

8. **Ba tshwarwe le bona** – subjunctive mood
   Let them also get arrested. (Laat hulle ook gearresteer word.)

9. **Mo tshwarele hle** – hortative mood
   Forgive him/her please. (Vergewe hom/haar asseblief.)

10. **Ha le ke le mo thuse** – subjunctive mood
    Please help him/her. (Help hom/haar asseblief.)

11. **Ba fihlile a bapala** – participial mood
    They found him/her playing. (Hulle het hom/haar gekry terwyl hy/sy gespeel het.)

12. **Seipone o bua a hlafuna** – participial mood
    Seipone talks while chewing. (Seipone praat terwyl sy kou.)

Exercises (Oefeninge)

Indicate the mood in each of the following sentences:

1. **Ngwana o a lla.**
   The child is crying. (Die kind huil.)

2. **Robalang hle.**
   Sleep, please. (Slaap asseblief.)

3. **Thola!**
   Keep quiet! (Bly stil!)

4. **Ka bula, ka kena.**
   I opened, I entered. (Ek het oopgemaak en ingegaan.)

5. **Moruti a ka nna a fihla.**
   The minister may still arrive. (Die predikant kan nog opdaag.)

6. **Ke re ba kene.**
   I say they may enter. (Ek sê hulle mag inkom.)

7. **Tloha mona sephoqo towe!**
   Go away from here, you fool! (Gaan weg hiervandaan, jou dwaas!)

8. **Ke a o bona.**
   I am seeing you. (Ek sien jou.)

9. **Nonyana e a fofa.**
   The bird is flying. (Die voël vlieg.)

10. **Ke bosiu.**
    It is night-time. (Dit is in die nag.)

11. **Mosuwe o ngola a tsheha.**
    The teacher writes while laughing. (Die onderwyser skryf terwyl hy/sy lag.)

12. **Re ba bone ba feta.**
    We saw them passing. (Ons het hulle gesien toe hulle verbygeloop het.)

13. **Ke a mo kopela hle.**
    I am pleading for him/her. (Ek pleit vir hom/haar.)

14. **Ba fumane le bona**
    Get them too. (Kry hulle ook.)

Increase your vocabulary (Verbreed u woordeskat)

ho bapala – to play (om te speel)
ho rapela – to pray (om te bid)
ho robala – to sleep (om te slaap)
ho ngola – to write (om te skryf)
ho tshwara – to hold (om vas te hou)
ho bua – to talk (om te praat)
ho tsamaya – to walk (om te loop)

ho dula – to sit (om te sit)

ho ja – to eat (om te eet)

ho nwa – to drink (om te drink)

ho sheba – to look,see (om te sien)

ho utlwa – to hear (om te hoor)

ho nkga – to smell (om te ruik)

ho betsa – to beat (om te slaan)

ho tsheha – to laugh (om te lag)

ho hlola – to defeat (om te verslaan)

ho nka – to take (om te vat)

ho bula – to open (om oop te maak)

ho senola – to reveal (om te openbaar)

ho amohela – to receive (om te ontvang)

ho hana – to refuse (om te weier)

ho anya – to suckle (om te laat drink)

ho rohaka – to swear (om te vloek)

ho utswa – to steal (om te steel)

ho kganna – to drive (om te bestuur)

ho hatella – to press down (om plat te druk)

22

The conjunction

(Die voegwoord)

Orientation (Oriëntering)

Communication would be boring if sentences were of a short nature. To offset this short-coming, other words are used to serve as a bridge between short sentences, e.g. and (**hape**), because (**hobane**), but (**empa**), since (**haesale**), etc. These words are called conjunctives or joiners.

Definition (Definisie)

The conjunction or conjunctive is a word that joins or connects sentences. It is used to avoid short sentences and thus links sentences in order to carry a fuller meaning or links two or more ideas to portray a better image.

Let us look at the following two sentences and see how they may be joined:

(i) **Modisa o sheba hohle.**
The shepherd looks everywhere. (Die skaapwagter kyk orals.)

(ii) **Ha a bone letho.**
He/she does not see anything. (Hy/sy sien niks nie.)

Now a conjunctive **empa**, "but", is used to link up the two sentences:

Modisa o sheba hohle empa ha a bone letho.
The shepherd looks everywhere but sees nothing. (Die skaapwagter kyk orals maar sien niks nie.)

Let us take another example:

(i) **Re bona bana.**
We see the children. (Ons sien die kinders.)

(ii) **Re bona sekolo.**

We see a school. (Ons sien 'n skool.)

Now we use the conjunctive **le**, "and", to join the two sentences:

Re bona bana le sekolo.

We see the children and a school. (Ons sien die kinders en 'n skool.)

N.B. In this construction, there is no need to repeat **re bona**

Exposition (Uitleg)

In Sesotho, the conjunctions fall into two main categories, namely the so-called primitive or basic conjunctions and the derivative conjunctions.

Typical examples of the basic or primitive conjunctions are:

ha – if (as)
kapa – either (of)
mme – and (en)
athe, anthe – whereas, yet (aangesien, tog)
kanthe, kathe – whereas, yet (aangesien, tog)
hanthe, hathe – whereas, yet (aangesien, tog)
hape – again (weer)

As can be seen from their structure, the above-mentioned conjunctions are original in nature. Hence they are called basic or primitive. The other types of conjunctions are derived, i.e. they are formed by other parts of speech. Examples of the derived conjunctions are:

hoba – so that, that (sodat, dat)
ho fihlela – until (tot)
hobane – because (want)
hore – in order that (sodat)
hola – if only (as ... net)
hoja – if only (as ... net)
kwana – however (egter, maar)
hoo – to the extent that (tot die mate dat)
jwale – and now (en nou)
leha – even if (al, selfs as)
ka hoba – by reason of (omrede van)
ka hoo – therefore (daarom, dus)
ke ha – it is when (dit is wanneer)

ke hona – it is only now that (dit is eers nou dat)

esita, esitana – even (selfs)

empa – nevertheless, but (nietemin, maar)

efela – really, indeed (werklik, inderdaad)

Clearly, the Sesotho conjunction takes many forms and has various applications, as more examples illustrate:

1. Conjunction **hape** – as well as (sowel as)

   (i) **Kgarebe e telele.**
   The lass is tall. (Die nooi is lank.)

   (ii) **Kgarebe e ntle.**
   The lass is beautiful. (Die nooi is mooi.)

   Kgarebe e telele hape e ntle.
   The lass is tall as well as beautiful. (Die nooi is lank sowel as mooi.)

2. Conjunction **ebile** – and, in addition (en, boonop)

   (i) **O bua haholo.**
   You talk too much. (Jy praat te veel.)

   (ii) **O sethoto.**
   You are stupid. (Jy is dom.)

   O bua haholo ebile o sethoto.
   You talk too much and are stupid. (Jy praat te veel en jy is dom.)

3. Conjunction **feela** – however (maar/egter)

   (i) **Ke a mo rata.**
   I love/like him/her. (Ek hou van hom/haar.)

   (ii) **Ha a lemohe.**
   He/she does not notice it. (Hy/sy is nie bewus daarvan nie.)

   Ke a mo rata, feela ha a lemohe.
   I love/like him/her, however, he/she does not notice it. (Ek hou van hom/haar maar hy/sy is nie bewus daarvan nie.)

Further examples of the conjunction (Verdere voorbeelde)

We shall build sentences using the conjunctions mentioned above in the same order.

Basic or primitive conjunctions

(i) **ha**– if (as)

Ha o rata a ka phela.

If you like, he/she can live.
(As jy wil hê, kan hy/sy lewe.)

(ii) **kapa**– either, or (of)

O batla tjhelete kapa phasele?

Do you want money or a parcel?
(Wil jy geld of 'n pakkie hê?)

(iii) **mme** – and (en)

Ke tla ba teng mme le wena o be teng.

I will be present and you must also be present.
(Ek sal teenwoordig wees en jy moet ook teenwoordig wees.)

(iv) **athe, anthe** – whereas, yet (terwyl)

Ke le batla mona athe le eme ka morao.

I am looking for you here whereas you are waiting at the back.
(Ek soek jou hier, terwyl jy daar agter wag.)

(v) **hape** – again (weer)

O futhumatse dijo hape o di je.

You must warm up the food (again) and you must eat it.
(Jy moet die kos weer warm maak en dit eet.)

The derivative conjunctions

(i) **hoba** – so that, that (sodat)

Ke mo tsebisa hoba a ba bolelle.

I am informing him/her so that he/she should let them know.
(Ek sê vir hom/haar sodat hy/sy hulle mag laat weet.)

(ii) **ho fihlela** – until (totdat)

Ema mona ho fihlela ke kgutla.

Wait here until I return.
(Wag hier tot ek terugkom.)

(iii) **hobane** – because (omdat, want)

Ke a mo rata hobane o a nthata.

I love him/her because he/she loves me.
(Ek hou van hom/haar want hy/sy hou van my.)

(iv) **hore** – in order that (sodat)

Ke boloka tjhelete hore ke hahe ntlo.

I save money in order that I should build a house.
(Ek spaar geld sodat ek 'n huis kan bou.)

(v) **hola** – if only (as)

Hola ka tseba.

If only I knew.
(As ek net geweet het.)

(vi) **hoja** – if only (as)

Hoja la mo tshwara.

If only you could have caught him/her.
(As julle hom maar net kon gevang het.)

(vii) **kwana** – however (maar, egter)

Ke lakatsa ho mo tjhakela, kwana ke hloka tjhelete.

I wish to pay him/her a visit, however, I lack money.
(Ek wil hom/haar besoek, maar ek het nie geld nie.)

(viii) **hoo** – to the extent that (in die mate, so)

O tahilwe hoo a sitwang ho ema.

He/she is drunk to the extent that he/she cannot stand.
(Hy/sy is so dronk dat hy/sy nie kan staan nie.)

(ix) **jwale** – now, and now (nou, en nou)

O lahlile tjhelete, jwale o kopa ho nna.

He/she has lost money and now borrows from me.
(Hy/sy het geld verloor en nou leen hy/sy by my.)

(x) **le ha** – even if (alhoewel)

Le ha o ka ntlhoya ha ke na taba.

Even if you may hate me, I do not care.
(Alhoewel jy my haat, gee ek nie om nie.)

(xi) **ka hoba** – by reason of (omrede van, vanweë)

Tshepo o nyala Dimakatso ka hoba a mo rata.

Tshepo marries Dimakatso by reason of love.
(Tshepo trou met Dimakatso omdat hy vir haar lief is.)

(xii) **ka hoo** – therefore (daarom, derhalwe)

O molato ka hoo o ya teronkong.

You are guilty, therefore you are going to prison.
(Jy is skuldig, daarom gaan jy tronk toe.)

(xiii) **ke ha** – it is then, when (toe)

Tshediso o ne a hlalosa, ke ha o mo thiba.

Tshediso was explaining, then you stopped him.
(Tshediso was besig om te verduidelik toe jy hom gestop het.)

(xiv) **ke hona** – it is only now that (dit is nou eers dat)

Ke hona o qalang ho bala.

It is only now that you start reading.
(Dit is nou eers dat jy begin lees.)

(xv) **Esita, esitana** – even (selfs)

E bobebe, esitana le ngwana a ka e jara.

It is light, even a child can carry it.
(Dit is lig, selfs 'n kind kan dit dra.)

(xvi) **empa** – but, nevertheless (nietemin, tog, maar)

Ke mametse empa ke a belaela.

I am listening but I am doubtful.
(Ek luister, maar ek twyfel.)

(xvii) **efela** – indeed (inderdaad)

Efela ho le jwalo.

Indeed it is like that.
(Inderdaad is dit so.)

(xviii) **etswe** – what is more, moreover (boonop, buitendien)

Mo tloheleng hle, etswe o kopile tshwarelo.

Leave him/her please, moreover, he/she has aked for forgiveness.
(Los hom/haar asseblief, hy/sy het om vergifnis gevra.)

Exercises (Oefeninge)

Use the correct conjunctions to join the following sentences:

1. **empa, le**

   Ke tsamaya — Tshepo.

   I walk — Tshepo. (Ek loop — Tshepo.)

2. **le, empa**

   Re bua — bana.

   We talk — children. (Ons praat — kinders.)

3. **empa, le**

   Ke a bua — ha o mamele.

   I am talking — you are not listening. (Ek praat — jy luister nie.)

4. **ha, kapa**

   — o ka pasa ke tla thaba.

   — you can pass, I will be happy. (— jy kan verbygaan, sal ek bly wees.)

5. **kapa, ha**
   O batla nna — o batla Ntswaki?
   You are looking for me — for Ntswaki? (Soek jy vir my — Ntswaki?)

6. **hoja, jwale**
   O bone — o sa batlang?
   You have seen — what are you looking for? (Jy het gesien — wat wil jy nog hê?)

7. **hore, le ha**
   Ke batla — a lebale.
   I want — he/she should forget. (Ek wil hê — hy/sy moet vergeet.)

   ke hona, kwana
   — ke qalang ho sebetsa.
   — I start to work. (— ek begin om te werk.)

8. **ka hoba, efela**
   — o le tsotsi.
   — you are a thief. (— jy is 'n dief.)

9. **Etswe, hoo**
   Mo leleke — ke leshodu.
   Chase him/her away — he/she is a thief. (Jaag hom/haar weg — hy/sy is 'n dief.)

Increase your vocabulary (Verbreed u woordeskat)

letshwao – mark (merk)
leoto – foot (voet)
bethe – bed (bed)
bobe – evil (bose)
botle – good (goed)
tala – green, raw (groen, rou)
kgubedu – red (rooi)
tshehla – yellow (geel)
ntsho – black (swart)
ho hlafuna – to chew (om te kou)
ho kuka – to carry (om te dra)
ho pepa – to carry on one's back (om op jou rug te dra)
ho pipitlelwa – to be constipated (om hardlywig te wees)
ho eka – to betray (om te verraai)
ho aka – to kiss, embrace (om te soen, omhels)
ho matha – to run (om te hardloop)
ho tseka – to contest (om te stry)
ho bapala – to play (om te speel)
ho ruta – to teach (om te leer)
ho lekola – to examine (om te ondersoek)
ho nka - to take (om te neem)
ho robala – to sleep (om te slaap)
ho kuta – to shave (om te skeer)
ho loma – to bite (om te byt)
ho tadima – to look, behold (om te kyk)

23

The enumerative

(The system of counting)

Die opsommende wyse (Die telwyse)

Orientation (Oriëntering)

In our daily lives, we are obliged to count the people we come across, objects we see and places we visit. In the study of language, the word that is used for counting is the enumerative.

Definition (Definisie)

The enumerative is a word that counts nouns or pronouns (substantive) in a sentence. A few simple examples of numerals from one to ten in Sesotho are:

1	–	**nngwe**	–	one (een)	6	–	**tshelela**	–	six (ses)
2	–	**pedi**	–	two (twee)	7	–	**supa**	–	seven (sewe)
3	–	**tharo**	–	three (drie)	8	–	**robedi**	–	eight (agt)
4	–	**nne**	–	four (vier)	9	–	**robong**	–	nine (nege)
5	–	**hlano**	–	five (vyf)	10	–	**leshome**	–	ten (tien)

Exposition (Uitleg)

Since the enumerative deals with the noun or pronoun, it conforms to the noun class system.

This means that the concordial agreement comes into play when counting is done. We use the following table to illustrate concordial agreement when counting things:

Table 23

Class	Noun	Concord	Numeral or counting word
1	**motho** (person)	**a le** (being)	**mong** (one)
2	**batho** (people)	**ba le** (being)	**babedi** (two)
3	**molomo** (mouth)	**o le** (being)	**mong** (one)
4	**melomo** (mouths)	**e le** (being)	**meraro** (three)
5	**lefielo** (broom)	**le le** (being)	**leng** (one)
6	**mafielo** (brooms)	**a** (being)	**tsheletseng** (six)
7	**sefefo** (storm)	**se le** (being)	**seng** (one)
8	**difefo** (storms)	**tse** (being)	**ngata** (many)
9	**nko** (nose)	**e le** (being)	**nngwe** (one)
10	**dinko** (noses)	**tse** (being)	**leshome** (ten)
Classes 11, 12 & 13 do not exist in Sesotho. These noun classes occur in other African languages such as Zulu, Xhosa, etc.			
14	**borotho** (bread)	**bo** (being)	**bong** (one)
15	**ho robala** (to sleep)	**ho le** (being)	**hongata** (much)
16	**fatshe** (down)		
17	**hodimo** (up)		
18	**morao** (back)		

In Sesotho, the numeral is largely based on the standard stem **-ng**, with the plural **ngata** from this primary stem. We shall use the following chart to illustrate how the standard or primary stem **ng** and the plural form **ngata** are created as part of the counting system in certain applications of the Sesotho language:

Please do not confuse the following table with that of the noun class system. The table is only used here to illustrate the point made above.

Table 24

Singular noun	Concordial agreement	Singular numeral	Plural noun	Concordial agreement	Plural numeral
mosadi wife, woman	**ya** being	**mong** one	**basadi** wives, women	**ba** being	**bangata** many
motse village	**o le** being	**mong** one	**metse** villages	**e** being	**mengata** many
lesiba feather	**le le** being	**leng** one	**masiba** feathers	**a** being	**mangata** many
serobe nest	**se le** being	**seng** one	**dirobe** nests	**tse** being	**ngata** many
ntwa war	**e le** being	**nngwe** one	**dintwa** wars	**tse** being	**ngata** man

Table 24 (continued)

Singular noun	Concordial agreement	Singular numeral	Plural noun	Concordial agreement	Plural numeral
borokgo bridge	**bo le** being	**bong** one	**marokgo** bridges	**a** being	**mangata** many
ho ja eat	**ho le** being	**hong** one	**ho ja** to eat	**ho** being	**hongata** too much

N.B. In the case of class 15, the plural form of the concord **ho** is duplicated.

Let us now continue with the counting system beyond ten.

11 – eleven (elf) – **leshome le motso o le mong**
Literary meaning (ten with root being one)

12 – twelve (twaalf) – **leshome le metso e mmedi**
(ten with root being two)

13 – thirteen (dertien) – **leshome le metso e meraro**
(ten with root being three)

14 – fourteen (veertien) – **leshome le metso e mene**
(ten with root being four)

15 – fifteen (vyftien) – **leshome le metso e mehlano**
(ten with root being five)

16 – sixteen (sestien) – **leshome le metso e tsheletseng**
(ten with root being six)

17 – seventeen (sewentien) – **leshome le metso e supileng**
(ten with root being seven)

18 – eighteen (agtien) – **leshome le metso e robedi**
(ten with root being eight)

19 – nineteen (negentien) – **leshome le metso e robong**
(ten with root being nine)

20 – twenty (twintig) – **mashome a mabedi**
(tens being two)

Beyond twenty, we carry on as follows:

21 – **mashome a mabedi a motso o le mong** – twenty one (een en twintig)

22 – **mashome a mabedi a metso e mmedi** – twenty two (twee en twintig)

Beyond thirty:

30 – **mashome a mararo** – thirty (dertig)

31 – **mashome a mararo a motso o le mong** – thirty one (een en dertig)

32 – **mashome a mararo a metso e mmedi** – thirty two (twee en dertig)

Beyond forty:

40 –	**mashome a mane**	– forty (veertig)
41 –	**mashome a mane a motso o le mong**	– forty one (een en veertig)
42 –	**mashome a mane a metso e mmedi**	– forty two (twee en veertig)

Beyond fifty:

50 –	**mashome a mahlano**	– fifty (vyftig)
51 –	**mashome a mahlano a motso o le mong**	– fifty one (een en vyftig)
52 –	**mashome a mahlano a metso e mmedi**	– fifty two (twee en vyftig)

Beyond sixty:

60 –	**mashome a tsheletseng**	– sixty (sestig)
61 –	**mashome a tsheletseng a motso o le mong**	– sixty one (een en sestig)
62 –	**mashome a tsheletseng a metso e mmedi**	– sixty two (twee en sestig)

Beyond seventy:

70 –	**mashome a supileng**	– seventy (sewentig)
71 –	**mashome a supileng a motso o le mong**	– seventy one (een en sewentig)
72 –	**mashome a supileng a metso e mmedi**	– seventy two (twee en sewentig)

Beyond eighty:

80 –	**mashome a robedi**	– eighty (tagtig)
81 –	**mashome a robedi a motso o le mong**	– eighty one (een en tagtig)
82 –	**mashome a robedi a metso e mmedi**	– eighty two (twee en tagtig)

Beyond ninety:

90 –	**mashome a robong**	– ninety (negentig)
91 –	**mashome a robong a motso o le mong**	– ninety one (een en negentig)
92 –	**mashome a robong a metso e mmedi**	– ninety two (twee en negentig)
100 –	**lekgolo**	– hundred (honderd)
1000 –	**sekete**	– thousand (duisend)
1,000,000 –	**milione**	– million (miljoen)

Further examples of the enumerative (Verdere voorbeelde)

1. The enumerative is used in various ways to express the idea of quantity or counting in Sesotho, as will be illustrated in the following sentences. It is also interesting to note that the numerals are used qualificatively, i.e. they qualify and basically represent various parts of speech.

(i) **motho a le mong**
a person being one or alone/one person (een persoon)

(ii) **batho ba le bang**
the same people or people only or by themselves (dieselfde mense, mense alleen)

(iii) **difate di le ding**
trees only or the same trees (bome alleen, dieselfde bome)

(iv) **Mong a re, nka!**
One said, take! (Een het gesê, vat!)

(v) **Bang ba re, nkang!**
Some said, take them! (Party het gesê, vat hulle!)

(vi) **motho ka mong**
each person (elke persoon)

(vii) **ntlo ka nngwe**
each house (elke huis)

(viii) **lesiba ka leng**
each feather (elke veer)

2. Sequence or numerical order is expressed in the following manner using the examples in table 15.

Class 1: **motho ya mong**
a person who is one, i.e. one person (een persoon)

Class 2: **batho ba babedi**
people being two, i.e. two people (twee persone)

Class 3: **molomo o le mong**
a mouth that is one, i.e. one mouth (een mond)

Class 4: **melomo e meraro**
mouths that are three, i.e. three mouths (drie monde)

Class 5: **lefielo le le leng**
a broom that is one, i.e. one broom (een besem)

Class 6: **mafielo a mane**
brooms that are four, i.e. four brooms (vier besems)

Class 7: **sefefo se le seng**
a storm that is one, i.e. one storm (een storm)

Class 8: **difefo tse hlano**
storms that are five, i.e. five storms (vyf storms)

Class 9: **nko e le nngwe**
a nose that is one, i.e. one nose (een neus)

Class 10: **dinko tse tsheletseng**
noses that are six, i.e. six noses (ses neuse)

Remember classes 11, 12 & 13 do not exist in Sesotho

Class 14: **borotho bo le bong**
bread that is one, i.e. one bread (een brood)

Class 15: **ho robala ho le hong**
to sleep being one, i.e. one sleep (een slaap)

Class 16: **fatshe ho le hong**
down being one (een minder)

Class 17: **hodimo ho le hong**
up being one (een meer)

3. We should also draw your attention to the fact that the adjectives are used in counting the sequencing or ordering of things, e.g.

(i) **Ke ntlo ya pele.**
It is the first house. (Dit is die eerste huis.)

(ii) **Ke ntlo ya bobedi.**
It is the second house. (Dit is die tweede huis.)

(iii) **Ke ntlo ya boraro.**
It is the third house. (Dit is die derde huis.)

(iv) **Ke ntlo ya bone.**
It is the fourth house. (Dit is die vierde huis.)

(v) **Ke ntlo ya bohlano.**
It is the fifth house. (Dit is die vyfde huis.)

(vi) **Ke ntlo ya botshelela.**
It is the sixth house. (Dit is die sesde huis.)

(vii) **Ke ntlo ya bosupa.**
It is the seventh house. (Dit is die sewende huis.)

(viii) **Ke ntlo ya borobedi.**
It is the eighth house. (Dit is die agste huis.)

(ix) **Ke ntlo ya borobong.**
It is the ninth house. (Dit is die negende huis.)

(x) **Ke ntlo ya boleshome.**
It is the tenth house. (Dit is die tiende huis.)

4. An uninterrupted counting from one to ten, will run as follows:

e le nngwe – being one (een wees)

tse pedi – being two (twee wees)

tse tharo – being three (drie wees)

tse nne – being four (vier wees)

tse hlano – being five (vyf wees)

tse tsheletseng – being six (ses wees)

tse supileng/supa – being seven (sewe wees)

tse robedi – being eight (agt wees)

tse robong – being nine (nege wees)

tse leshome – being ten (tien wees)

N.B. **e le**, denoting one, assumes the plural **tse**.

We can continue the sequence of counting as follows:

tse leshome le motso o le mong – being eleven (elf wees)

tse leshome le metso e mmedi – being twelve (twaalf wees)

tse leshome le metso e meraro – being thirteen (dertien wees)

tse mashome a mabedi – being twenty (twintig wees)

tse mashome a mabedi le motso o le mong – being twenty one (een en twintig wees)

tse mashome a mabedi a metso e mmedi – being twenty two (twee en twintig wees)

tse mashome a mararo – being thirty (dertig wees)

tse lekgolo – being one hundred (een honderd wees)

tse sekete – being one thousand (een duisend wees)

tse milione – being one million (een miljoen wees)

5. The ordering of things according to series is prefixed by **bo-** except in the first place as illustrated in the following examples:

(i) **pele** – the first (die eerste)

e.g. **motho wa pele**
a person of the first
the first person (die eerste persoon)

(ii) **bobedi** – the second

e.g. **motse wa bobedi**
a village of the second
the second village (die tweede dorp)

(iii) **boraro** – the third

e.g. **lesaka la boraro**
a kraal of the third
the third kraal (die derde kraal)

(iv) **bone** – the fourth

e.g. **ntlo ya bone**
a house of the fourth
the fourth house (die vierde huis)

(v) **bohlan**o – the fifth

e.g. **ngwana wa bohlano**
a child of the fifth
the fifth child (die vyfde kind)

(vi) **botshelela** – the sixth

e.g. **nku ya botshelela**
a sheep of the sixth
the sixth sheep (die sesde skaap)

(vii) **bosup**a – the seventh

e.g. **kgaolo ya bosupa**
a chapter of the seventh
the seventh chapter (die sewende hoofstuk)

(viii) **borobedi** – the eighth

e.g. **lekgetlo la borobedi**
a moment of the eighth
the eighth time (die agste keer)

(ix) **borobong** – the ninth

e.g. **kgwedi ya borobong**
a month of the ninth
the ninth month (die negende maand)

(x) **Leshome** – the tenth

e.g. **monyako wa leshome**
the door of the tenth
the tenth door (die tiende deur)

6. In signifying the frequency or number of times a particular thing happens, we use the prefix **ha-** as follows:

   (i) **hang** – once (een maal)

   (ii) **habedi** – twice (twee maal)

   (iii) **hararo** – thrice (drie maal)

   (iv) **hane** – four times (vier maal)

   (v) **hahlano** – five times (vyf maal)

   (vi) **hatshelela** – six times (ses maal)

   (vii) **hasupa** – seven times (sewe maal)

   (viii) **harobedi** – eight times (agt maal)

   (ix) **harobong** – nine times (nege maal)

   (x) **haleshome** – ten times (tien maal)

   (xi) **halekgolo** – a hundred times ('n honderd maal)

   (xii) **hasekete** – a thousand times ('n duisend maal)

   (xiii) **hamilione** – a million times ('n miljoen maal)

Exercises on the enumerative (Oefeninge)

1. Write the Sesotho numerals for the following:

1	6
2	7
3	8
4	9
5	10

2. Use the correct enumerative in each of the following sentences:

   (i) **monna wa** – the first (die eerste)
   (man of)

   (ii) **setulo sa** – the fourth (die vierde)
   (chair of)

   (iii) **ntwa ya** – the second (die tweede)
   (war of)

   (iv) **lehodimo la** – the third (die derde)
   (a heaven of)

(v) **kereke ya** – the fifth (die vyfde) (church of)

(vi) **lebokose la** – the sixth (die sesde) (a box of)

(vii) **monwana wa** – the seventh (die sewende) (a finger of)

(viii) **tshimo ya** – the eighth (die agste) (a farm of)

(ix) **letsatsi la** – the ninth (die negende) (a day of)

(x) **selemo sa** – the tenth (die tiende) (a year of)

Increase your vocabulary (Verbreed u woordeskat)

nomoro – number (nommer)
sefapamo – cross (kruis)
sekola – crown (kroon)
seporo – railway (spoorweg)
sefofane – aeroplane (vliegtuig)
leqhubu – wave (golf)
lehlaku – reed (riet)
seretse – mud (modder)
leshala – coal (steenkool, kole)
moro – gravy (sous)
lenaka – horn (horing)
phala – whistle (fluit)
leqeba – wound, sore (wond)
ho lla – to cry (om te huil)
ho tsheha – to laugh (om te lag)
ho kgumama – to kneel (om te kniel)
ho sesa – to swim (om te swem)
ho hopola – to remember (om te onthou)

24

The locative

(Die plekaanduidende naamval)

Orientation (Oriëntering)

When we refer to people or things, we always have in mind a particular place where they are. We think or speak of them as being above, below, on the side, in front, behind, etc. In the study of language, the word that is used to indicate place or location is called a locative.

Definition (Definisie)

A locative is a word that indicates a location or place. It can be said to be an adverb of place or location. A locative denotes prepositionally, a position at, on, into, to, from which, out of which a particular action is carried out.

In Sesotho, the locative is commonly indicated by adding the suffix or the formative **-ng** to the end of the noun.

Noun		**Locative**	
thaba	– mountain (berg)	**thabeng**	– at, to, on top of, the mountain (op, na, bo op die berg)
toropo	– town (dorp)	**toropong**	– to, in town (na die dorp)
sekolo	– school (skool)	**sekolong**	– at school (by die skool)

Exposition (Uitleg)

As can be seen from the above examples, the locative indicates a relationship between the verb and the noun or pronoun. In other words, the locative explains what the noun or pronoun is doing in terms of place or in relation to a particular destination or position.

Let us now see how the locative behaves in terms of the various noun classes in the following table.

Table 25

Class	Noun	Verb	Place	Locative
1	**moruti** minister	**ruta** preaches	**kereke** church	**kerekeng** in church
2	**baruti** ministers	**ruta** preach	**dikereke** churches	**dikerekeng** in churches
3	**mokopu** pumpkin	**mela** grows	**tshimo** field	**tshimong** in the field
4	**mekopu** pumpkins	**mela** grow	**ditshimo** fields	**ditshimong** in the fields
5	**lerumo** spear	**hlaba** stabs	**mobu** soil/earth	**mobung** on the soil/earth
6	**marumo** spears	**hlaba** stab	**mebu** soil/earth	**mebung** on the soil/earth
7	**sehlopha** class	**kena** attends	**sekolo** school	**sekolong** at school
8	**dihlopha** classes	**kena** attend	**dikolo** schools	**dikolong** at schools
9	**nko** nose	**otla** hit	**nko** nose	**nkong** on the nose
10	**dinko** noses	**otla** hits	**dinko** noses	**dinkong** on the noses
Classes 11, 12, & 13 do not exist in Sesotho. These noun classes occur in other African languages such as isiZulu, isiXosa, etc.				
14	**bohobe** bread	**tlotsa** spread	**bohobe** bread	**bohobeng** on the bread
15	**ho robala** to sleep	**robala** to sleep	–	–
16	**fatshe** down	**theoha** alight	**fatshe** down	**fatshe** down
17	**hodimo** up	**sheba** look	**hodimo** up	**hodimo** up
18	**motsheo** yonder	**dula** sit	**motsheo** yonder	**motsheo** yonder

However, in Sesotho the suffix or formative **-ng** is also used to indicate time, e.g.

ho sa	**hoseng**
to dawn	at sunrise, in the morning (in die môre)

Example:

Moeti o tsamaile ha ho sa.
A visitor left (departed) when the sun rose.
('n Besoeker het vertrek toe die son opkom.)

Moeti o tsamaile hoseng.
A visitor departed in the morning.
(d.w.s. Die besoeker het in die môre vertrek.)

In the case of personal nouns, i.e. names of people, the suffix or formative **-ho** is used to indicate the locative. Consider the following sentences:

(i) **Ngwana o kgasetsa ho mme.**
A baby crawls towards the mother. ('n Baba kruip na die moeder.)

It is wrong to say: **Ngwana o kgasetsa mmeng**. Instead, the formative **ho** is used as a substitute for **-ng**. Below are more examples:

(ii) **Ke ya ho ntate.**
I am going to father. (Ek gaan na pa toe.)

(iii) **Ntswaki o tjhakela ho Tshepo.**
Ntswaki visits Tshepo. (Ntswaki besoek Tshepo.)

(iv) The following sentences indicate location, however, they do not take the locative suffix **-ng**:

fatshe: **Senokwane se sheba fatshe.**
down: A crook looks down. ('n Skelm kyk neer.)

hodimo: **O rapela a shebile hodimo.**
upward, up: He/she prays while looking upwards.
(Hy/sy bid terwyl hy/sy boontoe kyk.)

hole: **Ba ile hole.**
far: They went far. (Hulle het ver gegaan.)

haufi: **Ba bapala haufi.**
nearby: They play nearby. (Hulle speel naby.)

(v) In the following cases, the names of these places take the locative suffix **-ng**:

Gauta – Gauteng – place of gold (die plek van goud)

Mangau – Mangaung – place of leopards (die plek van luiperds)

Maoka – Maokeng – place of the mimosa, i.e. long sharp thorns (die plek van die mimosa, d.w.s. lang skerp dorings)

Ditamati – Ditamating – place of tomatoes (die plek van die tamaties)

Mafika – Mafikeng – place of rocks (historically misspelt as Mafeking) (die plek van rotse)

N.B. In Sesotho, the locative can be found in numerous other cases that we cannot include here.

Further examples of the locative (Verdere voorbeelde)

1. The following original or so-called primitive nouns similar in character to **fatshe**, **hodimo** and **morao**, are also typical examples of the locative:

hole: far away:	**O ile hole.** He/she has gone far away. (Hy/sy het ver gegaan.)
hojana: a little far away:	**Ke e lahletse hojana.** I have thrown it a little far away. (Ek het dit taamlik ver gegooi.)
mose: across, abroad, overseas:	**Ntswaki o ile mose.** Ntswaki has gone abroad/overseas. (Ntswaki het oorsee gegaan.)

2. Other independent nouns are also used as locatives, e.g.

   (i) **kgotla** – court

   Ke ya kgotla.
   I am going to court. (Ek gaan hof toe.)

   (ii) **ifo** – fire-place, hearth

   Mosadi o beha pitsa ifo.
   A woman places a pot at the hearth. ('n Vrou sit 'n pot by die vuurmaakplek.)

   (iii) **monyako** – at the door, in the doorway

   Katse e rapaletse monyako.
   A cat is lying in the doorway. ('n Kat lê in die ingang.)

   (iv) **lewatle** – the sea, at sea

   Ntwa e lwanwa lewatle.
   The war is being waged at sea. (Die oorlog word op see gevoer.)

3. The four compass or cardinal points of the earth are also used as locatives:

   (i) **botjhabela** – east

   Letsatsi le tjhaba botjhabela.
   The sun rises in the east. (Die son kom op in die ooste.)

   (ii) **bophirima/bophirimela** – west

   Le dikela bophirima/bophirimela.
   It sets in the west. (Dit gaan onder in die weste.)

   (iii) **bokone/leboya** – north

   Sefefo se hlaha bokone/leboya.
   The storm rises from the north. (Die storm kom op in die noorde.)

(iv) **borwa** – south
Dinonyana di fofela borwa.
The birds are flying to the south. (Die voëls vlieg na die suide.)

Exercises (Oefeninge)

1. Use the suffix **-ng** to form the locative for the following words:

kereke – church (kerk)
setulo – chair (stoel)
tafole – table (tafel)
noka – river (rivier)
jwang – grass (gras)
sefate – tree (boom)
terene – train (trein)
kobo – blanket (kombers)
mokoti – hole (gat)
teronko – prison (tronk)

2. To which noun classes do the following locatives belong?

fatshe – down (onder)
hodimo – up, above (op, bo)
hole – far away (ver weg)
morao – at the back (agter)
motsheo – beyond (anderkant, oorkant)
mose – across, abroad (oorsee)
mosejana – a little far away ('n bietjie ver)

Increase your vocabulary (Verbreed u woordeskat)

nyooko – bile (gal)
mamina – mucus (slym)
mathe – saliva (spoeg)
dikeledi – tears (trane)
madi – blood (bloed)
metsi – water (water)
mofufutso – sweat (sweet)
moroto – urine (urine)
ho idibana – to pass out, to faint (om flou te word)
ho hlatsa – to vomit (om te vomeer)
ho ruruha – to swell (om te swel)
ho halefa – to get angry (om kwaad te word)
ho lwana – to fight (om te baklei)
ho befa – to be angry (om kwaad te wees)
ho kwata – to be angry (om kwaad te wees)
ho bipetsana – to get constipated (om te verstop)
ho taboha – to get torn (om te skeur)

25

The positive and negative forms of expression

(Die positiewe en die ontkennende vorms van uitdrukking)

Orientation (Oriëntering)

In our daily communication, we agree to certain things or reject certain statements. When we agree to or with a particular statement, this is called a positive form of expression and when we disagree, it is called a negative form of expression.

Definition (Definisie)

Any language has a way of saying "yes" and "no". This is known as the positive and negative forms of expression. It boils down to statements of confirming and denying in Sesotho. We use the prefix **ha** to form the negative. Consider the following simple examples:

Positive Form	**Negative Form**
Ke a ja. I am eating. (Ek eet.)	**Ha ke je.** I am not eating. (Ek eet nie.)
Pula e a na. The rain is falling. (Die reën val.)	**Pula ha e ne.** The rain is not falling. (Die reën val nie.)
Sekolo se a kena. The school is starting. (Die skool begin.)	**Sekolo ha se kene.** The school is not starting. (Die skool begin nie.)

Exposition (Uitleg)

From the above examples, it becomes evident that the verb undergoes a change or conjugation when the negative is formed. The usual Sesotho verb in the present tense ends with the vowel **a** as in **ja, na, kena.** However, when the negative form is made with the use of **ha,** this terminative vowel **a** changes or conjugates to **e**, i.e.

ja	becomes	**je**
na	becomes	**ne**
kena	becomes	**kene**

However, the verb changes in various ways as we shall see later. We shall now give more examples of how the negative is formed, using verbs in different tenses:

1. The present tense (Die teenwoordige tyd)

	Positive form (positiewe vorm)	Negative form (ontkennende vorm)
(i)	**Ngwana o a anya.** The child is sucking. (Die kind suig.)	**Ngwana ha a anye.** The child is not sucking. (Die kind suig nie.)
(ii)	**Mosadi o a roka.** A woman is sewing. ('n Vrou doen naaldwerk.)	**Mosadi ha a roke.** A woman is not sewing. ('n Vrou doen nie naaldwerk nie.)
(iii)	**Papadi e a qala.** A game is starting. ('n Spel of wedstryd begin.)	**Papadi ha e qale.** A game is not starting. ('n Spel of wedstryd begin nie.)
(iv)	**Re a tsamaya.** We are going. (Ons gaan.)	**Ha re tsamaye.** We are not going. (Ons gaan nie.)
(v)	**Banna ba phahamisa sefate.** Men lift a tree. (Mans tel 'n boom op.)	**Banna ha ba phahamise sefate.** Men are not lifting a tree. (Mans tel nie 'n boom op nie.)
(vi)	**Bohobe bo a butswa.** Bread is getting baked. (Brood word gebak.)	**Bohobe ha bo butswe.** Bread is not getting baked. (Brood word nie gebak nie.)
(vii)	**Ba a bona.** They see. (Hulle sien.)	**Ha ba bone.** They do not see. (Hulle sien nie.)

	Positive form	Negative form
(viii)	**Lesea le a robala.** A baby is falling asleep. ('n Babatjie slaap.)	**Lesea ha le robale.** A baby is not falling asleep. ('n Babatjie slaap nie.)
(ix)	**Re a ba nka.** We are taking them. (Ons vat hulle.)	**Ha re ba nke.** We are not taking them. (Ons vat hulle nie.)
(x)	**Sefate se a hola.** A tree is growing. ('n Boom groei.)	**Sefate ha se hole.** A tree is not growing. ('n Boom groei nie.)

2. The past tense (Die verlede tyd)

	Positive form	**Negative form**
(i)	**Ba ile ba haha.** They built. (Hulle het gebou.)	**Ha ba a ka ba haha.** They did not build. (Hulle het nie gebou nie.)
(ii)	**Sekepe se ile sa nwella.** A ship sank. ('n Skip het gesink.)	**Sekepe ha se a ka sa nwella.** A ship did not sink. ('n Skip het nie gesink nie.)
(iii)	**Bohloko bo ile ba fola.** An illness healed. ('n Siekte het gesond geword.)	**Bohloko ha bo a ka ba fola.** An illness did not heal. ('n Siekte het nie gesond geword nie.)
(iv)	**Feme e ile ya kwalwa.** A firm closed. ('n Firma het toegemaak.)	**Feme ha e a ka ya kwalwa.** A firm did not close down. ('n Firma het nie toegemaak nie.)
(v)	**Balemi ba ile ba jala.** The planters planted. (Die planters het geplant.)	**Balemi ha ba a ka ba jala.** The planters did not plant. (Die planters het nie geplant nie.)
(vi)	**Kopano e ile ya kwalwa.** The meeting closed. (Die vergadering het te einde geloop.)	**Kopano ha e a ka ya kwalwa.** The meeting did not close. (Die vergadering het nie ten einde geloop nie.)
(vii)	**Baeti ba ile ba fihla.** The visitors arrived. (Die besoekers het aangekom.)	**Baeti ha ba a ka ba fihla.** The visitors did not arrive. (Die besoekers het nie aangekom nie.)

(viii) **Lengolo le ile la ngolwa.**
A letter was written.
('n Brief was geskryf.)

Lengolo ha le a ka la ngolwa.
A letter was not written.
('n Brief was nie geskryf nie.)

(ix) **Matome o ile a tsamaya.**
Matome left.
(Matome het geloop.)

Matome ha a a ka a tsamaya.
Matome did not leave.
(Matome het nie geloop nie.)

(x) **Ho shwa ho ile ha ata.**
The dead increased.
(Die dooies het meer geword.)

Ho shwa ha ho a ka ha ata.
The dead did not increase.
(Die dooies het nie meer geword nie.)

3. The future tense (Die toekomende tyd)

	Positive form	**Negative Form**
(i)	**Ke tla kganna koloi.** I will drive a car. (Ek sal 'n kar bestuur.)	**Ha ke no kganna koloi.** I will not drive a car. (Ek sal nie 'n kar bestuur nie.)
(ii)	**Leeto le tla ba monate.** A trip will be pleasant. ('n Reis sal aangenaam wees.)	**Leeto ha le no ba monate.** A trip will not be pleasant. ('n Reis sal nie aangenaam wees nie.)
(iii)	**Morena o tla bua** The king will speak. (Die koning sal praat.)	**Morena ha a no bua** The king will not speak. (Die koning sal nie praat nie.)
(iv)	**Lehlwa le tla kgetheha.** Snow will fall. (Sneeu sal val.)	**Lehlwa ha le no kgetheha.** Snow will not fall. (Sneeu sal nie val nie.)
(v)	**Ho tla bata.** It will be cold. (Dit sal koud wees.)	**Ha ho no bata.** It will not be cold. (Dit sal nie koud wees nie.)
(vi)	**Dijo di tla fela.** The food will get finished. (Die kos sal klaar kom.)	**Dijo ha di no fela.** The food will not get finished. (Die kos sal nie klaar kom nie.)
(vii)	**Ba tla mmolella.** They will tell him/her. (Hulle sal vir hom/haar sê.)	**Ha ba no mmolella.** They will not tell him/her. (Hulle sal nie vir hom/haar sê nie.)

	Positive form	Negative form
(viii)	**Re tla rapela.** We will pray. (Ons sal bid.)	**Ha re no rapela.** We will not pray. (Ons sal nie bid nie.)
(ix)	**Sefofane se tla nyoloha.** An aeroplane will take off. ('n Vliegtuig sal opstyg.)	**Sefofane ha se no nyoloha.** An aeroplane will not take off. ('n Vliegtuig sal nie opstyg nie.)
(x)	**Lehlanya le tla baleha.** A lunatic will run away. ('n Kranksinnige sal weghardloop.)	**Lehlanya ha le no baleha.** A lunatic will not run away. ('n Kranksinnige sal nie weghardloop nie.)

4. The perfect tense (Die voltooide tyd)

	Positive form	Negative form
(i)	**Ba bapetse haholo.** They have played hard. (Hulle het hard gespeel.)	**Ha ba a bapala haholo.** They have not played hard. (Hulle het nie hard gespeel nie.)
(ii)	**Re jele nama.** We have eaten meat. (Ons het vleis geëet.)	**Ha re a ja nama.** We have not eaten meat. (Ons het nie vleis geëet nie.)
(iii)	**Le kgutlile ka pele.** You have come back soon. (Jy het vroeg teruggekom.)	**Ha le a kgutla ka pele.** You have not come back soon. (Jy het nie vroeg teruggekom nie.)
(iv)	**O shapile ngwana.** You have thrashed the child. (Jy het die kind geslaan.)	**Ha o a shapa ngwana.** You have not thrashed the child. (Jy het nie die kind geslaan nie.)
(v)	**Di fihlile maobane.** They have arrived yesterday. (Hulle het gister aangekom.)	**Ha di a fihla maobane.** They have not arrived yesterday. (Hulle het nie gister aangekom nie.)
(vi)	**Ntate o nnehile tjhelete.** Father has given me money. (Vader het my geld gegee.)	**Ntate ha a a nneha tjhelete.** Father has not given me money. (Vader het my nie geld gegee nie.)
(vii)	**Ke apere borikgwe.** I have worn a pair of trousers. (Ek het my broek aangetrek.)	**Ha ke a apara borikgwe.** I have not worn a pair of trousers. (Ek het nie my broek aangetrek nie.)

(viii) **Ba mpolelletse maobane.**
They have told me yesterday.
(Hulle het my gister vertel.)

Ha ba a mpolella maobane.
They have not told me yestersday.
(Hulle het my nie gister vertel nie.)

(ix) **Ba tlotse molao.**
They have broken the law.
(Hulle het die wet verbreek.)

Ha ba a tlola molao.
They have not broken the law.
(Hulle het nie die wet verbreek nie.)

(x) **O lelekilwe mosebetsing.**
He/she has been expelled from work.
(Hy/sy is uit die werk geskop.)

Ha a a lelekwa mosebetsing.
He/she has not been expelled from work.
(Hy/sy is nie uit die werk geskop nie.)

Further examples (Verdere voorbeelde)

The following sentences will help the learner get a firmer grip on the positive and negative construction by showing how a verb (e.g. **reka**) gets conjugated or changed according to the various tenses:

1. **Ke a reka.**
I am buying.
(Ek koop.)

Ha ke reke.
I am not buying.
(Ek koop nie.)

2. **Ke sa reka.**
I am still buying.
(Ek koop nog.)

Ha ke sa reka.
I am no longer buying.
(Ek koop nie meer nie.)

3. **Ke tla reka.**
I will buy.
(Ek sal koop.)

Ha ke no reka.
I will not buy.
(Ek sal nie koop nie.)

4. **Re a reka.**
We are buying.
(Ons koop.)

Ha re reke.
We are not buying.
(Ons koop nie.)

5. **Re sa reka.**
We are still buying.
(Ons koop nog.)

Ha re sa reka.
We are no longer buying.
(Ons koop nie meer nie.)

6. **Re sa tla reka.**
We are still going to buy.
(Ons sal nog koop.)

Ha re sa tla reka.
We are no longer going to buy.
(Ons sal nie meer koop nie.)

7. **O a reka.**
You are buying.
(Jy koop.)

Ha o reke.
You are not buying.
(Jy koop nie.)

8. **O sa reka.** – **Ha o sa reka.**
You are still buying. (Jy koop nog.) – You are no longer buying. (Jy koop nie meer nie.)

9. **O tla reka.** – **Ha o no reka.**
You will buy. (Jy sal koop.) – You will not buy. (Jy sal nie koop nie.)

10. **O sa tla reka.** – **Ha o sa tla reka.**
You will still buy. (Jy sal nog koop.) – You will no longer buy. (Jy sal nie meer koop nie.)

11. **Ba a reka.** – **Ha ba reke.**
They are buying. (Hulle koop.) – They are not buying. (Hulle koop nie.)

12. **Ba sa reka.** – **Ha ba sa reka.**
They are still buying. (hulle koop nog.) – They are no longer buying. (hulle koop nie meer nie.)

13. **Ba sa tla reka.** – **Ha ba sa tla reka.**
They will still buy. (Hulle sal nog koop.) – They will no longer buy. (Hulle sal nie meer koop nie.)

14. **Dibini di a reka.** – **Dibini ha di reke.**
The singers are buying. (Die sangers koop.) – The singers are no longer buying. (Die sangers koop nie meer nie.)

15. **Dibini di sa reka** – **Dibini ha di sa reka**
The singers are still buying. (Die sangers koop nog.) – The singers are no longer buying. (Die sangers koop nie meer nie.)

16. **Dibini di sa tla bina.** – **Dibini ha di sa tla bina.**
The singers will still sing. (Die sangers sal nog sing.) – The singers will no longer sing. (Die sangers sal nie meer sing nie.)

Exercises on the positive and negative forms of expression (Oefeninge)

Give the negative forms of the following sentences:

1. **Ke a bona.** – I see. (Ek sien.)
2. **O a bona.** – You see. (Jy sien.)
3. **O a bona.** – He/she sees. (Hy/sy sien.)
4. **Re a bona.** – We see. (Ons sien.)
5. **Le a bona.** – You see. (Julle sien.)

6. **Ba a bona.** – They see. (Hulle sien.)
7. **Nama e a tjha.** – The meat burns. (Die vleis brand.)
8. **Sefate se wele.** – The tree has fallen. (Die boom het geval.)
9. **Lebone le timile.** – The light has died. (Die lig is dood.)
10. **Thipa e bohale.** – The knife is sharp. (Die mes is skerp.)
11. **Hempe e tabohile.** – The shirt is torn. (Die hemp is geskeur.)
12. **Koloi e a duma.** – The car is idling – producing idling sound. (Die kar luier.)
13. **Dimpho o motle.** – Dimpho is beautiful. (Dimpho is mooi.)
14. **Nonyana e fofile.** – The bird has flown. (Die voël het gevlieg.)
15. **Thabo o tla sala.** – Thabo will remain. (Thabo sal agterbly.)
16. **Pula e sa na.** – The rain is still falling. (Die reën val nog.)
17. **Bana ba jele.** – The children have eaten. (Die kinders het geëet.)
18. **Kotsi e etsahetse.** – An accident has occured. ('n Ongeluk het plaasgevind.)
19. **Ba tla tla.** – They will come. (Hulle sal kom.)
20. **Borokgo bo tsepame.** – The bridge is sturdy. (Die brug is stewig.)
21. **Mo kadime katiba.** – Lend him/her the hat. (Leen hom/haar die hoed.)
22. **Rapolasi o a kotula.** – The farmer is reaping. (Die boer oes.)
23. **Ngwana o batla ho lla.** – The child wants to cry. (Die kind wil huil.)
24. **Ke mo romme.** – I have sent him/her. (Ek het hom/haar gestuur.)
25. **E kgutlise.** – Bring it back. (Bring dit terug.)

Increase your vocabulary (Verbreed u woordeskat)

boko – brain (brein)
boomo – on purpose (met opset)
phoofolo – animal (dier)
phoka – dew (dou)
phala – flute, whistle (fluit)
nokana – stream (stroom)
mosi – smoke (rook)
mosa – mercy (genade)
mmusi – governor (goewerneur)
mmutla – hare (haas)
ho mamola – to beat thoroughly (om hard te slaan)
ho tseka – to contest (om te betwis)
ho fuduwa – to stir (om te roer)
ho benya – to shine (om te blink)
ho ikgohomosa – to be proud, conceited (om trots, hoogmoedig te wees)
ho tseba – to know (om te ken/weet)
ho se tsebe – not to know (om nie te ken, weet nie)
ho se lebale – not to forget (om nie te vergeet nie)
ho se ngole – not to write (om nie te skryf nie)
ho se lefe – not to pay (om nie te betaal nie)
ho se rapele – not to pray (om nie te bid nie)
ho se tenehe – not to be fed up (om nie vies te wees nie)

ho se rate – not to like (om nie lief te hê nie)

ho se apare – not to dress up (om nie aan te trek nie)

ho se tshepe – not to trust (om nie te vertrou nie)

ho se natse – not to notice (om nie in ag te neem nie)

ho se mathe – not to run (om nie te hardloop nie)

ho se ithate – not to care for oneself (om nie vir jouself om te gee nie)

ho se ithute – not to learn (om nie te leer nie)

26

Synonyms

(Words with a similar meaning)

(Sinonieme)

Orientation and examples (Oriëntering en voorbeelde)

Languages are rich in vocabulary, so much so that each language has two or more words meaning the same thing. Such words are called synonyms. However, it is important to note that similar words do not necessarily convey exactly the same meaning. Sesotho has an abundance of synonyms. We give you a short list of these in order to show usage:

1. **sephiri/lekunutu** – secret, confidentiality (geheim)

   Taba ena ke sephiri sa ka le wena.
   This matter is the secret of me and you, i.e. this matter is between you and me. (Hierdie saak is tussen jou en my.)

2. **tulo/tao** – place, accommodation, domicile (woonplek)

   Ke tao e ntle ya ho phomola.
   It is a place which is fine for relaxing. (Dit is 'n plek wat reg is om te ontspan.)

3. **phoso/sepha/sekodi** – mistake, blemish (fout)

   Phoso ya ka e bile ho botsa.
   Mistake of mine was to ask, i.e. my mistake was to pose a question. (Dit was my fout om 'n vraag te stel.)

4. **hoseng/meso** – in the morning (in die oggend)

   Hoseng ho a bata mariha.
   In the morning it is cold in winter. (In die oggend is dit koud in die winter.)

5. **thapama, mantsiboya phirimana, shwalane** – at sunset, dusk, in the twilight (in die aand)

Letsatsi le dikela thapama.
The sun sets in the evening. (Die son gaan onder in die aand.)

6. **monyako, lemati, lehlafi** – door (deur)

Bula monyako re kene.
Open the door we must enter. (Maak oop die deur, ons moet inkom.)

7. **dikeledi, dikgapha, masodi, menyepetsi** – tears (trane)

Dikeledi di rothela dijong.
Tears drop onto the food. (Trane val in die kos.)

8. **metsi, manyabolo** – water (water)

Mphe metsi ke nyorilwe.
Give me water, I am thirsty. (Gee my water, ek is dors.)

9. **bohobe, papa, borotho** – bread, porridge (pap, brood)

Ke ja bohobe ba mabele.
I eat bread of mealies (i.e. I eat porridge). (Ek eet mieliepap.)

10. **bohato, kgato** – step (tree, stap)

Morena o nkile bohato bo boholo.
The king has taken a big step. (Die koning het 'n groot tree gegee.)

11. **thala, tweba** – draw a line ('n streep trek)

Mosuwe o thala mola fatshe.
The teacher draws a line on the ground. (Die onderwyser trek 'n streep op die grond.)

12. **tshasa, neta, tlotsa** – smear, apply (smeer)

Morwetsana o tshasa sefahleho sa hae ka oli.
A lass applies on the face of hers oil (i.e. a young woman applies oil on her face). ('n Meisie smeer olie op haar gesig.)

13. **tshosa, nyarosa** – be afraid, fear, scare, frighten (vrees, skrikmaak, verskrik)

Ntja e tshosa mmutla.
A dog scares a hare. ('n Hond verjaag 'n haas.)

14. **qhowa, tlhoro, sehlohlolo** – peak of a mountain, apex (hoogtepunt, bergpiek)

Ho boima ho fihlela qhowa.
It is difficult to reach a peak. (Dit is moeilik om 'n bergpiek te bereik.)

15. **tsela, mmila** – way, road, street (straat, pad)

Tsela ena e telele.
Road this is long, i.e. This road is long. (Hierdie pad is lank.)

16. **kgoro, heke** – gate (hek)

Ha dikgomo di felletse, modisa o kwala kgoro.
When the cows are all in the shepherd closes the gate. (Wanneer al die beeste in die kraal is, maak die beeswagter die hek toe.)

17. **kou, huku** – corner (hoek)

Ke tla o emela koung ya tsela.
I will wait for you at the corner of the street. (Ek sal vir jou op die hoek van die straat wag.)

18. **otla, betsa, shapa** – beat (slaan)

Ke tla o otla.
I will you beat, i.e. I will beat you. (Ek sal jou slaan.)

19. **pola, mamola** – thrash (pak gee, uitklop)

Moshemane o pola e mong.
A boy he thrashes the other one, i.e. a boy thrashes the other one. ('n Seun slaan die ander seun.)

20. **tabola, harola** – tear, mangle (skeur, afskeur)

Ngwana o tabola pampiri.
A child he/she tears a paper, i.e. a child tears a paper. ('n Kind skeur 'n papier op.)

21. **otlolla, sarolla, tamolla** – stretch (rek)

Ke otlolla maoto ha ke matha.
I stretch (my) legs when I run. (Ek rek my treë wanneer ek hardloop.)

22. **rokahanya, hokahanya** – link up, sew up, co-ordinate (verbind, aanwerk, inryg)

Nkgono o rokahanya difaha.
Grandmother sews up the beads. (Ouma ryg die kraletjies in.)

23. **tsamaya, ya** – walk, go (loop, gaan)

Tsamaya ka kgotso.
Go in peace. (Gaan in vrede.)

24. **botha, paqama** – lie, rest (lê, rus)

Katse e botha hodima bethe.
A cat lies on the bed. ('n Kat lê op die bed.)

25. **tjapalla, qheama** – lie clumsily (lomp lê)

    Motho ya botswa o tjapalla fatshe.
    A person who is lazy lies clumsily on the ground. ('n Persoon wat lui is, lê lomp op die grond.)

26. **sheba, bona, leba, tadima** – see, look (kyk, sien)

    Ke bona ka mahlo.
    I see with the eyes. (Ek sien met die oë.)

27. **hema, phefomoloha** – breathe (asemhaal)

    Ngaka e re ho mokudi, "hema"!
    The doctor says to a patient, "breathe in!" (Die dokter sê vir die pasient, "asem in!")

28. **ja, hlafuna, ho phomosetswa** – eat, chew (eet, kou)

    Monna o ja apole.
    A man eats an apple. ('n Man eet 'n appel.)

29. **phatlalatsa, pepesa** – publicise, advertise (bekend stel)

    Mongodi o phatlalatsa ditsebiso.
    A secretary publicises the notices. (Die sekretaris maak die aankondigings bekend.)

30. **nyolla, phahamisa** – raise, elevate, lift (optel, oplig)

    Monna o nyolla tshepe e boima.
    A man lifts up an iron which is heavy. ('n Man tel 'n swaar yster op.)

31. **diha, wesa** – drop, cause to fall, trip (laat val)

    Sebapadi sa bolo se diha se seng.
    A player of soccer trips the other one. ('n Sokkerspeler pootjie 'n ander speler.)

32. **dintlo, matlo** – houses (huise)

    Ho hlokahala dintlo tse ngata.
    It is required houses which are many, i.e. many houses are required. (Baie huise word benodig.)

33. **dinku, manku** – sheep (skape)

    Dinku tse ngata di bolailwe ke lehlwa.
    Sheep which are many have been killed by snow, i.e. many sheep have been killed by snow. (Baie skape is deur die sneeu doodgemaak.)

34. **dikgomo, makgomo** – cattle, cows (koeie)

    Molefe o ruile dikgomo tse nonneng.
    Molefe has reared cattle which are fat. (Molefe het vet beeste geteel.)

35. **tsotsi, senokwane, sekebekwa** – thug, hooligan (skelm)

Mapolesa a tshwere tsotsi e tshwenyang.
The police have arrested a thug who is troublesome. (Die polisie het 'n skelm, wat moeilikheid veroorsaak het, gearresteer.)

36. **bolotsana, bofelekwane** – crookery, mischief (skelmstreke)

Bolotsana ha bo batlehe bathong .
Mischief is not required among people. (Skelmstreke is nie nodig tussen mense nie.)

37. **bofumanehi, tlhopheho** – poverty, indigence (armoede)

Ha re fediseng bofumanehi.
Let us obliterate (end) poverty. (Laat ons armoede beëindig.)

38. **kgora, nala** – prosperity (voorspoed)

Setjhaba se thabile hobane kgora e tlile.
The nation is glad because prosperity has come. (Die nasie is bly oor voorspoed wat gekom het.)

39. **matjeke, madungwadungwane** – at dawn (met sonop/vroeg in die oggend)

Badisa ba tsoha ka matjeke.
The shepherds they wake up at dawn, i.e. the shepherds wake up at dawn. (Die herders staan vroeg in die oggend op.)

40. **morubisi, sephooko** – owl (uil)

Morubisi o robala motsheare.
An owl sleeps during the day. ('n Uil slaap gedurende die dag.)

41. **ntja, nyalasi** – dog (hond)

Ntja e bohola leshodu.
A dog barks at a thief. ('n Hond blaf vir 'n dief.)

42. **noha, monyabalatsi** – snake (slang)

Ke bona noha sefateng.
I see a snake in the tree. (Ek sien 'n slang in die boom.)

43. **mealo, diphate, bethe** – bedding, sleeping place (beddegoed)

Mealo ya mokudi e hlwekile.
The bedding of a patient is clean. (Die beddegoed van 'n pasiënt is skoon.)

44. **fuparela, tlapurela** – clasp, grab, grip onto (vasklem/styf vashou)

Ke fuparela tjhelete hore e se ke ya utsuwa.
I clasp the money so that it is not stolen. (Ek hou die geld styf vas sodat dit nie gesteel word nie.)

45. **mamarela, namathela** – stick onto, glue onto (vasklou)

Boka bo mamarela seeteng.
Tar sticks onto the shoe. (Teer klou aan die skoen vas.)

46. **potapota, dikadika** – go around, beat about (rondloop, rondgaan)

Leshodu le potapota lebenkele.
A thief goes around the shop. ('n Dief loop in die winkel rond.)

47. **tsekela, lelera, solla** – move aimlessly, roam (swerf)

O se ke wa tsekela, eya sekolong.
Do not roam, go to school. (Moenie dwaal/swerf nie, gaan skool toe.)

48. **hahlaula, hlahlathela** – traverse, travel all over (deurreis, orals rondloop)

Motho ya lahlehileng o hahlaula dithota.
A person who is lost traverses the fields. ('n Persoon wat verdwaal het, loop in die veld rond.)

49. **nahathote, lefelleng** – barren place, waste land (woesteny)

Ke nahathote, ha ke bone le batho.
It is a waste land, I do not see people. (Dit is 'n woesteny, ek sien nie mense nie.)

50. **thola, fumana** – find, get, obtain, acquire (kry, vind)

Modisa o ile a thola nku e lahlehileng.
A shepherd found a sheep that was lost. ('n Herder het 'n skaap wat verdwaal het, gevind.)

51. **Bolwetse, lefu** – disease, illness, sickness (siekte)

Lepera ke bolwetse bo sehloho.
Leprosy is a cruel disease. (Melaatsheid is 'n wrede siekte.)

52. **ho shwa, ho ya boya-batho** – to die (doodgaan, sterf)

Ho shwa ho bohloko.
To die is painful, i.e. dying is painful. (Om te sterf is pynlik.)

53. **ditshila, dikgwerekgwere, mamphemphe** – dirt, filth (vuilgoed)

Tlosa ditshila tafoleng.
Remove the dirt from the table. (Verwyder die vuilgoed van die tafel af.)

54. **dithole, matlakala** – rubbish, refuse, waste (gemors)

Ngwanana o fiela dithole.
A girl sweeps or wipes up the rubbish. ('n Meisie vee die gemors op.)

55. **eta, tjhaka** – visit (kuier)

Ha ke rate ho eta mariha.
I do not like to visit in winter. (Ek hou nie daarvan om in die winter te kuier nie.)

56. **lekola, hlahloba** – examine, test (ondersoek, toets)

Lefokisi le lekola maemo.
A detective examines the conditions. ('n Speurder ondersoek die toestande.)

57. **ema, phahama** – stand up, rise (staan op)

Ema o tsamaye!
Stand up and walk! (Staan op en loop!)

58. **kgaotsa, emisa** – stop, end (stop)

Ngwana o tla kgaotsa ho lla ha mme a fihla.
A child will stop crying when his/her mother arrives. ('n Kind sal ophou huil wanneer sy/haar moeder aankom.)

59. **lefa, patala** – pay (betaal)

Ke lefa rente ka tjheke.
I pay rent by cheque. (Ek betaal die huur met 'n tjek.)

60. **dila, neta** – smear, apply (smeer)

Mosadi o dila lebota ka boloko.
A woman smears a wall with cow-dung. ('n Vrou smeer die muur met koeimis.)

61. **lehadima, letolo, tladi** – lightning (weerlig)

Lehadima le otlile sefate.
Lightning has struck a tree. (Die weerlig het 'n boom getref.)

62. **mookodi, molalatladi** – rainbow (reënboog)

Mookodi o hlaha ka mora pula.
A rainbow appears after the rain. ('n Reënboog verskyn na die reën.)

63. **mofufutso, sethito** – sweat, perspiration (sweet)

Semathi se tswa mofufutso.
A runner (athlete) sweats. ('n Hardloper sweet.)

64. **hatsela, bata** – become or feel or get cold (koud kry)

Kwala monyako, ke a hatsela.
Close the door, I am getting cold. (Maak die deur toe, ek kry koud.)

65. **fothola, tsomula, motsula** – rip off, uproot (ontwortel/uitroei)

Setsokotsane sa fothola sefate.
A whirlwind uprooted a tree. ('n Warrelwind het 'n boom ontwortel.)

66. **kakalla, pheama** – slouch (slordig sit)

Motho ya botswa o a kakalla.
A person who is lazy slouches. ('n Persoon wat lui is, sit op 'n slordige manier.)

67. **potoloha, dikoloha** – go round (rondom loop)

    Tau e potoloha lesaka.
    A lion is going round the kraal. ('n Leeu loop rondom die kraal.)

68. **sesefa, kwekwetla** – avoid (vermy)

    Motho ya lokileng o sesefa bobe.
    A person who is good avoids evil. ('n Persoon wat goed is, vermy die bose.)

69. **thiba, kiba, topa** – stop, block (stop)

    Ntate o thiba fenstere e patsohileng ka poti.
    Father blocks a window that is cracked with putty. (Pa stop 'n gekraakte venster met stopverf.)

70. **ritsa, phetjha** – slither, drag (seil)

    Noha e ritsa jwanng.
    A snake slithers in the grass. ('n Slang seil deur die gras.)

71. **thuha, tjhwatla** – smash, break (breek)

    Ngwana o thuha lehe la kgoho.
    A child breaks a hen's egg. ('n Kind breek 'n eier van 'n hen.)

72. **nanara, kgukgunela** – stalk, creep, move stealthily (bekruip)

    Nkwe e nanarela phoofolo.
    A tiger stalks an animal. ('n Tier bekruip 'n dier.)

73. **hora, leka, latswa** – lick (lek)

    Ha ke lapile haholo, ke hora sejana.
    When I am very hungry, I lick out a dish. (Wanneer ek baie honger is, lek ek 'n bord uit.)

74. **halefa, kwata** – become angry (kwaad word)

    Batswadi ba a halefa ha bana ba utswa.
    Parents get angry when children steal. (Ouers word kwaad as kinders steel.)

75. **disa, alosa** – to shepherd, tend, look after (oppas)

    Moshemane o disa dinku.
    A boy tends the sheep. ('n Seun pas die skape op.)

76. **kgwedi, ngwedi** – moon (maan)

    Kgwedi e tolokile.
    The moon is glowing, i.e. it is full moon. (Dit is volmaan.)

77. **hama, peteta** – milk, squeeze, force liquid out (melk)

    Modisa o hama kgomo.
    A herdsman is milking a cow. ('n Beeswagter melk die koei.)

78. **phetshela, ripitla** – squash, crush, press (pap druk)

Kariki e phetshela mokopu tshimong.
A cart squashes the pumpkin in the field. ('n Wa druk die pampoen pap in die veld.)

79. **fodisa, phekola** – to heal, to cure (genees, gesond maak)

Moriana ona o tla fodisa leqeba.
Medicine this will heal the wound, i.e. this medicine will heal the wound. (Hierdie medisyne sal die wond gesond maak.)

80. **meriana, methokgo** – medicines, traditional drugs (medisyne)

Meriana ya setho e ntse e thusa.
Medicine of tradition still helps, i.e. traditional medicine still helps. (Tradisionele medisyne help steeds.)

81. **bola, senyeha** – go off, decay, rot (vrot wees of word)

Nama e tla bola ha e sa hatsetswe.
Meat (it) will go off if it is not refrigerated. (Vleis sal vrot word as dit nie verkoel word nie.)

82. **bodila, bohla** – sour, rancid (suur)

Lebese le se le le bodila.
The milk is already sour. (Die melk is alreeds suur.)

83. **potlaka, tata, haba** – hurry up, be hasty (gou maak, haastig wees)

Potlaka terene e tla o siya.
Hurry up the train (it) will (you) leave, i.e. hurry up, the train will leave you behind. (Maak gou, jy sal die trein verpas.)

84. **ruta, rupella** – teach, train (onderwys gee, leer)

Mosuwe o ruta bana.
A teacher (he/she) teaches children. ('n Onderwyser leer kinders.)

85. **sefonthwane, sehanyata, rankahadi** – gigantic person, muscle man ('n sterk man, reusagtige persoon)

Lesole lane ke sefonthwane sa motho.
Soldier that is a giant of a person, i.e. that soldier is a gigantic person. (Daardie soldaat is 'n reusagtige persoon.)

86. **lamola, arohanya** – separate from a fight, intervene, arbitrate (as bemiddelaar optree)

Moruti o lamola batho ba lwanang.
A minister separates people who are fighting. ('n Predikant tree op as bemiddelaar tussen mense wat baklei.)

87. **arohanya, kgaohanya** – divide, separate (verdeel)

Ha o arohanya leshome ka pedi o thola hlano.
If you divide ten by two you get five. (As jy tien deur twee deel, kry jy vyf.)

88. **tsholla, qhala** – spill, throw out (stort, mors, uitgooi)

Butle, o se ke wa tsholla lebese.
Be careful not to spill the milk. (Wees versigtig om nie die melk uit te gooi nie.)

89. **thothomela, tshereana** – shiver, quiver, tremble (bewe, bibber)

Mokudi o a thothomela.
A patient is shivering. ('n Pasiënt bewe.)

90. **tonela, tjamela** – cast eyes upon furiously (met streng oë aankyk)

Lefokisi le tonela leshodu mahlo.
A detective casts his/her thief eyes, i.e. a detective casts his/her eyes furiously upon the thief. ('n Speurder kyk die dief met streng oë aan.)

91. **phoqa, tlontlolla** – embarrass, humiliate (in die verleentheid bring)

Jo, wa tla wa phoqa batswadi ba hao!
Oh, you have embarrassed the parents of yours! Oh, you have embarrassed your parents! (Ag nee, jy het jou ouers in die verleentheid gebring!)

92. **lefotha, monko** – smell, scent, aroma, fragrance (geur, reuk)

Dikgomo di utlwa monko wa tau.
The cattle are smelling the scent of a lion. (Die beeste kry die reuk van 'n leeu.)

93. **monate, hlabosa** – delicious, nice, pleasant, tasty (lekker)

Dijo tsena di monate.
Food this is delicious, i.e. this food is delicious. (Hierdie kos is lekker.)

94. **fothola, rutla** – uproot, wrest, blow off (ontwortel, uitroei)

Setsokotsane se fothola sefate.
The whirlwind uproots a tree. (Die warrelwind ontwortel 'n boom.)

95. **pata, boloka** – bury (begrawe)

Re tla pata mofu ka Moqebelo.
We will bury the deceased on Saturday. (Ons sal die oorledene Saterdag begrawe.)

96. **solla, lelera** – roam, move aimlessly (swerf, dwaal)

Lehlanya le solla diterateng.
A lunatic roams the streets. ('n Mal persoon dwaal deur die strate.)

97. **ikgantsha, qhosha** – brag, swank (trots/spog)

Ngwanana o a ikgantsha.
A girl is proud. ('n Meisie is trots.)

98. **ikgohomosa, ikakasa** – conceited, haughty (hoogmoedig)

Morui o a ikgohomosa.
A rich person is conceited. ('n Ryk persoon is hoogmoedig.)

99. **fosa, fanya** – miss, make a mistake ('n fout maak)

O a fosa.
You miss the point. (Jy maak 'n fout.)

100. **phutha, bokella** – collect, gather, assemble (versamel)

Phutha diaparo pula e a tla.
Collect the clothes, the rain is coming. (Maak die klere bymekaar, die reën kom.)

101. **seboka, kopano** – gathering (vergadering)

Ke seboka sa dipapadi tsa bolo.
It is a gathering of the players of soccer, i.e. it is a gathering of soccer players. (Dit is 'n vergadering van sokkerspelers.)

102. **silla, sidila** – massage, rub (vryf)

Ke silla nkgono mokokotlo.
I rub granny's back. (Ek vryf ouma se rug.)

103. **ratha, rema, kapa, hlatha** – chop, axe (kap)

Ratha patsi.
Chop the wood. (Kap die hout.)

104. **fata, epa, tjheka** – scratch the ground/dig a hole (skrop/grawe 'n gat)

Kgoho e fata thotobolo.
A fowl scratches the dump. ('n Hoender skrop op die hoop.)

105. **phumula, hlakola, sola** – wipe off, erase, clean (afvee)

Semathi se phumula mofufutso.
A runner wipes off the sweat. ('n Hardloper vee die sweet af.)

106. **belaela, sola** – suspect (verdink)

Lepolesa le belaela motshwaruwa.
The police suspects the convict. (Die polisie verdink die gevangene.)

107. **kgotsa, babatsa, tsota** – praise, admire (bewonder)

Baahlodi ba kgotsa botle ba Moipone.
The judges admire the beauty of Moipone, i.e. the judges admire Moipone's beauty. (Die beoordelaars bewonder Moipone se skoonheid.)

108. **hapeletsa, qobella** – compel, force (dwing)

O se ke wa hapeletsa motho.
Do not force a person. (Moenie 'n persoon dwing nie.)

109. **dumellana, kgema** – agree with, consent to (saamstem)

Ke dumellana le wena tabeng ena.
I agree with you issue this, i.e. I agree with you on this issue. (Ek stem saam met jou oor hierdie kwessie.)

110. **hlalosa, qaqisa** – explain, elucidate (verduidelik)

Mosuwe o hlalosa pale.
A teacher explains a story. ('n Onderwyser verduidelik 'n verhaal.)

111. **manala, dinala** – nails (naels)

Ntatemoholo o kuta manala a setloholo.
Grandfather cuts the nails of the grandchild. (Oupa sny die naels van die kleinkind.)

112. **tshwarela, leballa** – forgive (vergewe)

Modimo o re tshwarela melato ya rona.
God (He) forgives trespasses of ours, i.e. God forgives our trespasses. (God vergewe ons oortredings.)

113. **Tlalellana, pipitlelwa** – to be constipated (hardlywig raak)

Lesea le a tlalellana.
A baby gets constipated. ('n Baba raak hardlywig.)

114. **tsitsipana, honyela, finyela** – contract (saamtrek)

Mosifa wa leoto o a tsitsipana.
A muscle of the foot contracts. ('n Spier van die voet trek saam.)

115. **ata, ngatafala** – multiply, increase (vermeerder)

Setjhaba se a ata ha ho na le kgotso.
The nation increases when there is peace. (Die nasie vermeerder as daar vrede is.)

116. **pepeneneng, pontsheng, phatlalatsa** – obvious, in public (in die openbaar)

O se ke wa phoqa motho pepeneneng.
Do not disgrace a person in public. (Moenie 'n persoon in die openbaar beledig nie.)

117. **re tjho** – we say, mention (ons sê)

Ke tjho jwalo.
I say so. (Ek sê so.)

118. **lenqosa, moromuwa** – messenger (boodskapper)

Lenqosa ha le tsekisetswe molaetsa.
A messenger should not be accused for the message. ('n Boodskapper moet nie beskuldig word vir die boodskap nie.)

119. **lelapa, lehae** – home, family (tuis, huis)

Lelapa la hae le qhalehile.
His/her home is disrupted. (Sy/haar huis is ontwrig.)

120. **mathata, ditsietsi, makaqabetsi** – problems, difficulties (probleme, moeilikhede)

Ha ho bophelo bo se nang mathata
There is no life without problems. (Daar is geen lewe sonder probleme nie.)

121. **mahlomola, masisapelo** – sadness (droefheid)

Kgutsana e dikilwe ke mahlomola.
An orphan is surrounded by sadness. ('n Weeskind is omring deur droefheid.)

122. **phaposi, kamore** – room (kamer)

Kamore ya nkgono e hlwekile.
Grandmother's room is clean. (Ouma se kamer is skoon.)

123. **molemo, betere** – better, advantageous (beter)

Ho molemo ho se nwe jwala.
It is better not to drink liquour. (Dit is beter om nie sterk drank te drink nie.)

124. **sekoto, halofo** – half (helfte)

Ke abetse sekoto sa bohobe mofutsana.
I gave half of the bread to the needy person. (Ek het die helfte van die brood aan 'n behoeftige persoon gegee.)

125. **kgesa, nyatsa, nyefola** – despise, treat scornfully (verag)

O se ke wa kgesa basebeetsi ba hao.
Do not treat scornfully workers of yours; i.e. do not treat your workers scornfully. (Moenie jou werkers minag nie.)

126. **lehlakore, thoko** – side, flank (sy)

Lehlakore la mokudi le shwele.
One side of a patient is paralysed. (Een kant van 'n pasiënt is verlam.)

127. **leboha, boka, tankisa** – thank (dankie sê)

Re leboha Modimo ka pula.
We thank God for the rain. (Ons sê dankie aan God vir die reën.)

128. **boka, sekontiri** – tar (teer)

Seroto sa Moshe se ne se ditswe ka boka.
The basket of Moses was smeared with tar. (Die mandjie van Moses was met teer gesmeer.)

129. **hatisa, tlapisa** – print, press (druk)

O tla hatisa buka ya hao neng?
You will print the book of yours when?, i.e. When will you print your book? (Wanneer sal jy jou boek druk?)

130. **tlama, bofa** – tie (vasmaak)

Semathi se tlama borikgwe
The runner ties his/her trousers. (Die hardloper maak sy/haar broek vas.)

131. **tlamella, tantella** – bind securely (vasbind)

Banna ba tlamella sesenyi sefateng ho fihlela mapolesa a tla.
The men tied the wrongdoer to a tree until the police arrived. (Die mans het die kwaaddoener aan die boom vasgebind tot die polisie opgedaag het.)

132. **qeta, fedisa** – to finish, complete (klaarmaak)

O se ke wa qeta dijo, bo!
Do not finish the food, please! (Moenie al die kos opeet nie, asseblief!)

133. **lelekisa, mathisa** – to chase (wegjaag)

Ntja e lelekisa mmutla.
A dog chases a hare. ('n Hond jaag 'n haas.)

134. **phura, bjabjaretsa** – to chew hard substance, masticate (kou)

Tau e phura masapo a qwaha.
A lion chews the bones of a zebra. ('n Leeu kou die bene van 'n sebra.)

135. **bitsa, hwehla** – to call, beckon (roep)

Bitsa mapolesa.
Call the police. (Roep die polisie.)

136. **rohaka, hlapaola** – to swear at, verbally abuse (vloek)

Ngwana ya seleng o rohaka motho e moholo.
A naughty child swears at an elderly person. ('n Stout kind vloek ouer mense.)

137. **akgeha, idibana** – to faint (flou word)

Eitse ha a utlwa ditaba, a akgeha.
When he/she heard the news, he/she fainted. (Toe hy/sy die nuus gehoor het, het hy/sy flou geword.)

138. **tena, apara** – to dress (aantrek)

Tena mose, rwala dieta re ntano tsamaya.
Put on your dress and your shoes so that we may go. (Trek jou rok en jou skoene aan sodat ons kan gaan.)

139. **letsa, teya** – to blow a whistle ('n fluitjie blaas)

Letsa phala papadi e fele.
Blow the whistle, the game must end. (Blaas die fluitjie, die spel moet eindig.)

140. **tiya, thatafala** – to become hard or strong (sterk word)

Masapo a lesea a se a tiya.
The bones of a baby are now becoming strong. (Die bene van 'n baba word nou sterk.)

141. **akgela, lahlela** – to throw, hurl (gooi)

Akgela bolo kwano.
Throw the ball here. (Gooi die bal hiernatoe.)

142. **bophara, botenya** – breadth, width, roundness (breedte, wydte)

Bophara ba tshimo ke dimitara tse sekete.
The width of a farm is metres which are a thousand, i.e. The width of a farm is a thousand metres. (Die breedte van 'n plaas is een duisend meter.)

143. **baka, tseka** – to contest (stry)

Basadi bao ba tseka eng?
Women those are contesting what? i.e. What are those women arguing about? (Waaroor stry daardie vrouens?)

144. **sokoloha, baka** – to repent (berou hê, spyt voel)

Baetsadibe ba sokoloha ka bongata.
Sinners repent in large numbers. (Sondaars kom tot inkeer in groot getalle.)

145. **busa, rena, laola** – to rule, govern (regeer)

Morena o a busa.
The king rules. (Die koning regeer.)

146. **sitwa, hloleha** – to fail (druip, om iets nie te kan doen nie)

Ke sitwa ho utlwisisa lebaka la hao.
I fail to understand the reason of yours, i.e. I fail to understand your reason. (Ek kan nie jou rede verstaan nie.)

147. **imela, sita** – to be burdened by, to be heavy for (om swaar te kry)

Melato e a mo imela.
Debts are heavy for him/her. (Hy/sy het baie skuld.)

148. **shwa, hlokahala** – to die (om dood te gaan)

A shwa.
He/she died. (Hy/sy het doodgegaan.)

149. **sudubana, kudupana** – to roll in the dust, mud (om in die stof of modder te rol)

Kolobe ya sudubana seretseng.
A pig rolls in the mud. ('n Vark rol in die modder.)

150. **nyaroha, tshoha** – to become afraid, terrified (bang word)

Ke ile ka nyaroha ha ke utlwa seboko.
I became scared when I heard the screaming. (Ek het bang geword toe ek die geskreeu hoor.)

151. **pere, katola** – horse (perd)

Pere e raha ha bohloko.
A horse kicks painfully. ('n Perd skop seer.)

152. **nku, kgatala** – sheep (skaap)

Boya ba nku bo bongata.
The wool of a sheep is much, i.e. a sheep has much wool. ('n Skaap het baie wol.)

153. **honyela, finyela** – contract (trek saam)

Rekere e a honyela mme e otlolohe.
Rubber contracts and then stretches. (Rubber trek saam en dan rek dit.)

154. **paka, buella** – testify for or against someone (getuig)

Ke a paka hore o utswitse koloi.
I testify that he/she stole the car. (Ek getuig dat hy/sy die kar gesteel het.)

155. **seso, leqeba, selota** – wound, sore (wond)

Seso ha se fole.
A wound does not heal. ('n Wond word nie gesond nie.)

156. **teteka, rabella** – hit with heavy blows (hard slaan)

Rampa o ile a teteka motho ka ditebele.
Rampa hit a person with fists. (Rampa het 'n persoon met die vuis geslaan.)

157. **thethefatsa, kokobetsa** – soften, relieve (verlig)

Pidisi ena e thethefatsa lehlaba.
Pill this one tones down the pain, i.e. this pill relieves the pain. (Hierdie pil verlig die pyn.)

158. **sello, seboko** – cry (gehuil)

Mosadi o tsositswe ke sello sa lesea.
A woman was awakened by the cry of the baby. ('n Vrou is deur die gehuil van 'n baba wakker gemaak.)

159. **fuama, alama** – lie on the eggs, to guard or protect jealously (op die eiers lê)

Sethole se fuama ditsuonyana.
A hen lies on the chickens. ('n Hen lê op die kuikens.)

160. **kgwele, bolo** – (soccer)ball (bal)

Bashemane ba raha kgwele.
The boys kick the ball. (Die seuns skop die bal.)

161. **setebele, feisi** – fist (vuis)

Matlala o akgela setebele se boima.
Matlala throws a powerful blow. (Matlala slaan 'n harde hou.)

162. **qalong, tshimolohong** – in the beginning (in die begin)

A re ye qalong ya pale.
Let us go to the beginning of the story. (Laat ons by die begin van die storie begin.)

163. **matha, titima** – to run (om te hardloop)

Bana ba sekolo ba matha hoseng.
Children of the school run in the morning, i.e. school children run in the morning. (Skoolkinders hardloop in die môre.)

164. **kotama, kotsomala, tsorama** – squat, to sit in a perched position (neerhurk)

Dula setulong o tlohele ho kotama lejweng.
Sit on a chair and stop squatting on a stone. (Sit op 'n stoel en moenie op 'n klip neerhurk nie.)

165. **lebenkele, shopo** – shop (winkel)

Lebenkele le rekisa diphahlo tse ntle.
A shop sells beautiful goods. ('n Winkel verkoop mooi goedere.)

166. **dumela, ananela** – to agree, concur with (saamstem)

Ke dumela ha o bua nnete.
I agree with you when you tell the truth. (Ek stem saam met jou as jy die waarheid praat.)

167. **monahano, mohopolo** – thinking, thought (mening, gedagte)

Monahano wa hao o ditshila.
The thinking of yours is dirty, i.e. your thinking is dirty. (Jou gedagtes is vuil.)

168. **raoha, thakgoha** – to stand up like soldiers or rush out as if chasing something or running away from something (opstaan, weghardloop)

Lesole la raoha ha le utlwa sethunya.
A soldier got up quickly, when he/she heard a gunshot. ('n Soldaat het opgestaan toe hy/sy 'n geweerskoot hoor.)

169. **tjheha, tshwasa** – to trap, snare ((in 'n strik) vang)

Bashanyana ba tjheha dinonyana.
The boys trap the birds. (Die seuns stel 'n strik vir die voëls.)

170. **sotleha, hlopheha** – to suffer, struggle (om swaar te kry)

Ke ile ka sotleha haholo bonyaneng.
I suffered a lot in my childhood. (Ek het baie swaar gekry in my kinderdae.)

171. **satalla, tsetalla** – to be determined (om vasberade te wees)

Morutwana o ile a satalla le ha ho le thata .
A student was determined even if it was tough. ('n Student was vasbeslote, al was dit moeilik.)

172. **jabela, tlelapa** – to slap, smack (om te klap)

Ntswaki o ile a jabela Dimakatso.
Ntswaki slapped Dimakatso. (Ntswaki het Dimakatso geklap.)

173. **honohela, fufela** – to be jealous of (om jaloers te wees)

O se ke wa honohela ya atlehileng .
Do not be jealous of him/her who has been successful. (Moenie jaloers wees op hom/haar wat suksesvol was nie.)

174. **nyemotsa, qekotsa** – to look askance at, look scornfully upon, frown at (om minagtend te kyk na)

O se ke wa nyemotsa batho .
Do not look scornfully at people. (Moenie minagtend na ander mense kyk nie.)

175. **fofa, rura** – to fly (om te vlieg)

Ditsie di fofa ka bongata.
Locusts fly in large numbers, i.e. in a swarm. (Sprinkane vlieg in groot swerms.)

176. **kuka, nka** – to take, carry away (wegvat of -dra)

Phiri e kuka lesea.
A hyena carries a baby away. ('n Hiëna dra 'n baba weg.)

27

Antonyms

(Words with opposite meanings)

(Antonieme)

Orientation and examples (Oriëntering en voorbeelde)

As noted in chapter 26 on synonyms, language is rich in words that have the same meaning. In this chapter, we deal with those words with opposite meanings. In the study of language, such a word is called an antonym. Sesotho has many interesting antonyms, as will be seen in the following examples:

1. **bosiu** – night (nag); **motsheare** – day (dag)

   Sephooko se fofa bosiu. – The owl flies at night. (Die uil vlieg in die nag.)

   Bana ba a robatswa motsheare. – Children must sleep during the day. (Kinders moet gedurende die dag slaap.)

2. **tshweu** – white (wit); **ntsho** – black (swart)

   hempe e tshweu – a shirt that is white ('n hemp wat wit is)

   kobo e ntsho – a blanket that is black ('n kombers wat swart is)

3. **mafolofolo** – activeness (bedrywigheid); **botswa** – laziness (luiheid)

   Rakgadi o na le mafolofolo. – Aunt has activeness, i.e. aunt is energetic. (Tannie is bedrywig.)

   Tlohela botswa bona ba hao. – Leave/stop laziness this of yours, i.e. stop your laziness. (Staak jou luiheid.)

4. **monna** – man (man); **mosadi** – woman (vrou)

   Tshepo ke monna ya sebete. – Tshepo is a man who is brave. (Tshepo is 'n dapper man.)

Seipone ke mosadi ya makgethe. – Seipone is a woman who is neat. (Seipone is 'n vrou wat netjies is.)

5. **moshemane** – boy (seun); **ngwanana** – girl (meisie)

   Moshemane o a matha. – A boy is running. ('n Seun hardloop.)

   Ngwanana o a tola. – A girl is bathing. ('n Meisie spoel af of bad.)

6. **robala** – sleep (slaap); **tsoha** – wake up (wakker word, opstaan)

   Nkgono o a robala. – Grandmother is sleeping. (Ouma slaap.)

   Badisa ba tsoha hoseng. – The shepherds wake up in the morning. (Die veewagters word wakker in die oggend.)

7. **tutubala** – shut eyes (oë toemaak); **sheba** – look, see (kyk, sien)

   Tutubala ha o rapela. – Shut your eyes when you pray. (Maak jou oë toe as jy bid.)

   Sheba moo o tsamayang. – Look where you go. (Kyk waar jy loop.)

8. **bata** – cold (koud); **tjhesa** – hot (warm)

   Ho a bata. – It is cold. (Dit is koud.)

   Ho a tjhesa. – It is hot. (Dit is warm.)

9. **kula** – ill, sick (siek); **fola** – be well, healed (gesond wees)

   Mpho o a kula. – Mpho is ill. (Mpho is siek.)

   O tla fola. – He/she will get well. (Hy/sy sal gesond word.)

10. **matla** – strong (sterk); **fokola** – weak (swak)

    Ke ntlha e matla. – It is a point which is strong, i.e. it is a strong point. (Dit is 'n sterk punt.)

    Mabaka a hao a a fokola. – Reasons of yours are weak, i.e. your reasons are weak. (Jou redes is swak.)

11. **tona** – male (manlik); **tshehadi** – female (vroulik)

    Ke phoofolo e tona. – It is an animal which is male, i.e. it is a male animal. (Dit is 'n manlike dier.)

    Ke phoofolo e tshehadi. – It is an animal which is female, i.e. it is a female animal. (Dit is vroulike dier.)

12. **thata** – hard (hard); **bonolo** – soft (sag)

    Mosifa o thata. – A muscle is hard. ('n Spier is hard.)

    Botoro e bonolo. – Butter is soft. (Botter is sag.)

13. **hwama** – curdle (stol); **qhibidiha** – melt (smelt)

Ha ho bata, mafura a a hwama. – When it is cold, fat curdles. (Wanneer dit koud is, stol die vet.)

Ha ho tjhesa, mafura a a qhibidiha. – When it is hot, fat melts. (Wanneer dit warm is, smelt die vet.)

14. **tlama** – tie, lock (vasmaak); **tlamolla** – untie, unlock (losmaak)

Ke tlama lefito. – I tie a knot. (Ek maak 'n koop vas.)

Ke tlamolla lefito. – I untie a knot. (Ek maak 'n knoop los.)

15. **silafatsa** – make dirty (vuil maak); **hlwekisa** – make clean (skoonmaak)

Lerole le a silafatsa. – Dust makes dirty, i.e. dirties. (Stof maak vuil.)

Metsi a a hlwekisa. – Water makes clean, i.e. cleans. (Water maak skoon.)

16. **nona** – to be fat (om vet te wees); **ota** – to be lean (om maer te wees)

O tla nona ha o ja haholo. – You will be fat if you eat a lot. (Jy sal vet word as jy te veel eet.)

Ha o sa je hantle, o tla ota. – If you do not eat well, you will be lean. (As jy nie goed eet nie, sal jy maer wees.)

17. **kgutshwane** – short (kort); **telele** – tall, long (lang, lank)

pale e kgutshwane – a story which is short, i.e. a short story ('n kortverhaal.)

thero e telele – a sermon which is long, i.e. a lengthy sermon ('n lang preek)

18. **phahama** – rise up (op staan, opstyg); **wa** – fall (val)

Letsatsi le a phahama. – The sun rises. (Die son kom op.)

Lemoha, o tla wa. – Beware, you will fall. (Pas op, jy sal val.)

19. **fumana** – find (vind, kry); **lahla** – lose (verloor)

Fumana phahlo ya ka. – Find the parcel of mine, i.e. find my parcel. (Soek my pakkie.)

O tla lahla phahlo eo ha o sa hlokomele. – You will lose that parcel if you are not careful. (Jy sal die pakkie verloor as jy nie versigtig is nie.)

20. **bua** – talk (praat); **thola** – keep quiet (stilbly)

Bua nnete. – Speak the truth, i.e. tell the truth. (Praat die waarheid.)

Thola o etsa lerata. – Keep quiet, you are making a noise. (Bly stil, jy maak geraas.)

21. **tsamaya,** – walk, move, go (loop, weggaan); **ema** – stand (staan)

Koloi e a tsamaya. – A car moves away, goes away. ('n Kar ry weg.)

Koloi e a ema. – A car stops. ('n Kar stop.)

22. **kadima** – borrow (leen); **kgutlisa** – return, repay (terugbetaal)

    Mofutsana o kadima tjhelete. – A poor person borrows money. ('n Arm persoon leen geld.)

    Tshepo o kgutlisa tjhelete. – Tshepo repays the money. (Tshepo betaal die geld terug.)

23. **motjha** – a young person ('n jong persoon); **Motsofe** – an old person ('n ou persoon)

    Motjha o rata ho tantsha. – A young person likes to dance. ('n Jong persoon hou daarvan om te dans.)

    Motsofe o kgathala ka pele. – An old person tires soon. ('n Ou persoon word gou moeg.)

24. **dumela** – to agree (saamstem); **hana, latola** – to refuse (weier)

    Moqosuwa a dumela molato. – An accused agreed to the crime, i.e. the accused pleaded guilty. (Die beskuldigde het skuldig gepleit.)

    Pere e hana ho matha. – A horse refuses to run. ('n Perd weier om te hardloop.)

25. **nnete** – truth (waarheid); **leshano** – lies, deceit (leuens)

    Ke bua nnete. – I am telling the truth. (Ek praat die waarheid.)

    O se ke wa bua leshano. – Do not tell lies. (Moenie leuens vertel nie.)

26. **futhumatsa** – to warm up (om warm te maak); **hatsetsa** – to make cold (om koud te maak)

    Mosadi o futhumatsa dijo. – A woman warms up the food. ('n Vrou maak die kos warm.)

    Pula ya mariha e hatsetsa diphoofolo. – Rain of winter makes animals cold, i.e. Animals feel the cold after winter rain. (Winter maak dat die diere koud kry.)

27. **rata** – like, love (hou van, liefhê); **hloya** – hate (haat)

    Ke rata mmino. – I like music. (Ek hou van musiek.)

    Ke tla o hloya. – I will hate you. (Ek sal jou haat.)

28. **bolaya** – kill (doodmaak); **phedisa** – bring to life (lewendig maak)

    Sekoloto se a bolaya. – Debt it kills, i.e. debt kills. (Skuld maak dood.)

    Thapelo e a phedisa. – Prayer it brings to life, i.e. prayer enlivens. (Gebed maak lewendig.)

29. **fodisa** – to heal (om gesond te maak); **kudisa** – to cause to become sick (om siek te word)

    Moriana ona o a fodisa. – Medicine this one heals, i.e. this medicine heals. (Hierdie medisyne maak gesond.)

Tjhefu e a kudisa. – Poison it sickens, i.e. poison causes illness. (Gif veroorsaak siekte.)

30. **lahla** – lose, throw away (verloor, weggooi); **thola** – retrieve (vind, kry)

    Ngwana o lahla tjhelete. – A child loses money. ('n Kind verloor geld.)

    Mapolesa a thola koloi e utswitsweng. – The police retrieved a car that was stolen. (Die polisie het 'n gesteelde kar gevind.)

31. **timana** – be stingy (om suinig te wees); **fana** – be generous (om vrygewig, edelmoedig te wees)

    Sello o a timana. – Sello is stingy. (Sello is suinig.)

    Mohau o a fana. – Mohau is generous. (Mohau is edelmoedig.)

32. **thaba** – to be happy (om bly te wees); **hlonama** – to be sad (om treurig te wees)

    Pontsho o thabile. – Pontsho is happy. (Pontsho is bly.)

    Teboho o a hlonama. – Teboho is sad. (Teboho is treurig.)

33. **kgothetse** – industrious (bedrywig); **botswa** – lazy (lui)

    Ngwanana o kgothetse. – A girl is industrious. ('n Meisie is bedrywig.)

    Mpho o botswa. – Mpho is lazy. (Mpho is lui.)

34. **makgethe** – decent (ordentlik); **bohlaswa** – careless (sorgeloos)

    mosebetsi o makgethe – work which is decent, i.e. decent work (ordentlike werk)

    karabo e bohlaswa – A reply which is careless, i.e. a careless reply ('n sorgelose antwoord)

35. **palama** – climb, ride (opklim); **theoha** – come down, alight, dismount (afklim)

    Palama pere ya hao. – Ride your horse. (Ry jou perd.)

    Theoha pere. – Come down from your horse. (Klim van jou perd af.)

36. **rwesa** – burden, put on hard (belas); **rola** – to take off load (las wegneem)

    Ke o rwesa morwalo wa ho hodisa ngwana. – I am burdening you with a responsibility to bring up the child. (Ek belas jou met 'n verantwoordelikheid om die kind groot te maak.)

    Rakgadi o rosa mme morwalo. – Aunt takes off mother, burden, i.e. aunt takes off the burden from mother. (Tannie neem die las van moeder weg.)

37. **tsitsipana** – contract, be tense (gespanne); **phutholloha** – to relax (om te ontspan)

Ka tshoha ka tsitsipana. – I got scared and became tense. (Ek het geskrik en gespanne geraak.)

Ka thaba, ka phutholloha. – I became happy and relaxed. (Ek was bly gewees en het ontspan.)

38. **kgora** – become satiated, full (versadig); **lapa** – become hungry (honger)

Ha o ja haholo o tla kgora. – If you eat too much you will be satiated. (As jy te veel eet, sal jy versadig wees.)

Ha o le botswa o tla lapa. – If you are lazy you will be hungry. (As jy lui is, sal jy honger word.)

39. **tenya** – thick (dik); **tshesane** – thin, slim (dun)

sefate se setenya – a tree which is thick ('n boom wat dik is)

thupa e tshesane – a stick that is thin ('n stok wat dun is)

40. **atleha** – to succeed, pass (om te slaag); **hloleha** – fail (om te misluk)

Dikeledi o tla atleha dithutong. – Dikeledi will succeed in her studies. (Dikeledi sal in haar studies slaag.)

Ratau o ile a hloleha mojahong. – Ratau failed in the race. (Ratau het in die wedren misluk.)

41. **lehlohonolo** – luck, fortune (geluk); **bomadimabe** – ill luck, misfortune (ongeluk)

O lehlohonolo hakaakang! – You are so lucky! (Jy is so gelukkig!)

Ba madimabe hakaakang! – They are so unlucky! (Hulle is so ongelukkig!)

42. **tshwara** – hold, catch (vashou, vang); **tlohela** – leave, release (los, vrylaat)

Lepolesa le tshwere leshodu. – A policeman has caught a thief. ('n Polisieman het 'n dief gevang.)

Lepolesa le tlohela moqosuwa. – A policeman leaves the accused on his own. ('n Polisieman laat die beskuldigde alleen.)

43. **nolofatsa** – make easy (eenvoudig maak); **thatafatsa** – make difficult (moeilik maak)

Mosuwe o ile a nolofatsa tshomo. – The teacher made easy the story, i.e. the teacher made the story easy. (Die onderwyser het die verhaal eenvoudig gemaak.)

Faro o ile a thatafatsa molala wa hae. – Pharaoh hardened the neck of his, i.e. Pharaoh hardened his neck (to be stubborn). (Farao het sy nek verhard.)

44. **ntshofatsa** – blacken (swart maak); **sweufatsa** – whiten (wit maak)

Leshala le ntshofatsa mose. – Coal blackens a dress. (Kool maak 'n rok swart.)

Lehlwa le sweufatsa dithaba. – Snow whitens the mountains. (Sneeu maak die berge wit.)

45. **tabola** – tear off (skeur); **roka** – sew together (vaswerk, aanwerk)

Ntja e tabola kobo. – A dog tears a blanket. ('n Hond skeur 'n kombers.)

Nkgono o roka jase. – Granny sews an overcoat. (Ouma werk 'n oorjas vas.)

46. **lerato** – love (liefde); **lehloyo** – hatred (haat)

Modimo o lerato. – God is love. (God is liefde.)

Lehloyo ha le hahe batho. – Hatred does not build people. (Haat bou nie mense nie.)

47. **tiisa** – toughen (versterk); **nyehlisa** – lessen (verswak)

Sehahi se tiisa moaho ka tshepe. – A builder toughens the building with steel. ('n Bouer versterk die gebou met staal.)

O tla nyehlisa mathata a hao ha o sebetsa. – You will lessen your problems if you work. (As jy werk, sal jy jou probleme verminder.)

48. **atamela** – come near, approach (nader); **furalla** – turn one's back on, abandon (verlaat, die rug na iemand draai)

Batsamai ba atamela toropo. – The travellers are approaching the town. (Die reisigers nader die dorp.)

Batshehetsi ba furalla dibapadi. – The supporters are abandoning the players. (Die ondersteuners verlaat, draai hulle rug na die spelers.)

49. **lla** – cry, (huil); **tsheha** – laugh (lag)

Lesea le a lla. – A baby is crying. ('n Baba huil.)

Ke tla o tsheha ha o ka wa. – I will laugh at you if you fall. (Ek sal vir jou lag as jy val.)

50. **fadimeha** – be awake (wakker wees); **otsela** – be drowsy (slaperig wees)

Masole a lokela ho fadimeha. – Soldiers are supposed to be awake or on the alert. (Soldate moet wakker wees.)

Ntatemoholo o a otsela. – Grandfather is drowsy. (Oupa is slaperig.)

51. **nyala** – marry (trou); **hlala, nyalolla** – divorce (egskeiding verkry)

Pule o nyala Matshediso. – Pule marries Matshediso. (Pule trou met Matshediso.)

Pule o hlala Matshediso. – Pule divorces Matshediso. (Pule verkry 'n egskeiding van Matshediso.)

52. **haha** – build (bou); **heletsa** – destroy (vernietig)

Monna o haha ntlo. – A man is building a house. ('n Man bou 'n huis.)

Sesenyi se heletsa ntlo. – A wrongdoer destroys a house. ('n Kwaaddoener vernietig 'n huis.)

53. **kgathala** – to get tired (om moeg te word); **hlasimoloha** – to get refreshed and lively (verfris word)

Ha o sebetsa haholo o tla kgathala. – If you work too much you will get tired. (As jy te veel werk, sal jy moeg word.)

Ha o nwa metsi a phodileng o tla hlasimoloha. – If you drink cold water, you will be refreshed. (As jy koue water drink, sal jy verfris word.)

54. **lokisa** – fix up (regmaak); **senya** – mess up (deurmekaar krap)

Lokisa phoso ya hao. – Fix up mistake of yours, i.e. fix up your mistake. (Maak jou fout reg.)

Ntwa e senya lefatshe. – War messes up the world. (Oorlog krap die wêreld deurmekaar.)

55. **pholla** – stroke gently (streel); **ngwapa** – scratch (krap)

Ke pholla katse. – I am stroking a cat gently. (Ek streel 'n kat saggies.)

Ntja e ngwapa leqeba. – A dog scratches the wound. ('n Hond krap die wond.)

56. **bula** – open (oopmaak); **kwala** – close (toemaak)

Bula monyako. – Open the door. (Maak oop die deur.)

Kwala lemati. – Close the door. (Maak toe die deur.)

57. **dumela** – agree (saamstem); **hana** – refuse (weier)

Ke a dumela hore ke nnete. – I agree that it is true. (Ek stem saam dat dit waar is.)

Ke hana ho bua leshano. – I refuse to tell a lie. (Ek weier om 'n leuen te vertel.)

58. **phela** – alive (lewendig); **shwa** – (dood)

Tlisa kgoho e phela. – Bring a fowl that is alive. (Bring 'n lewendige hoender.)

Ha ke batle ho shwa pele ho batswadi ba ka. – I do not want to die before my parents. (Ek wil nie voor my ouers doodgaan nie.)

59. **butswa** – to be cooked, ripe (gaar, ryp); **tala** – raw, green (rou, groen)

Nama e a butswa. – The meat is getting cooked, i.e. it is almost ready for eating. (Die vleis is amper gaar.)

Diperekisi di sa le tala. – The peaches are still green. (Die perskes is nog groen.)

60. **bobebe** – light (lig); **boima** – heavy (swaar)

Joko e bobebe. – A yoke is light. ('n Juk is lig.)

Tshepe e boima. – Iron is heavy. (Yster is swaar.)

61. **fatshe** – down (neer); **hodimo** – up (op)

Beha buka fatshe. – Put the book down. (Sit die boek neer.)

Sheba hodimo. – Look up. (Kyk op.)

62. **apesa** – clothe, wrap up, dress (aantrek, toemaak); **tsola/hlobola** – undress (uittrek)

Apesa ngwana leleiri. – Clothe the baby in a napkin, i.e. wrap up the baby in a cloth. (Maak die baba toe met 'n doek.)

O se ke wa tsola pontsheng. – Do not undress in public. (Jy moenie in die openbaar uittrek nie.)

63. **kopanya** – unite (verenig); **arola** – divide (verdeel)

Moruti o kopanya mahlakore a lwanang. – A minister unites sides which are fighting. ('n Predikant verenig die partye wat baklei.)

Ntwa e arola setjhaba. – War divides a nation. (Oorlog verdeel 'n nasie.)

64. **atisa** – enlarge (vergroot); **ngotla** – reduce (verklein, verkort)

Rapolasi o atisa lesaka la mohlape. – A farmer enlarges a pound of the flock. ('n Boer vergroot die skutkraal van die skape.)

Seroki se ngotla mose. – A dressmaker shortens a dress. ('n Rokmaker maak 'n rok korter.)

65. **hloma** – blossom (bloei); **pona** – wither (kwyn)

Dipalesa di a hloma selemo. – Flowers blossom in spring. (Die blomme blom in die lente.)

Jwang bo a pona mariha. – Grass withers in winter. (Gras kwyn in die winter.)

66. **halefa** – to be angry (om kwaad te wees); **hauhela** – to pity (om te bejammer)

Mosuwe o a halefa ha bana ba etsa lerata. – The teacher gets angry when children make a noise. (Die onderwyser word kwaad as kinders 'n geraas maak.)

Modimo o hauhela baetsadibe. – God is merciful upon sinners. (God vergewe sondaars.)

67. **phoqa** – to ridicule (om te bespot); **rorisa** – to praise (om te prys)

Ke eng o rata ho phoqa batho? – Why do you like to ridicule people? (Hoekom hou jy daarvan om mense te bespot?)

Bakudi ba rorisa baoki le dingaka. – The patients praise the nurses and doctors. (Die pasiënte prys die verpleegsters en dokters.)

68. **tsitsa** – to be firm (om ferm te wees); **thekesela** – to shake (om te bewe)

O tsitse ha o le mathateng. – Be firm when you are in difficulties. (Jy moet ferm wees wanneer jy in die moeilikheid is.)

Letahwa le a thekesela. – A drunk person shakes. ('n Dronk persoon bewe.)

69. **robatsa** – cause to sleep (laat slaap); **tsosa** – to awaken (laat wakker te word)

Dipidisi di robatsa ngwana. – Pills cause to sleep child, i.e. the pills make the child sleep. (Die pille laat die kind slaap.)

Ha mokoko o lla, o tsosa basebetsi. – When the cock crows, it awakens the workers. (Wanneer die haan kraai, maak hy die werkers wakker.)

70. **ja** – to eat (eet); **hlatsa** – to throw up, vomit (vomeer)

Ke ja dijo. – I eat food. (Ek eet kos.)

Ke hlatsa tjhefu. – I vomit poison. (Ek vomeer gif.)

71. **tshela** – to pour in (ingooi); **tsholla** – to spill (mors, uitgooi)

Mosadi o tshela teye. – A woman pours tea. ('n Vrou gooi tee in.)

Ngwanana o tsholla metsi a ditshila. – A girl spills water which is dirty. ('n Meisie gooi die vuil water uit.)

72. **nepa** – to aim (om te mik, korrel); **fosa** – to miss (om te mis)

Sebapadi sa nepa penele A player scored a penalty, i.e. he aimed well. ('n Speler het 'n strafskop ingeskop.)

Kulo e ile ya mo fosa. – A bullet missed him/her. ('n Koeël het hom/haar gemis.)

73. **nnete** – truth (waarheid); **leshano** – lie (leuen)

Bua nnete feela. – Tell the truth plainly. (Praat net die waarheid.)

O leshano! – You are a liar! (Jy lieg of jy is 'n leuenaar!)

74. **botshepehi** – trustworthiness (betroubaarheid); **bofelekwane** – untrustworthiness (onbetroubaarheid)

Mpho o hloka botshepehi. – Mpho lacks trustworthiness. (Mpho is onbetroubaar.)

Bofelekwane bo tla o kenya kgathatsong. – Untrustworthiness will put you into trouble. (Onbetroubaarheid sal jou in die moeilikheid beland.)

75. **ikokobetsa** – to humble oneself (om jouself te verneder); **ikgohomosa** – to be conceited (om hoogmoedig te wees)

Motshwaruwa o ikokobetsa pela moahlodi. – A prisoner humbles himself/herself before the judge. ('n Gevangene verneder homself/haarself voor die regter.)

O a ikgohomosa. – He/she is conceited. (Hy/sy is verwaand.)

76. **paka** – to attest to (getuig van); **latola** – to deny (ontken)

Ke paka hore Thabo o ne a le teng. – I attest to the fact that Thabo was present. (Ek getuig van die feit dat Thabo teenwoordig was.)

Moqosuwa o latola molato. – The accused denies the accusation. (Die beskuldigde ontken die aanklag.)

77. **boholo** – bulk, bigness (grootheid); **bonyenyane** – smallness (kleinheid)

Boholo ba tshimo bo kotutswe. – The largest part of the field has been reaped. (Die grootste deel van die land is geoes.)

Ho setse bonyenyane feela. – It is left the small part only, i.e. only a small part is left. (Net 'n klein deeltjie bly oor.)

78. **botle** – beauty (mooiheid); **bobe** – ugliness (lelikheid)

Botle ba hao bo a makatsa. – Beauty of yours is stunning, i.e. your beauty is stunning. (Jou skoonheid is oorweldigend.)

Batho ba tsota bobe ba ketso tsa hao. – People remark about the badness of deeds of yours, i.e. people remark about your bad deeds. (Mense maak opmerkings oor jou slegte dade.)

79. **nala** – prosperity (voorspoed); **bokaota** – famine (skaarste)

Pula e nele, nala e tla ba teng. – The rain has fallen, prosperity will be there, i.e. it has rained, prosperity will come. (Dit het gereën, voorspoed sal kom.)

Ka nako ya difaqane ho ile ha ba le bokaota. – At a time of **difaqane** (war) there was famine. (Gedurende die tyd van **difaqane** (oorlog) was daar hongersnood.)

80. **kgora** – abundance of food (oorvloed van kos); **tlala** – hunger (hongersnood)

Kgora e teng hoba kgotso e le teng. – Abundance of food is there because peace is there, i.e. there is an abundance of food because peace prevails. (Daar is 'n oorvloed van kos, want vrede heers.)

Tlala e tshaba matsoho. – Hunger is afraid of hands i.e when people are industrious, hunger disappears. (Wanneer mense bedrywig is, verdwyn hongersnood.)

81. **botjha** – youth (jeug); **botsofadi** – old age (ouderdom)

Botjha ke bokgabane. – Youth is wonderful. (Jeug is wonderlik.)

Nkgono o imetswe ke botsofadi. – Grandmother is overpowered by decrepitude or age. (Ouma is deur ouderdom oorweldig.)

82. **ntatemoholo** – grandfather (oupa); **nkgono** – grandmother (ouma)

Ntatemoholo o dilemo di lekgolo. – Grandfather is the years that are a hundred, i.e. grandfather is a hundred years old. (Oupa is een honderd jaar oud.)

Nkgono o tsoha hoseng. – Grandmother wakes up early in the morning. (Ouma staan vroeg op.)

83. **kgaitsedi** – brother (broer); **kgaitsediye** – sister (suster)

Mokone ke kgaitsedi ya Malebo. – Mokone is a brother to Malebo. (Mokone is Malebo se broer.)

Ntswaki ke kgaitsediye ya Molefi. – Ntswaki is a sister to Molefi. (Ntswaki is Molefi se suster.).

84. **rangwane** – uncle (oom); **mangwane** – aunt (tante)

Mokete ke rangwane wa ka. – Mokete is an uncle of mine. (Mokete is my oom.)

Nnuku ke mangwane wa ka. – Nnuku is an aunt of mine. (Nnuku is my tante.)

85. **moholwane, abuti** – elder brother (ouer broer); **monyane** – small brother (jonger broer)

Modise ke moholwane wa Modisenyane. – Modise is a big brother to Modisenyane. (Modise is 'n ouer broer van Modisenyane.)

Modisenyane ke monyane wa Modise. – Modisenyane is small brother to Modise. (Modisenyane is 'n jonger broer van Modise.)

86. **hopola** – remember (onthou); **lebala** – forget (vergeet)

Hopola batswadi ba hao. – Remember parents of yours, i.e. think of your parents. (Onthou jou ouers, d.w.s. dink aan jou ouers.)

Lebala ka boshodu. – Forget about theft. (Vergeet van diefstal.)

87. **ikemisetsa** – to be determined (om vasberade te wees); **tsilatsila** – to be hesitant (om te aarsel)

Dibapadi di ikemisetsa tlholo. – The players are determined for victory. (Die spelers is vasberade om te wen.)

Mohahlaudi o a tsilatsila. – A traveller is hesitant. ('n Reisiger is aarselend.)

88. **tshwanela** – to become (om te pas); **rona** – not to be suited for (om nie te pas nie)

Seaparo sena se a o tshwanela. – This garment becomes you. (Hierdie kledingstuk pas jou.)

Katiba eo e a o rona. – Hat that one does not become you, i.e. that hat does not become you. (Daardie hoed pas jou nie.)

89. **isa** – take (vat, neem); **kgutlisa** – bring back/return (terugbring)

Ke isa ngwana sekolong. – I am taking a child to school. (Ek vat 'n kind skool toe.)

Morutwana o kgutlisa buka. – A student returns a book. ('n Student bring 'n boek terug.)

90. **kwekwetla** – avoid (vermy); **toba** – confront (konfronteer)

Bebele e re ruta ho kwekwetla bobe. – The Bible us teach to avoid evil, i.e. the Bible teaches us to avoid evil. (Die Bybel leer ons om kwaad te vermy.)

Toba mathata a hao. – Confront your problems. (Konfronteer jou probleme.)

91. **tsetela** invest, conceal (belê); **utulla** unearth (uithaal, opgrawe)

Mohwebi o tsetela leruo naheng ya habo. – A trader invests his/her wealth in the country of his/hers. ('n Sakeman belê sy rykdom in sy land.)

Mafokisi a ile a utulla dibetsa. – The detectives unearthed the weapons. (Die speurders het die wapens uitgehaal.)

92. **kata** – to compact (vastrap); **epolla** – to dig out, up (opgrawe, uitgrawe)

Tlou e kata lefatshe. – An elephant compacts the ground. ('n Olifant trap die grond vas.)

Phiri e epolla masapo. – A hyena digs up the bones. ('n Hiëna grawe die bene op.)

28

General vocabulary

(Algemene woordeskat)

Sesotho vocabulary is rich and varied. We have selected the following words to expose the Sesotho learner to some useful words and concepts.

Sesotho	*English*	*Afrikaans*
aba	allocate	toeken, aanwys
ahlola	sentence	vonnis, veroordeel
ahlola	judge, adjudicate	beoordeel, uitspraak lewer
akere	acre	akker
ala	make a bed	bed opmaak
amanya	associate	assosieer
amohela	receive	ontvang
araba	respond	reageer
atamela	approach	nader, naderkom
aterese	address	adres
atleha	succeed	slaag
baahi	population	bevolking, populasie
badimo	ancestors	voorouer, stamvader
bahlabani	armed force	gewapende mag
baka	bake	bak
bala	read, count	lees, tel
banka	bank (for money)	bank
batla	require	vereis, nodig hê, vorder
beke	week	week
besa	make fire	'n vuur maak
bese	bass	bas
bete	beetroot	beet
bethe	bed	bed
boditse	bristle	borsel, borselhaar
bodumedi	religion	godsdiens, geloof

boemo ba lehodimo	weather	weer
boemo	position, condition	posisie, stand, toestand
bohareng	inland	binneland
bohata	insincerity	onopregtheid, valsheid
bohlale	intelligence	intelligensie
bohlaswa	carelessness, negligence	agtelosigheid, nalatigheid
bohlwa	white ant, termite	rysmier, termiet
boholo	magnitude	grootte
boiketlo	comfort	gemak
boima	weight (tare)	gewig, eiegewig, tarra
boithutelo	qualification	kwalifikasie
boitshwaro	conduct	gedrag
boka	pitch, bitumen	bitumen, pik
bokaakang	quantity	kwantiteit, hoeveelheid
bokaalo	number (quantity)	aantal, hoeveelheid
bokahodimo	plane (surface)	vlak
boko	brain	brein, harsings
boladu	pus	etter (van 'n wond)
bolelele	length	lengte
bolo	ball	bal
boloka	maintain, save	handhaaf, spaar
bomong	individual	individu
bong	sex	geslag
bongata	majority	meerderheid
bonolo, bobebe	easy	maklik, eenvoudig
bontsha	reflect	weerkaats, weerspieël
boomo	wilfullnes	eiesinnigheid, opsetlikheid
bophirima	west	wes
bora	antagonism	antagonisme
borena	monarchy	monargie
borokgo	bridge	brug
borwa	south	suid
bosesane	thinness	dunheid
boshodu	theft	diefstal
botala	indigenous	inheems
botenya	thickness	dikte
bothata	difficulty	moeilikheid, haakplek
botho	personality, African humanness	persoonlikheid, menslikheid van die Swartes
botjhabela	east	oos
botle	beauty	skoonheid
botlokotsebe	crime, delinquency	misdaad, oortreding

botlolo	bottle	bottel
botshepehi	honesty	eerlikheid
buisana	negotiate	onderhandel
buka	book	boek
busa	reign	heers, regeer
dibeso	wood	hout
dibetsa	armament	krygstoerusting, wapentuig
dieta	footwear	skoene, skoeisel
difaha	beadwork	kraalwerk
dihwete	carrots	wortels
dijana	crockery	breekgoed
dijo	foodstuffs	eetware, voedselware
diketso	action	handeling
dikgetho	elections	verkiesings
dikgomo	cattle	vee, beeste
dikgopo	ribs	ribbes
dikweqe/dihoro	rickets	Engelse siekte, ragitis
dinala	claws	kloue, naels
dinaledi	stars	sterre
dipalo	arithmetic	rekenkunde
ditaba	news	nuus
ditho	organs	organe
dithunya	artillery, guns	geskut, artillerie
dithusathuto	teaching aids	hulpmiddels by onderwys
ditshiba	quill	pennetjie
duma	thunder	donder, bulder
dumela	acknowledge, agree	erken, toegee
ebola	paring	skil, skaafsel
eie	onion	ui
eketsa	increase (knitting)	vermeerder (brei)
emisa	suspend	suspendeer, skors
enta	inoculate	ent, inent
erekisi	pea	ertjie
fantisi	auction	vendusie, veiling
faro	Pharoah	Farao
fatuku	dishcloth	vadoek
fedisa	abolish	afskaf
fenetha	assassinate	vermoor
fenstere	window	venster
fereko	fork	vurk
feta	surpass	oortref, uitblink bo
fetisetsa	pass	aangee

fetola	modify, change	wysig, verander
fiela	sweep	vee
fokotsa	reduce (lessen)	reduseer, verminder
folouru	flour	meelblom
foufala	become blind	blind word
foufatsa	make blind	verblind
fuluru	floor	vloer
fumana	obtain, acquire	verkry. verwerf, aanleer ('n taal), aanskaf
furu	fodder	veevoer
futuhela	attack	aanval
halalelang	sacred, holy	heilig
hapa	annex	annekseer
haraka	rake	hark
hatella	stress	beklemtoon, aksentueer
hatisa	print (by hand)	in drukskrif skryf
haufi, bohaufi	neighbourhood	buurt, omgewing, nabyheid
hlaba/ tofa	inject	inspuit
hlabolla	civilise	beskaaf
hlafuna	chew	kou
hlaha	savage, wild	wild, woes, barbaars
hlaha	originate	ontstaan
hlahlobo ya setopo	post-mortem	lykskouing
hlahola	weed	skoffel, onkruid uitroei
hlaka	clear	helder, duidelik, skoon, oop
hlakileng	plain	eenvoudig, duidelik
hlama	dough	deeg
hlapi	fish	vis
hlatswa	wash up	afwas, uitspoel
hlokofatso	passion (intense emotion)	hartstog, passie
hlola	win	wen
hloma	pitch (tent)	opslaan
hlopha	arrange	rangskik
hlwekile	clean	skoon
hlwekisa	refine, purify	raffineer, reinig
ho arola	to divide	om te verdeel
ho beisa	to race	om resies te jaag, om vinnig te loop
ho bintsha	to conduct	om te dirigeer
ho boha	to admire	om te bewonder
ho boloka	to conserve	om te bewaar, om in stand te hou

ho botsa	to enquire	om te ondersoek, om navraag te doen
ho butswa	to mature	om ryp te word
ho diha	to knock down	om plat te slaan, om neer te slaan
ho disa	to herd	om vee op te pas
ho fahla	to dazzle	om te verblind
ho falla	to emigrate	om te emigreer
ho fihla	to arrive	om aan te kom
ho fihlella	to attain	om te bereik
ho hana	to refuse	om te weier, om te verwerp
ho hana	to deny	om te ontken
ho hapa	to confiscate	om te konfiskeer
ho hlahloba	to assess	om te skat, om te beraam
ho hlomela	to shoot/bud	om te bot, om uit te loop
ho hlophisa	to classify	om te klassifiseer
ho hobela,	to dance	om te dans
ho hodisa	to amplify	om uit te brei, om te versterk
ho idibana	to be unconscious	om bewusteloos te wees
ho ipolela	to confess (sins)	om te bely (sonde)
ho ja	to eat	om te eet
ho jala	to plant	om te plant
ho kala	to weigh	om te weeg
ho kgangwa	to be asphyxiated	om te versmoor
ho kokota	to knock, tap	om te klop
ho kolobetsa	to baptise	om te doop
ho kwenya	to swallow	om in te sluk
ho lakatsa	to covet, wish, desire	om te begcer
ho laola	to administer, control	om te bestuur, administreer
ho leka	to try, to attempt	om te probeer, om te poog
ho lema	to plough	om te ploeg
ho loha	to plait	om te vleg
ho lotha, qaka	to puzzle	om te verwar, om dronk te slaan
ho mema	to hemstitch	om te soomsteek
ho mena	to fold	om te vou, plooi
ho nama	to sit with your legs stretched out	om te sit met jou bene voor jou uitgestrek
ho ngala	to desert/abandon	om weg te loop/te verlaat
ho ngwapa	to scratch	om te krap
ho nwa	to drink	om te drink
ho otla	to assault, beat	om aan te rand
ho paka	to certify	om te sertifiseer

ho phahama/ ho nyoloha	to rise	om te styg
ho pheha/ho tlhatleha	to cook	om te kook
ho phunyeletsa	to penetrate	om deur te dring, om te penetreer
ho qosa	to charge (accuse)	om aan te kla
ho rerisa	to consult	om te raadpleeg
ho ruta	to teach	om te leer, onderrig
ho senya	to damage, to ruin	om te beskadig, verwoes
ho sila	to grind	om te maal
ho sitela	to trespass	om te oortree
ho supa	to indicate	om aan te dui, om aan te wys
ho tataisa	to guide	om te lei, stuur
ho tebela	to expel, sack	om te ontslaan, om in die pad te steek
ho tepella	to be listless	om lusteloos te wees
ho thabisa	to entertain	om te onthaal
ho thapisa	to domesticate	om mak te maak
ho timana/ bokgonatha	to be stingy	om suinig, inhalig te wees
ho tseka	to claim, contest	om te eis, om aanspraak te maak op, om te betwis
ho tshwaya	to correct, mark	om te korrigeer, verbeter
ho tjhona	to be insolvent or broke	om insolvent te wees
ho tuka	to burn	om te verbrand
hodisa	enlarge, magnify	vergroot
hohola, fala	abrade	afvryf, afskuur
hokela	attach	aanheg, vasheg
hora	hour	uur
hotetsa	kindle	aansteek
huku, kou	angle, corner	hoek
hwetla	autumn	herfs
ikana	swear	sweer
ineela	yield, surrender	oorgee
jeke	jack	domkrag
jeme	jam	(fyn) konfyt
Jenale	journal	tydskrif
jeresi	jersey	trui
jute	jute	jute, goiing
ka nako	in time	betyds
kadima	borrow	leen
kahlolo	verdict	uitspraak, beslissing

kama	comb	kam
kamano	contact	kontak, aanraking
kano	oath	eed
kantle	outside	buitekant
karabo	answer, reply	antwoord
karolo	division, part, section	verdeling, afdeling (van boek)
katara	guitar	kitaar
katiba	hat	hoed
katleho	success	sukses, welslae
kausu	stocking (hose)	kous
kelello	quick-witted	slagvaardig, skerpsinnig
keletso	advice	advies, raad
kenomoya	ventilation	ventilasie
kenyeletsa	include	insluit, omvat
kereke	church (denomination)	kerk
ketlele	kettle	ketel
ketsahalo	occurrence, incident	gebeurtenis, voorval
ketso	act	handeling
ketso mpe	malpractice	wanpraktyk
kgaba	spoon	lepel
kgabisa	adorn	versier
kgabisa	make attractive	aantreklik maak, versier
kgabiso	decoration	versiering
kgahlamelo	influence	invloed, inwerking
kgalefo	anger	woede
kgaolo	chapter	hoofstuk
kgatiso	printing-press	drukpers
kgauta	gold (substance)	goud
kgefutso	truce	wapenstilstand
kgetho	selection	keuse, seleksie
kgetla	shell	skulp
kgitla	midnight	middernag
kgohlo	valley, ravine	vallei, laagte, dal, ravyn, kloof
kgosana	prince	prins
kgotso	peace	vrede
kgutsufatso	abbreviation	afkorting
kgwebo	business (trade)	besigheid (handel)
kgwedi	moon	maan
kitjhine	kitchen	kombuis
kokobela	abate, subside	bedaar
kokwana	insect, micro-organism	insek, mikro-organisme

koloi	wagon, car	wa, bokwa, motor(kar)
komello	drought	droogte
komiti	committee	komitee
konopo	button	knoop
kontane	cash	kontant
kopano	assembly	vergadering
kopanya	add	optel, bytel
kopi	cup (tea), copy	koppie (tee), afskrif
kopo	application	aansoek, aanwending
koporo	copper	koper
koranta,	newspaper	koerant, nuusblad
koro	corn	koring, graan
korone	crown (coin)	kroon (muntstuk)
kotara	quarter	een kwart, 'n kwart
kotlo	plague, suffering	plaag
kotsi	accident	ongeluk
kotula	reap	oes, maai, insamel
kou	bay	baai
kounyana	quay	kaai, hawehoof
kutlwelo-bohloko	sympathy	simpatie, medelye
kutu	stem, stump	stam, stomp
kwae	tobacco	tabak
kweetsa	whirlpool	maalstroom, draaikolk
kwepere	quince	kweper
lakane	sheet	laken
laolla	unload	afpak, aflaai
latela	follow, ensue	volg, voortvloei
laya	moralise	moraliseer
lebaka, sesosa	cause	oorsaak
lebaka	reason	rede, motief, dryfveer
lebanta	band, belt	(dryf)band
lebatowa	area, region, constituency	landboustreek, streek, kiesafdeling
lebelo	velocity, speed	snelheid, spoed
lebenkele	shop (store)	winkel
lebese	milk, latex	melksap, lateks
lebitso	name	naam
lebopo	coast	kus, strand
leboya	north	noord
leeme	prejudice	vooroordeel
leeto	journey, voyage	reis, seevaart
lefa	heritage	erfnis, erfdeel
lefapha	department	departement

lefatla	bald crown	kaalkop
lefatshe	earth, world	aarde, wêreld
lehaba	lamina leaf	blaarskyf
lehadima	lightning	weerlig
lehafi	armpit	armholte
lehaha	cave	grot
lehano	mouth cavity	mondholte
lehare	razor blade	skeermeslem
lehata	skull	skedel, kopbeen
lehe	egg	eier
lehlabathe	sand	sand
lehlabathe/tetebedi	quicksand	dryfsand
lehlabula	summer	somer
lehlaka	reed, stalk	riet, steel, stingel
lehlasedi	beam (of light)	straal (lig)
lehlatso	vomiting	braking, vomering
lehlwele	blood clot	bloedklont
lehoho/bofalo	crust	kors
lehola	noxious weed	skadelike onkruid
lehwatata	plain	vlakte
leifo	hotbed	broeikas
leihlo	eye	oog
leino	tooth	tand
leka	make an effort	'n poging aanwend
lekgalo	pass, cutting	bergpas, deurgrawing
lekgapetla	peel, scale	skil, skub
lekgathe	tense	tyd
lekgetho	duty, tax	belasting, heffing
lekgoba	slave	slaaf
lekgopho	acne	puisies
lekgotla	council	raad
lekgowa	white (person)	blanke (persoon)
lekunutu	confidential, secret	vertroulik, geheim
lekweba	foam	skuim
leleme	tongue	tong
lelente	ribbon	lint
leloko	social unit	sosiale eenheid
lengeloi	angel	engel
lengolo	letter	brief
lengope	donga	sloot, donga
lenqosa	ambassador	ambassadeur, gesant
leoka	mimosa tree	mimosa, doringboom

leoto	foot (human)	voet (menslik)
lepera	leprosy	melaatsheid
lepetjo	motto	motto, leuse
lephela	cockroach	kakkerlak
leqaqailana	ankle	enkel
leqeba	wound	wond
leqephe	page, leaf	bladsy, pagina, blaar
leqhaama	waist band	gordel
leqhubu	breaker, wave (sea)	brander, golf
leqhwa	ice, block (of ice)	ys, ysblok
leqwetha	attorney	prokureur
lera	membrane	membraan, vlies
leralla	hill	randjie, bult, heuwel
lerama	cheek	wang
lerato	love	liefde
lere	ladder	leer
lereo	term (expression)	term (uitdrukking)
lerole	dust	stof
lerothodi	drop	druppel
leru	cloud	wolk
leruarua	whale	walvis
leruo	possession, property	besitting, eiendom
lesapo	bone	been
lesedinyana	periodical, newspaper	tydskrif, koerant
lesela	cloth	kledingstof
lesiba, pene	pen	pen
lesoba	hole	gaatjie
lesupi	ruin (of building)	ruïne, bouval, murasie
letamo	dam (of water)	dam
letanta	gauze	gaas
letata	duck	eend
letheba	blemish, spot, blot, stain	letsel, vlek, klad, smet
lethopa	boil (tumour)	sweer, pitsweer
lethopo	hose (pipe)	rubberpyp, tuinslang
letlalo	skin	vel
letlao, tang	pincers	knyptang
letlapa	slate, blackboard	lei, swartbord
letlojana	petty cash	kleinkas, kleingeld
letlowa	net	net
letona	councillor	raadslid
letsa	dial	skakel
letsatsi la phomolo	public holiday	openbare vakansiedag

letsatsi	day	dag, etmaal
letsha	lake	meer
letshollo	diarrhoea	buikloop, diarree
letsoho	hand	hand
letsopa	clay	klei
letswai	salt	sout
letswalo	conscience, diaphragm	gewete, diafragma
letswalo	shock	skok
letswapo	hillside	heuwelhang, skuinste
lewatle	ocean	oseaan
lokisa	improve	verbeter
lokolla	absolve	kwytskeld, vryspreek
loto	lead	lood
madi	blood	bloed
maele	proverbs	spreekwoorde
maemo	circumstances	omstandighede
mafelo a beke	weekend	naweek
mafi	curd	dikmelk
mafolofolo/matjato	active	aktief, bedrywig
mafome, rusi	rust	roes
mafome	brown rust	rooiroes
mahetla	back (of shoulders)	rug, blaaie
mahlasedi	ray (of sunlight)	sonstraal
mahloko	poison	gif
mahlomola	sadness (suffering)	lyding
mahwashe	rough	ru, grof
maikemisetso	aim	doel, oogmerk
maikutlo	attitude, feelings	houding, gevoelens
makgulo	pasture	weiveld, grasveld
mariha	winter	winter
marulelo	roof	dak
mashala/leshala	coal	steenkool
maswebeswebe	wrinkles	plooie, rimpels
matekwane/sabonkgi	dagga	dagga
mathe	saliva	speeksel
mathuleng	verandah	veranda, stoep
matla	power	mag
matla ohle	omnipotence	almag, alvermoë
matla	authority, force	gesag, volmag, krag, dwang
matlakala	rubbish	vuilgoed, afval, gemors
matlotlo	assets	bates
matokomane	peanuts	grondboontjies
meedi	boundaries	grense

mefutafuta	variety	verskeidenheid
meraka	ranching area	veestreek
meso	daybreak	dagbreek, daglumier
metsi	water	water
mmadi	reader	leser
mmala	colour	kleur
mmaraka	market	mark
mmele	body	liggaam
mmetso	gullet	slukderm
mmila	public road	openbare pad
mmino	music	musiek
mmolai	murderer	moordenaar
mmopi	creator	skepper, maker
moahisani	neighbour	buurman
moahlodi	judge	regter
moahlodi	adjudicator	beoordelaar
moaho	building	gebou
moalo	bedding	beddegoed
moamohẹdi	receiver	ontvanger
mobu	soil	grond
modisa	shepherd	herder, skaapwagter
moditjhaba	foreigner	uitlander
modumo	sound	klank, geluid
moduwane,	weeping willow	treurwilger
moedi	border (boundary)	grens
moepa	incline, gradient	helling, skuinste
moeti	guest	kuiergas, gas
moferefere	riot	oproer, opstand
mofetshe	cancer	kanker
mofo	vassal	ondergeskikte
mofu	deceased	afgestorwene
mofumahadi	queen/wife	koningin/vrou
mofuta	breed	ras, geslag
mofuthu	warmth, warm weather/ climate	warmte, warm weer/ klimaat
mohale	hero	held
mohatiso	script	handskrif, skrif
mohla	date	datum
mohlahare	cheekbone	wangbeen
mohlahlobi	assessor (assistant to judge)	assessor (assistent van regter)
mohlaka	swamp	vlei

mohlala	clue, track, sign	leidraad, spoor, bewys, teken
mohlape	herd, flock	kudde, trop
mohlodi	winner	wenner
mohlolo	miracle	wonder, wonderwerk
mohoma	plough, hoe	ploeg, skoffelpik
mohwebi	merchant	handelaar
moithaopi	volunteer	vrywilliger
mokgwa	manner	manier, wyse
mokitlane	credit	krediet
moko	marrow of bone	beenmurg
mokoka	stamina	uithouvermoë
mokokotlo	ridge, back	rug, rif
mokola	nosebleed	neusbloeding, neusbloei
mokoloko	queue	ry, tou
mokotla	bag	sak
mokudi	patient	pasiënt
molala	neck	nek, hals, kraag
molao	act (law)	wet, akte
molaodi	administrator (of province)	administrateur (van provinsie)
molebedi	warder, guard	bewaarder
molefi	payer	betaler
molekgetho	receiver of revenue	ontvanger van inkomste
moleko	temptation	versoeking
molemo	value	waarde
molomo	mouth (of river)	riviermonding
molora	ash	as
molotsana	villain	skurk, skobbejak
mona	here, local	lokaal, hier, plaaslik
mongodi	author, writer	skrywer
mongolo	orthography, writing	ortografie, skrif
monkgo/lephoka	odour	reuk, geur
monko	fragrance	geur
monontsha	fertiliser	messtof
monoto	lower leg	onderbeen
monwana	finger, toe	vinger, toon
monya	swab, absorb	skrop, opvee, skoonmaak, absorbeer
monyetla	opportunity	geleentheid
mookodi	rainbow	reënboog
moomo	shin bone	skeenbeen
moputso	wage, salary	loon, salaris
moqoqo	narrative, essay	verhaal, vertelling, opstel

morabe	tribe, race	stam, ras
moreki	customer	kliënt
morena	monarch, chief, king	koning, vors, kaptein, hoofman
Morena	Lord, the	Here, die
morero	project, plan	plan, skema, projek, voorneme
moriri	hair	hare
moriti	shade	skaduwee, koelte
moroba	leisure	vrye tyd
moropa	bass drum	groot trom
moru	jungle, forest, plantation, bush	bos, ruigte. plantasie, bos
moruti	minister, clergyman	predikant, dominee
morutuwa	disciple	dissipel, volgeling
morwalo	freight (cargo)	vrag, lading
morwetsana	virgin	maagd
mosa	benevolence	welwillendheid, liefdadigheid
mosa, lereko	kindness	vriendelikheid
mosadi	housewife (woman)	huisvrou (vroumens)
mosamo	cushion	kussing
mosebetsi	occupation, employment	beroep, werk
moseme/mmete	mat	mat
moseneke	crisis	krisis
mosesisi	sailor	matroos
mosha	meercat	meerkat
mosifa	muscle, tendon	spier, sening
mosuwe	teacher	onderwyser
mothamo	capacity	inhoud, volume
mothapo	nerve	senuwee
motheo	base, foundation	basis, fontdament
motho	person	persoon
motjhafofane	runway, airstrip	landingstrook, aanloopbaan
motjhotjhisi	public prosecutor	staatsaanklaer
motlakase	electricity	elektrisiteit
motoho	soft porridge	sagte pap
motsara	skim(med) milk	afgeroomde melk
motse	village, city	dorp, stad
motseki	plaintiff	eiser, klaer
motsheare	daylight	daglig
motshepuwa	stalwart, trustee	staatmaker, trustee
motshwaruwa	captive	gevangene

motswako	mixture	mengsel
moya	breath, air	asem, lug
mpa	abdomen	maag, buik
mpho	gift	geskenk
naha	country	land
nahana	think	dink
nako/mohla	period	periode, tydvak
nako	duration, time	tydsduur, tyd
nakwana	interim, temporary	tussentyds, voolopig, tydelik
nala	boom	oplewing, voorspoedgolf
nale/nalete	needle	naald
naledi	star	ster
nama ya nku	mutton	skaapvleis
nawa	bean	boontjie
neo	gift (see talent)	gawe, talent
nepo	accuracy	noukeurigheid
nese/mooki	nurse (of sick)	verpleegster
ngaka	doctor	dokter
ngata	numerous	talryk
ngatana	batch	bondel, stel
ngola	write	skryf
nkgo	clay pot	kleipot
nko	nose	neus
nku	sheep	skaap
noka	hipbone	heupbeen
nomoro	number	nommer
nonyana	bird	voël
noto	nil	nul
nta	louse	luis
ntho	thing, matter	ding, stof, materie
ntjhafatso/ phetoho	reform	hervorming
ntlha	apex	toppunt, spits
ntlo	house	huis
ntlwana	toilet, privy	toilet, kleinhuisie, latrine
ntwa	battle	slag
nyalana	integrate	integreer
nyehelo tsa teboho	thanksgiving offer	dankoffer
nyewe	court case	hofsaak, regsgeding
nyoloha	ascend	opstyg
nyolohelo	ascension	hemelvaart
nyooko	bile	gal
oli	oil	olie

oma	dry	droog, uitdroog, verdroog
otla	penalise	straf
paki	witness	getuie
Palamente	Legislative Assembly	Wetgewende Vergadering
pale	story	storie, verhaal
palesa	flower	blom
pallo	predestination	uitverkiesing
palo	number	getal
pampiri	paper	papier
papadi	match, game	wedstryd, spel
papiso	comparison	vergelyking
parafine	paraffin	paraffien, lampolie
paseka	passover	paasfees
patata	sweet potato	patat
peiso	running game	hardloopspeletjie
peke	pick (tool)	pik
pele	beforehand	vooraf
pelo	heart	hart
peni	penny	pennie
peo	seed	saad
perekisi	peach	perske
peterolo	petrol	petrol
peto	rape	verkragting, ontering
phaello	gain	baat, wins
phala	bugle/whistle	beuel, horing/fluitjie
phalo/lehare	plane blade, plane-iron	skaafbeitel, skaafmes
phate	rug (travelling)	reisdeken
phatla	forehead	voorkop
phatlalatso	declaration	verklaring
phatsimo	shine	glans
pheko/sehlare	remedy	geneesmiddel
phema	avert	keer, afwend
phepompe	malnutrition	ondervoeding, wanvoeding
pheta	revise, repeat	hersien, verbeter, herhaal
phetho/qeto	resolution	voorneme, besluit
phio	kidney	nier
phofudi	vapour	damp, wasem
phokolo/bolwetse	ailment	kwaal, siekte
pholoho	salvation	verlossing, saligheid
pholoso/topollo	deliverance	verlossing
phomolo	rest, holiday	rus, vakansie
phoofolo	animal	dier

phororo	cascade, waterfall	waterval
phoso	mistake, error	fout
phoso	incorrectness	onjuistheid, verkeerdheid
phutheho	congregation	gemeente
piano	piano (instrument)	klavier
pitsa	pot	pot
polane/leqheka	plan	planne beraam, beplan
polao	murder	moord
pompo	pump	pomp
pona	wither	verwelk
pono	vision, eyesight	visioen, gesig
poone	maize	mielies
poso	post (mail)	pos
potlako	rapidly	vinnig, gou
puisano	discussion	bespreking
pula	rain	reën
puo	language	taal
qapa	compose	komponeer, toonset
qeto	decision	besluit
qhaqha	dissect, dismantle	ontleed, uitmekaar haal
qhaqholla	parse	ontleed (woorde)
qhoma	explode	ontplof
qoba	avoid	vermy
qomatsi	state of emergency	noodtoestand
qoqotho	trachea	lugpyp
qosa	accuse	aankla, beskuldig
qotso	quotation	aanhaling, sitaat
radio	radio	radio, draadloos
raka	shelf	rak
ramatlotlo	treasurer	tesourier, penningmeester
ranta	rand	rand
rateha	likeable	innemend, gaaf
reberebe	pulp	pulp, pap
reka	buy	koop
rephaboliki	republic	republiek
roba rekoto	break a record	'n rekord slaan
roka	sew	naai, naaldwerk doen
ruri	really	rêrig
ruruha	swell (as bruise)	swel, opswel
saena	sign	teken
saense	science	wetenskap
sakga	jigsaw	figuursaag

sakramente/selallo	sacrament	sakrament
samente	cement	sement
satalla	rigid (not flexible)	styf, onbuigsaam
seaparo	mantel (clock)	mantel
sebaka	locality	plaaslikheid, omgewing
sebalwa	reading matter	lektuur, leesstof
sebata	predator	roofdier
sebete	liver	lewer
sebetsa	weapon	wapen
seboba	tsetse fly	tsetsevlieg
seboko	outcry, worm	geskreeu, lawaai, wurm
sediba	well (spring)	put, fontein
seemo	posture	liggaamshouding, postuur
seeta	shoe	skoen
sefaha	necklace, bead	halssnoer, kraal
sefahleho	countenance	gesig, voorkoms
sefako	hail	hael
sefe	mesh, sieve	maas, sif
sefefo	thunderstorm,anti-cyclone, hurricane	donderstorm, antisikloon orkaan
sefela	hymn-book, hymnal	gesangboek
sefi/leraba	trap	lokval
sefofane	aircraft	vliegtuig
sefofu	blind man	blinde man
sefuba	breast	bors
seha	make a cut	’n snit maak
sehahabi	reptile	reptiel
sehahi	builder	bouer
sehlaba	tableland	tafelland, plato
sehlabelo	offering	offerande
sehlaha	nest	nes
sehlahla	bush, shrub	bos, struik
sehlekehleke	island	eiland
sehlopha	standard	standerd
sehlopha	category	kategorie, soort
sehole	palsied person	verlamde persoon
seipone	mirror	spieël
sejana	dish, utensil	skottel, werktuig
sekaja	sprint	naelloop
sekama	slant	skuinste, helling
sekepe	ship	skip
sekgeo	blank	oop ruimte, spasie

sekolo	school	skool
sekontiri	tarmac	teerblad
sekwahelo	covering	oortreksel
selao	den	lêplek, hol
selekane	covenant (theology)	verbond
selemo	spring year, season	lente
seletsa	musical instrument	musiekinstrument
sello	complaint	klagte
selotho	riddle	raaisel
selotho, qaka	puzzle	raaisel, vraagstuk
semela	plant	plant
seno	drink	drank
senoko	inch	duim
senotlolo	key	sleutel
sente	cent	sent (geldeenheid)
senya	waste, bladder, urinary bladder	verkwis, vermors, blaas urineblaas
senyeha	perish	bederf, vergaan
seolo	antheap	miershoop
seotlwana	courtyard	binneplein, binneplaas, binnehof
sepatjhe	wallet	portefeulje, geldbeursie
sepekere	wire-nail	draadspyker
sepele	pin	speld
sepetlele	hospital	hospitaal
sephaka	fore arm	voorarm
sephara	broad	breed, wyd
sepheo	aim, goal	doel
sephetho	result	resultaat
seqo	mealie stalk (dry)	mieliestronk
sera	enemy	vyand
serame	frost	ryp
serethe	heel	hakskeen, polvy
serope	thigh, upper leg	dy, bobeen
seroto	basket	mandjie
serotswana	quarter evil	sponssiekte
Sesebediswa	tool	gereedskap
sesedi/seboko sa poone	stalk-borer	stamrusper, stronkboorder
sesehi	cutter (tool)	snyer (beitel, mes)
sesepa	soap, bar of soap	seep, steen seep
sesiu	grain-elevator	graansuier
seso, sebebe	abscess	abses, sweer

seso/alsa	ulcer	oop seer
sesomo	sarcasm	sarkasme
sesupo	reflection	refleksie, weerkaatsing
setempe	stamp	posseël
setene	brick	blok, baksteen
seterata	street	straat
sethetsamahlo	mirage	lugspieëling
setho	morals	sedes, sedelike gedrag
setho	member	lid, lidmaat
sethwathwa	epilepsy	vallende siekte
setjhaba	nation	nasie
setlama	herb	kruid, bossie
setlapedi	ringworm	omloop
setlolo	ointment	salf
setofo	stove	stoof
setsebi	expert, authority	ekspert, deskundige, outoriteit
setsha	site	ligging
setshwantsho	picture	prent, skildery
setswe	elbow	elmboog
setulo	chair	stoel
setumo	repute	aansien
sewelo	coincidence	toeval
sibolla	discover	uitvind, ontdek
sireletsa	protect	beskerm
sireletsa	secure (make safe)	verseker, waarborg, beskerm
sopho	soup	sop
sotha/sotheha	warp, twist	skeef- of kromtrek
sotha	contort (writing)	verdraai
swaya	swerve	swenk
tabataba	subject matter	leerstof, stof, onderwerp
tabola	tear	skeur
tadimo	point of view	gesigspunt
taelo	command	bevel
tahi	alcohol	alkohol
tang	flat-nose pliers	platbektang
tapeiti	linoleum	linoleum
tataiso	guidance	leiding
tatso	flavour	geur
tebela	banish	verban
teboho	thanksgiving	danksegging
tefo	payment	betaling

tema	plot (of ground)	kleinhoewe, stuk grond
temana	passage	uittreksel, gedeelte
temo	agriculture	landbou
temoso	signal	sein, teken
terekere/katakata	tractor	trekker
terone	throne	troon
teye	tea	tee
thabo	pleasure	genot, plesier
thakgiso	crucifixion	kruisiging
thapedi	petition	petisie, versoekskrif
thapelo ya teboho	thanksgiving prayer	dankgebed
thapelo	prayer	gebed
thapo	rope	tou, lyn
thebe	shield	skild
thekiso	sale, marketing	uitverkoping, bemarking
theko	cost	koste, prys
theolelo	discount	korting, afslag, diskonto
thibela	restrain	bedwing, beteuel
thipa	knife, penknife	mes, knipmes
thomo	organ	orrel
thonyo	nomination	nominasie, benoeming
thota	open veld	oop veld
thuisa	digest	verteer
thunya	shoot, bloom	skiet, uitbot, blom
thupa/leswai	rod (for chastisement)	lat, rottang
thusa	help	help
thuso	aid, assistance	hulp
thuto	education, course, teaching	opvoeding, onderwys, kursus, onderrig
tjhai	crop	oes
tjheke	cheque	tjek
tjhelete	money	geld, munt
tjhentjhe	change (money)	kleingeld
tjhoko	chalk	kryt
tjotjo	bribery	omkopery
tlanya/thaepa	type	tik
tlhahlobo	examination	eksamen
tlhalo	divorce	egskeiding
tlhaloso	definition	definisie
tlhohonolofatso	blessing	seëning
tlhokeho	necessity	noodsaaklikheid
tlhokomelo	maintenance, care	onderhoud, instandhouding sorg

tlholo	victory	oorwinning
tlhompho	courtesy	hoflikheid
tlhoriso	persecution	vervolging
tlhweko	cleanliness	sindelikheid
tlwaelo	habit	gewoonte
tlwaetsa	accustom	gewoond maak
toka	justice	regverdigheid, geregtigheid
tokollo	acquittal	vryspraak
tomoso	yeast	suurdeeg
tora	tower	toring
toropo/motse	town	dorp
tsebe	ear	oor
tsebiso	notice (attention)	aandag, notisie
tsebo	knowledge	kennis
tsekisana	dispute	twis, betwis, redetwis
tsenene	sting	angel
tshehetsa	maintain, patronise	handhaaf, ondersteun
tshehla	yellow	geel
tshenyo	damage	skade
tshepe	iron (element)	yster
tshephe	springbok	springbok
tshepo	confidence	vertroue, selfvertroue
tshila	filth	vullis, vuilgoed
tshimo	land (cultivated)	land
tshita	obstacle	hindernis, struikelblok
tshitshidi	bedbug	wandluis, weeluis
tshiya/pilara	column, pillar	pilaar, suil, kolom
tshomo	fable	fabel, sprokie
tshupa	weevil	kalander
tshwara	arrest	arresteer, in hegtenis neem
tshwarelo	pardon, forgiveness	vergifnis, kwytskelding
tsie	brown locust	bruinsprinkaan
tsoho	resurrection	opstanding
tsokotsa	rinse	uitspoel, afspoel
tsukunya	rinse mouth	mond uitspoel
tumelo	faith	geloof
tumello	admission	toegang, toelating